Intercultural Learning in Modern Language Education

LANGUAGES FOR INTERCULTURAL COMMUNICATION AND EDUCATION

Series Editors: Michael Byram, *University of Durham,* UK and Alison Phipps, *University of Glasgow,* UK

The overall aim of this series is to publish books which will ultimately inform learning and teaching, but whose primary focus is on the analysis of intercultural relationships, whether in textual form or in people's experience. There will also be books which deal directly with pedagogy, with the relationships between language learning and cultural learning, between processes inside the classroom and beyond. They will all have in common a concern with the relationship between language and culture, and the development of intercultural communicative competence.

Full details of all the books in this series and of all our other publications can be found on http://www.multilingual-matters.com, or by writing to Multilingual Matters, St Nicholas House, 31-34 High Street, Bristol BS1 2AW, UK.

LANGUAGES FOR INTERCULTURAL COMMUNICATION AND
EDUCATION: 28

Intercultural Learning in Modern Language Education

Expanding Meaning-Making Potentials

Erin Kearney

MULTILINGUAL MATTERS
Bristol • Buffalo • Toronto

Library of Congress Cataloging in Publication Data
A catalog record for this book is available from the Library of Congress.
Kearney, Erin.
Intercultural Learning in Modern Language Education: Expanding Meaning-Making Potentials/Erin Kearney.
Languages for Intercultural Communication and Education: 28
Includes bibliographical references and index.
1. Language and languages–Study and teaching. 2. Intercultural communication–Study and teaching. 3. Language and culture–Study and teaching. 4. Multicultural education. I. Title.
P53.45.K43 2015
418.0071–dc23 2015023401

British Library Cataloguing in Publication Data
A catalogue entry for this book is available from the British Library.

ISBN-13: 978-1-78309-467-7 (hbk)
ISBN-13: 978-1-78309-466-0 (pbk)

Multilingual Matters
UK: St Nicholas House, 31-34 High Street, Bristol BS1 2AW, UK.
USA: UTP, 2250 Military Road, Tonawanda, NY 14150, USA.
Canada: UTP, 5201 Dufferin Street, North York, Ontario M3H 5T8, Canada.

Website: www.multilingual-matters.com
Twitter: Multi_Ling_Mat
Facebook: https://www.facebook.com/multilingualmatters
Blog: www.channelviewpublications.wordpress.com

Copyright © 2016 Erin Kearney.

All rights reserved. No part of this work may be reproduced in any form or by any means without permission in writing from the publisher.

The policy of Multilingual Matters/Channel View Publications is to use papers that are natural, renewable and recyclable products, made from wood grown in sustainable forests. In the manufacturing process of our books, and to further support our policy, preference is given to printers that have FSC and PEFC Chain of Custody certification. The FSC and/or PEFC logos will appear on those books where full certification has been granted to the printer concerned.

Typeset by Deanta Global Publishing Services Limited.
Printed and bound in Great Britain by Short Run Press Ltd.

For Eric, Scarlett and Ray

Contents

1	**The Challenges of Addressing Culture in Modern Language Education**	1
	The Ideological Landscape of Modern Language Education in the United States	5
	The Global Challenge	13
	Conceptions of Culture and Approaches to Culture in Modern Language Education in the United States	19
	Rethinking Meaning-Making in Modern Language Classrooms	28
	Overview of Chapters in this Book	30
2	**The Culture Learning Target: Engagement with Meaning Potentials**	31
	Models of Intercultural and Symbolic Competence Informing Culture Pedagogy	32
	Empirical Studies of the Development of Intercultural and Symbolic Competences in Modern Language Education	50
	An Ecological, Social Semiotic View of Modern Language Learning	57
3	**Creating and Investigating Intercultural Worlds in a Modern Language Classroom**	70
	Establishing the Global Simulation in Emilie's Class	71
	Methods for Investigating Meaning-Making in a Modern Language Classroom	94
	Everyday Narrative Sense-Making and Storying to Make Meaning at Grander Scale	97

4	Understanding Signification and Interpretive Acts Through Engagement with Cultural Representations	100
	Identifying Cultural Reference Points and Symbolic Forms	102
	Hypothesizing about the Meanings of Culturally Symbolic Forms	118
	Repositioning Classroom Actors and Animating Cultural Texts through Voicing and Embodiment	125
	Developing a Metalanguage for Engaging in Interpretation	138
5	Realizing Meaning Potentials Through Narrative Writing	146
	Writing Through a Culturally Different Voice and Exploiting Affordances of Semiotic Resources	149
	Two *Mémoires* Projects	151
	The References, Stories and Stances in Brina's Project	153
	The References, Stories and Stances in Katie's Project	160
	Students' Take on Perspective-Taking	169
6	Sense-Making in a Web of Meanings: Implications for Theory, Research and Practice	176
	A Web of Meanings	176
	Renegotiating 'Negotiation of Meaning'	180
	Translating a Social Semiotic Model of Intercultural Learning into Practice	182
	Future Directions	192
References		194
Index		201

1 The Challenges of Addressing Culture in Modern Language Education

In the early weeks of a first semester French class I was teaching, I asked students about where they lived, following a short lesson on the question form 'D'où viens-tu?' (Where are you from?) and the basic vocabulary necessary for responding. The problem arose that a student wanted to say that she was from a town in the suburbs of Austin, Texas. I hesitated, yet went to the chalkboard, wrote the word 'banlieue' (suburb), then modeled how the student could make a full sentence using the term, and waited for her to repeat. I then took care to note to the class, in English, that the word carried different connotations in French, that the 'banlieue' was not as coveted a place to live as in the US (as some people sometimes refer to 'suburban bliss' for example). In France, I explained, moderate-income housing in the form of tall apartment buildings was located on the outskirts of the main cities and for decades has been a place where immigrant families and families in financial difficulty have lived in higher concentrations than in other places, like inside cities (although ethnic neighborhoods obviously exist in Paris and elsewhere in France). But as I spoke I realized the essentialization of culture that was occurring as I tried to succinctly deal with a very complex word and meaning. I knew, first of all, that discussions of social housing in French society differ from those in the US, with important conceptions of assimilation and integration being talked about in very different ways in the two societies. I also knew that living in a 'cité' (a grouping of tenement buildings in the French suburbs and another lexical item that is enormously complex) and being from the 'banlieue' evoke images of a very particular nature for speakers of French and that even within the category of 'French speakers,' understandings of this word are rooted in various social realities; yet, relating the complexity of the interrelated linguistic and social situation in this introductory-level course seemed at odds with the purpose of the class – to get the basics of the French language.

> *My student's question made me think of the gross generalities that are sometimes made in presenting the vocabulary for talking about where one lives, ostensibly for the sake of getting students to master linguistic elements themselves, outside of their social and cultural context, before delving into the complex meanings around such words as 'banlieue'. This moment signaled to me more generally as well the complicated task of communicating meaning to my students. It led me to consider what other instructors might have done in the same situation, and it seems that in at least some cases, this discussion would have been completely glossed over or the complexity of the term entirely ignored, with a translation being supplied and no further discussion ensuing. On the other hand, perhaps instructors had effective strategies for addressing the social and cultural weight of language even in the introductory-level classroom. What was also striking to me shortly after this classroom experience was that in another class that I was teaching, a fifth semester, intermediate French level, life in the 'banlieue' was taken up in much more detail, with three and a half hours of class time over several days devoted to examining the historical, artistic, social and linguistic aspects of life for 'banlieusards' (people who live in the 'banlieue'). In this content-based course, the learners' language skills were assumed to be stable enough to allow for much more substantive discussion of social and cultural reality and were conducted entirely in French. Ultimately, this classroom moment and many others that occurred in the course of my own teaching practice, led me to wonder about the place of culture in language learning and how, in a modern language (ML) classroom especially, culture is taught and learned. (Kearney, 2008: 1–3).*

These episodes from my own teaching inspired the classroom ethnography reported in this book. Upon learning of another university-level French classroom, from which students apparently emerged not only with improved linguistic abilities but also deep cultural knowledge and competence, I became interested in studying Emilie[1] – a reportedly outstanding ML teacher – her students, and the impact her pedagogical approach had on their learning. The challenge I faced in the classroom and the one Emilie faced in teaching culture is indeed the challenge faced by many ML educators these days – how to engage students in more deeply meaningful learning in the language classroom, how to connect them with culture and hopefully, in the process, how to spur change in their worldviews.

The ML classroom, for me, for Emilie and for many others increasingly, is a site where students not only learn to speak, read, listen or write a new language but where they also can learn to understand, to feel and to be in new ways and to potentially transform themselves and the world around them through language study. Transformative ML education is, I will argue, intimately tied to a view of language learning as an engagement in meaning-making activity or what we might refer to as semiotic practice. Reconceptualization along these lines is already occurring in some ML classrooms but also in theorizing of what language education is as an individual and group activity. Research, too, increasingly attempts to document and analyze classroom interactions, learners' subjective and personal experiences with language learning, and the broader policy and political environment in which language education occurs, all in an effort to foreground the meaning and meaningfulness of language learning as an activity. All of this work underscores the argument that rethinking the meaning of ML education and meaning-making in ML education is the major issue language teachers, theorists and researchers grapple with today.

What we need above all in order to continue moving these efforts forward is to more clearly connect meaning-based theories language with actual classroom environments and practices so that a range of contexts and experiences with meaning-making in ML classrooms becomes visible. Research that produces nuanced descriptions of the overarching conditions and the specific teaching and learning interactions that foster deep cultural learning will form the basis for generating a more robust set of curricular and pedagogical options when it comes to teaching culture in ML education.

In this book, cultural learning – or better intercultural learning[2] – and meaning-making practices in language education are taken to be closely linked. The complicated enterprise of making meaning in ML classrooms is assumed to involve linguistic and other semiotic resources and meaning-making processes at both individual and collective levels (what we recognize as cultures). While it has been common to take up referential meanings in ML education and to think of cultural meaning as a code of sorts that can be acquired by learners, linguistic and cultural forms have yet to be taken up in the curriculum and pedagogy for the broad range of significances we personally and collectively assign to them. Nor have the individual and shared processes through which meanings are generated, negotiated and transformed been a major focus of ML education.

Particularly important in meaning-making processes is the shifting of meaning potentials. Meaning potentials figure prominently in this book (as the title suggests), as they are relevant to language learners in two ways. First, learners must access and develop an understanding of the more or less conventionalized meaning potentials that the forms of a new language offer them. Second, they must expand their own personal meaning potential and shape a voice that may sometimes use language in ways that express expected meanings but that may at times also stretch the meaning potentials of linguistic resources to forge novel meanings. These ideas will be taken up in much more detail further on in the book, but at the outset, it is essential to know that, based on theories of meaning potential and on empirical research that analyzed a group of learners' engagements with meaning, I ultimately advocate for a *pedagogy of potentials* in ML education; this refers on one hand to the need to focus learners' attention on developing understandings of new symbolic resources, but on the other, and quite crucially, to the need to foster learners' engagements with the languages they are learning in ways that engender deep and personal connections to those languages, that create varied opportunities for expressing symbolic meanings of their own and that ultimately make possible new options for speakerhood.

The challenges of addressing culture in the ML education classroom stretch far beyond those made salient in the vignette at the start of this chapter, though my own teaching experiences do highlight the crux of the issue facing university-level instructors and primary and secondary school teachers alike. These challenges in intercultural pedagogy in ML education, at the core, have to do with meaning – not only understanding others' ways of referring to the world and of construing and attributing significance to it but also understanding meaning-making as a process of selecting symbolic forms from a range of options and doing so purposefully in order to establish, negotiate or advance a perspective. In this book, and with Emilie's and other teachers' dilemmas in mind, my goals are (1) to demonstrate, by drawing on the in-depth study of one classroom, that intercultural learning of substance can and does occur in ML classroom settings; (2) to illuminate the features of the classroom environment and processes of interactional engagement that support meaningful culture-in-language-learning; (3) to illustrate the impact of in-class teaching and learning interactions on students' meaning-making repertoires; and (4) to connect the empirical evidence I present and analyze to both the theorizing of culture-in-language-teaching and to the practical concerns of teaching. In the remainder of this chapter, I describe the ideological landscape in which ML education occurs in the United States, since challenges in culture teaching and learning in language classrooms are significantly shaped by this environment. Given the way ML education is situated in the United States and also taking into account some other general trends in conceptualizations of language teaching and learning, I explain how culture pedagogy has come to be characterized in particular ways. Finally, I argue at the end of the chapter that, based on the way culture pedagogy has come to be practiced in ML education in the United

States, a reconsideration of the meaning of ML education and meaning-making in ML education is urgently needed.

The Ideological Landscape of Modern Language Education in the United States: Broad Orientations and Impact on Practices

To fully appreciate the challenges of addressing culture in ML classrooms of any educational level in the United States, one must take into account the broader ideological terrain in which particular classrooms find themselves. In this section, I discuss powerful societal and professional discourses that impact the structure and practice of ML education in the United States, from teachers' and students' classroom experiences, teacher education and professional development to the public imagination about the purpose and value of learning languages. My purpose in doing so is not only to contextualize the challenges ideology poses to culture pedagogy in particular but also to suggest that, even though ideologies are strong and endemic to the organization of ML education and practices within it, there are countercurrents and practices in play, including the approach described in this book. Ultimately, the quality of the experience students have in ML classrooms is greatly impacted by strong ideological flows, which influence the degree to which the curricular area most expected to support development of individual and societal multilingualism and to promote intercultural knowledge and understanding actually delivers on those assumptions.

Monolingual ideologies

By and large, monolingual ideologies dominate in the United States and permeate the organization and practice of all education but of ML education in particular (Reagan & Osborn, 1998; Stanton, 2005). From the relatively late start to ML education common in the United States to a lack of articulation of the curriculum and goals for ML learning across educational levels to a host of classroom practices (such as the heavy use of English and a tendency toward rote and decontextualized language exercises as opposed to abundant opportunities for creative language use), structural constraints and interactional routines in ML education have come to limit and undermine the ostensible mission of the field and ultimately sustain monolingualism as a value and as a reality for many in the United States. It is important to keep in mind that language ideologies are common sense notions of what language is, what it does and who language users are

(Woolard & Schieffelin, 1994) but that these notions operate in a subtle fashion to produce very real consequences, most often in favor of powerful groups in society.

Monolingual ideologies do not just promote the notion that one language is preferable to many; they also circulate messages about who speakers are – either native or nonnative – and what languages are – contained and separate linguistic systems (L1, L2, L3, etc.). It has been uncommon in our field to conceive of ML learning as the expansion of *one* meaning-making repertoire in an individual, for example, as is now advocated in theories of dynamic bilingualism and translanguaging that have arisen in the field of English as a second language in the United States and elsewhere around the world (e.g. Canagarajah, 2011; García & Sylvan, 2011). These scholars view language users as drawing on a range of linguistic features and discursive practices that are all part of one meaning-making system; rather than having separate, relatively fixed languages in the mind, language users are seen to flexibly and situationally deploy features of one broad, integrated semiotic system. Learning new languages, then, amounts to growing the linguistic and discursive features available in an individual's system and ideally involves a vast expansion of that flexible repertoire of meaning-making potential. It is equally uncommon to view the goal of ML education as the development of students as *multilingual* speakers; instead, we speak mostly about learners becoming native-like in their use of an L2, imagining an idealized native speaker as the measure against which we might discern whether or not a learner has reached some level of proficiency or competence (Kramsch, 1997). When such rigid understandings of languages and speakers prevail, we see practices in language classrooms like the strict separation of languages and the insistence on exclusive use of the L2 being studied, for example, as opposed to more flexible, multilingual approaches (Levine, 2011). What a native/nonnative speaker binary, fueled by monolingual bias, means for the intercultural learning we envision for ML learners is also problematic. In all cases, this dichotomy seems to facilitate prescriptivism when it comes to both linguistic and cultural knowledge, skills and meanings and to present a considerable roadblock to truly engaging with the dynamism and complexity of language use and both individual and intercultural meaning-making.

The native speaker/nonnative speaker distinction

The rigid native speaker/nonnative speaker and L1/L2 dichotomies that are treated as normal in and that are further naturalized through ML education in the United States create conditions for the construction of foreignness in ML classrooms (Levine, 2014; Osborn, 2005; Reagan, 2002). Indeed, 'foreign' language is the more common term used to refer to the field, although I opt for 'modern' language in a conscious effort to reject the distancing and othering that accompanies this construction of foreignness in language education. Given that ML education is often treated as an elite, enrichment type of activity that rounds out the educations of a privileged class of citizens, it is not all that surprising that foreignness is ideologically built into ML education and that it is rarely challenged as an organizing principle for what occurs in language classrooms.

We might say that ML education in the United States often reinforces dominant cultural and societal norms as it sets up anything 'other' as 'foreign' and therefore different and possibly strange or inferior. The prevalence of comparative types of activities in ML classes as teachers and students engage with culture are an example of how foreignness gets constructed and how distance is maintained between students (assumed to be all the same and to share a unified culture) and the 'other' culture. These activities also point to the ramifications of the construction of foreignness in ML classes for intercultural learning.

In these types of classroom exercises, cultures are usually first essentialized, generally in national terms (i.e. the American way, the Russian way, the Chinese way, etc.), and are then treated in a largely oppositional and universalizing manner as students are asked to articulate differences and similarities between two apparently monolithic ways of being. There is nothing inherently problematic about comparison as a pedagogical exercise, but if it starts from the premise that the world is carved up into black and white, us and them, and then fails to question these divisions through the comparative exercise, then it stops short of engaging students in critical dialogue and dealing with the actual complexity of intercultural life and belonging. Rather, broad comparison establishes what is 'normal' and 'foreign' in sweeping ways, usually without any context, and rarely with any follow-up or further probing to question what may at first seem natural or foreign.

Foreign language crisis

A powerful monolingual orientation and construction of foreignness are interestingly coupled in the United States with a discourse about a 'foreign language crisis' (Wiley, 2007a), referring to a perceived paucity of speakers of languages other than English (although demographic data show that there is in fact considerable and rapidly growing linguistic diversity in the United States). Wiley (2007b) rightly points out that in the current moment of 'crisis', an ever-growing resource in terms of multilingualism and linguistic diversity – immigrant and so-called 'heritage' language speaking populations – is completely ignored. Along with this perceived problem, there is widespread belief in the 'failure of foreign language education' (Osborn, 2005; Reagan, 2002). Reagan (2002) writes that the 'social expectation of failure is in fact the thread that holds together the other structural, institutional, and pedagogical constraints' that mark ML education in the United States (p. 37). From a critical theory perspective, Osborn (2005) writes that

> *foreignness*, or the ideological construction of an extra-national language identity in service of the dominant culture, is an agenda at which some success has been evident [in the US]. Remembering that critical theorists reject the claim that students have not learned simply because educational programs seem to fail, one can see that the failure of an educational program (in this case foreign language education) may in fact represent a success in terms of hegemony. (p. 81–2, emphasis in original).

The portrayal of ML education as a perpetually failing educational enterprise then masks the ideological forces supporting hegemony at work in the field while also feeding into stagnation in terms of the evolution of instructional practices or shifts in participants' attitudes. Considering the ramifications for intercultural teaching and learning, the expectation of failure allows for the bar to be set extremely low in terms of what kinds of intercultural competence and critical abilities students will take away from their ML education experiences.

Modern language learners and teachers

As I have alluded to above, the field of ML education in the United States has furthermore been influenced by a set of assumptions about who learners are and what expectations there are for their language learning, and this too contributes to a challenging environment for teachers, learners and advocates of change in US ML education. As Ortega (1999) notes,

> [T]he [foreign language] FL teaching profession has traditionally assumed an understanding of language and education premised on the alleged neutrality of FLs regarding the relative power and status of languages within the larger society. Moreover…FL professionals have traditionally associated themselves with the educational needs of

English native-speaker students. The reasons for this apolitical stance and linguistic elitism may be found in ideological as well as structural aspects of the FL profession. (p. 245)

That different languages enjoy different status in society, that whether one is learning a new language as a so-called 'foreign' language or English as a second language in school makes a difference, or that languages (English and all others) are claimed by various social and cultural groups in the United States for a range of ideological reasons is rarely taken into account in discussing, planning for and carrying out ML education. Nor is the alleged homogeneity of the ML classroom challenged, despite the growing linguistic and cultural diversity of all classrooms in all schools in the United States.

Since Ortega wrote in 1999, there has been some increased attention to so-called 'heritage' learners, especially of Spanish, who come to the ML classroom with some connection to or proficiency in the language already. However, there is still an overwhelming sense that ML education in the United States is intended to enrich the education of monolingual, majority speakers of English. Nevertheless, these learners are never expected to reach any considerable level of language proficiency in their MLs. The act of ML learning for majority speakers of English in the United States has more of a symbolic than a practical currency (Darvin & Norton, 2015). This is in stark contrast to the expectations society has for minority language speakers in the United States, who, in short amounts of time and with little prestige gained for their efforts, are expected to learn English to high degrees of competency. Essentially, Ortega names this state of affairs as 'the myth of foreign language education as an elite endeavor' (p. 247), a myth that is clearly buoyed by the monolingual ideologies discussed above and endorsed by the stance that ML learning is somehow a neutral act.

An apolitical view of language in relationship to society and a limited view of who learners are in the ML classroom represent a major problem for culture pedagogy in that consideration of difference remains very superficial, and given the strong feeling that ML classrooms are homogeneous and neutral, it is even more likely that instruction and interaction can sidestep development of critical self-awareness or inward reflection. Viewing ML education as apolitical avoids issues of power differences (among learners and other language users) and misses the opportunity to cultivate in learners the 'power to speak' (Darvin & Norton, 2015). These misunderstandings of students as language learners and users will be revisited in further depth in Chapter 2 when discussing the work of Claire Kramsch, who proposes we see learners as multilingual subjects.

Modern language teachers and the profession

While the myth of who students of MLs are flattens the reality of cultural and linguistic diversity that exists in US classrooms and outside of them and limits the vision of what learners might become through their language study, little attention is accorded to who teachers in these classrooms are. They are, arguably, a more homogeneous group than their students. While it is true that the teaching profession in the United States is marked in gender-, race- and class-based ways, with white middle-class women working as teachers much more often than other groups, the ML profession in the United States is also characterized, especially at the primary and secondary level of education, by the language histories of teachers. Most speak English as a first language and only acquired their ML(s) through schooling in the United States (and possibly through some study abroad and/or travel experiences). Perhaps more important than the fact that ML teachers speak the languages they teach as a second rather than a first language is the effect the teachers' own language learning experiences have on their professional practices; having come through the US ML education system themselves, teachers are likely to carry into their instruction many of the same practices that have, taken together, undermined the development of multilingualism and interculturality in learners. This is not at all to suggest that teachers intentionally work to suppress the development of linguistic or intercultural competence; on the contrary, we might well argue that most ML teachers speak enthusiastically of their mission to open the world to their students through language study, to support development of linguistic proficiency and fluency so that students can use language in communication, and to help students connect to speakers of other languages. The nature of ideology, however, is that it acts on individual and collective practice in subtle, subversive ways (Bourdieu & Passeron, 1990). ML teachers are, generally, quite well-intentioned; but the practices they themselves experienced as ML learners that get reproduced once they become teachers, end up – if left unquestioned and unchallenged – being hegemonic and maintaining the status quo. The general lack of diversity in the ML teaching corps as well as the nature of teachers' language-learning histories may skew learning objectives, conceptions of the goals of language learning and intercultural teaching in important ways.

Monolingual ideologies and the belief in the homogeneity and neutrality of ML classrooms are strong and have an important impact on what occurs in classrooms, including how intercultural teaching and learning get done. In addition, very deeply held beliefs about what language learning consists of and what purposes it serves play out in instructional practice and learning interactions. By and large, language learning as a process is still conceived of in narrow ways in ML education in the United States. Perhaps because of the strong influence of so-called 'mainstream' second language acquisition research on language curricula and teachers' beliefs, language learning in ML education is often discussed as and assumed to be a linear process, the staged acquisition of linguistic (mostly grammatical and lexical) forms, with learners moving from one well-defined phase to another and, eventually, from the concrete, immediate and referential to the abstract and symbolic. This is, of course, a view of the language learning process that delimits language itself in important ways, treating it as a collection of forms, rules and sometimes functions. This narrow conception of language learning as the staged acquisition of linguistic forms and the subsequent fitting of these forms to situations of use, based on quite static notions of situational and contextual factors, is not without problems. There seems to be a widespread transfer-of-knowledge issue – that is, that students do not seem to be able to apply the forms and rules they have 'learned' through their ML instruction to contexts outside of controlled practice or highly structured role plays. Larsen-Freeman (2003) calls this the 'inert knowledge problem' and cites the 'individual and social consequences' (2003: 108) that should call into question the notion that the acquisition of forms is all there is to ML learning. But again, ideology is likely at work, and shifting practices away from the deeply entrenched traditions in ML education that are driven by such a view of language learning is a daunting prospect in practical terms. The impact of this constrained concept of language on classroom practice is detailed further in the next section, but it is worth reiterating that overall, narrow views of language limit the scope of content for ML education to linguistic forms and a very narrow range of communicative contexts and functions. In turn, certain kinds of instruction become privileged as they are viewed as potentially supportive of the staged acquisition of forms (rule learning, form-focused practice, application of forms in some kinds of tightly controlled communicative situations, etc.). All of this impacts classroom practice and the nature of students' language abilities and competences (or lack thereof, as Larsen-Freeman points out). Of course, when language learning is considered in these constrained ways, the role of culture too is impacted. Culture is largely sidelined in favor of a focus on linguistic form or is seen simply as the broad backdrop against which language use occurs. The relationship between language and culture, however, is not addressed in a substantive fashion when language learning focuses so squarely and exclusively on linguistic forms.

Beliefs about what language is and who is involved in ML education in the United States certainly shape the nature of practice in ML classrooms. Ideologies about the purpose of ML education do as well. Reagan and Osborn (2002) cite the kinds of common rationales that are offered for

ML study in the United States, including the cognitive, cultural and pragmatic. Arguments for the cognitive benefits of language study include the notion that learning a ML will engender critical thinking skills, for example. Cultural rationales may speak to the benefit of language study for individuals (personal growth, ability to appreciate other cultures) or for society (enhanced multiculturalism, acceptance of diversity). Several of these oft-cited justifications for ML study actually contribute to the construction of foreignness in ML education, however; for example, pragmatic arguments that ML study can serve economic and national security interests clearly set up an us/them configuration, in which the learning of a new language is only viewed as useful insofar as it allows US citizens to gain a competitive or strategic political edge over 'others' who pose some type of threat to the nation-state. Even rationales rooted in arguments for the possible personal and cultural benefits ML study might bestow on learners and society may have unintended effects. For example, articulation of more humanistic, diplomatic and peace-oriented goals still may create an othering or distancing of the 'foreign'. In all cases, the common rationales offered up for ML education in the United States imply that knowing about culture is for dealing with some 'other' but maybe not in deep ways, and intercultural learning is not an activity through which learners will be prompted to reflect critically on themselves or the world. In contrast to those rationales for ML study that circulate more widely in US society, Reagan and Osborn (2002) argue that

> For us, perhaps the most powerful argument for the need for students to study languages, other than their own is that the point of education is to introduce and initiate the individual into our common, human social and cultural heritage, and that this cannot be done adequately without some exposure to the different ways in which human beings, in various times and places, have constructed an amazingly wide variation of languages to meet their needs. If becoming educated is, as many scholars have suggested, the process by which one learns to join in the human conversation, then language skills will inevitably be required if one wishes to join the conversation on anything other than the most trivial level. (p. 12)

Such a rationale is in line with the meaning-based approach to intercultural learning presented in this book and expressed by others. Phipps and Levine (2012), for example, in advocating more critical and intercultural approaches to ML education, identify 'the conviction that there is a deeper ethical basis for language pedagogy, one that teachers in the classroom know and feel daily but that often is not reflected systematically in the larger discourses about teaching and learning' (2). Few examples, however, are available of the ways in which ML education might enhance learners' ability to 'join in on the human conversation' in meaningful ways.

The Global Challenge

While the rationales described above still hold considerable sway and surface in discussion of language study in both popular and professional arenas, ascendance of a new argument for ML study emphasizes the need for learners in the United States to be prepared for participation in a 'globalized' world and to be equipped with '21st century skills,' including language competence. The central proposition is that study of languages can raise students' awareness of difference and equip learners with readiness to interact with others, faraway and near, that may have different worldviews and experiences than themselves. The problem with this rationale for ML study, however, lies in the underlying assumption that it is by sheer virtue of learning a ML that 'global' skills or orientations will naturally develop. Decades ago, Robinson (1978) deemed this type of thinking the 'magic-carpet-ride-to-another-culture syndrome'; yet the notion persists in professional and popular discourse that language learning inevitably leads to intercultural learning. This is not to say that there is no merit in the globalization argument as a rationale for ML study. Scholars have problematized basic notions of language, culture and communication in the context of globalization (Kramsch, 2014) and proposed that late modern tenets of mobility, cultural hybridity and increased diversity conflict deeply with the modernist anchors of ML education as it is practiced in the United States. Kramsch (2014) writes that in today's globalized environment, 'semiotic fluidity presents a challenge to the traditional normativity of [ML] education, which is expected to teach usable skills but is increasingly outpaced by the changes brought about by global means of communication' (p. 300); she also points to a series of other normativities and rigidities with which ML education operates but that do not make sense in current times (such as language purity and correctness and the association of languages with particular localities, among others). Beyond theorizing, though, and despite the reliance on globalization-based rationales for ML study in professional standards and policy documents (discussed further in the next section of this chapter), there has been no widespread adjustment of language teaching practice that might prepare learners in new ways specifically for necessarily intercultural encounters in the current day context, a key aspect of which is the ability to interpret and make meaning and to exercise agency in using language. A further complication is that, while many associate interaction in a globalized environment as necessitating communication across cultures and experiences, there is a concurrent belief among learners, teachers and others that English use is so dominant in a 'globalized' world that there is no real need to learn other languages, even if they do desire to participate in 'global' life. Of course, this is another reduction of real-world social and communicative complexity, and as Kramsch (2006) stresses, in order to interact in a context that does indeed facilitate and make much more likely communication that represents more fluid configurations of social belonging, 'it is not sufficient for learners to know how to communicate meanings; they have to understand the practice of meaning making itself' (p. 251). The extent to which ML education in the United States promotes such understanding is highly questionable at present, however, and if no move is made to adjust thinking and practice in the field, learners' capacities are unlikely to qualify as '21st century skills'. Notably absent in public discourse and the societal imaginary around ML education is any mention of the growth of an individual's meaning-making repertoire through language education or the transformation of communication potentials on the broader scale of social groups and communities of language users.

Understanding the ideological backdrop against which ML education in the United States occurs is key for understanding what then happens in individual classrooms, especially with regard to intercultural learning and the sorts of meanings teachers and learners engage with, expect to encounter and generate through their joint activity. The main ideological challenges in ML education as a field in the United States are that language study and multilingualism are undervalued, in individuals and in society at large. As a result, the exercise of ML education has been able to remain somewhat fixed in its traditions, structures and practices and to continue operating at a superficial and falsely apolitical level. This poses major problems when it comes to intercultural learning and attempts to reconceptualize ML education as the expansion of learners' meaning-making repertoires.

Typifying ML classroom interactions: Challenges in the classroom

The ideological is always connected to the interactional, such that taken-for-granted notions about languages, language users, language learning or anything else are indexed and reproduced or challenged in localized ways and through local practices (Schieffelin et al., 1998;

Woolard & Schieffelin, 1994). What we know about the interactions that occur in ML classrooms in the United States, however, is fairly limited. Of those empirical studies of classroom discourse in the United States that exist, many have been driven by a desire to identify what features of teacher talk and other input as well as various forms of interactions create conditions for second language acquisition, as conceived of from a cognitivist point of view (Hall & Verplaetse, 2000); that is, researchers have attempted to identify what in classroom discourse and interaction promotes learners' noticing, negotiation and production of various linguistic systems and the integration of these features into their own developing interlanguages. Of particular interest is the specification of discourse conditions and circumstances that promote second language acquisition of particular features (e.g. Kang, 2010), elements of teacher talk that are facilitative of language development (e.g. Toth, 2004, 2011; Waring, 2008), the range (or lack of range) of linguistic or pragmatic features in classroom discourse when compared with 'real-world' discourse (e.g. Ellis 1992), and so on. Studying and characterizing ML classroom interactions with regard to the way they promote intercultural learning and how instructional discourse in ML classrooms might address language and intercultural meaning in integrated fashion has been less prevalent. Recommendations for curricular approaches that might generate such classroom interactions, however, are convincingly argued in Byrnes (2008), Swaffar and Arens (2005) and Kramsch's (1993) work.

From the studies that do exist and drawing on other resources (extensive observation in schools, discussions with many teacher educators, consideration of professional policies that speak to perceived needs in the profession), it is possible to characterize in a broad way the interactions that have come to typify ML education in the United States and to do so with an eye not to detailing the opportunities for language acquisition this discourse either affords or constrains but rather with a concern for understanding the discourse environment in which *meaning* is taken up and engaged with (or not) and to what extent and in what ways. It is of course the case that not all classrooms will fit the profile I sketch; however, the fact that many learners who enter the ML education system in the United States continue to emerge from years of instruction with little productive competence in MLs tends to support the claim that interactions in these classrooms merit our attention and are likely to be dominated by the patterns described below, namely less than adequate levels of use of the target language and teaching and learning interactions that are focused on form over meaning; and on meaning, when it is taken up, only in limited ways.

A first discursive characteristic of ML classrooms in the United States has to do with levels of ML or 'target language' use when compared with use of English. A recent effort by the American Council on the Teaching of Foreign Languages to advocate for 90% or more target language use in American ML classrooms (ACTFL, 2010) presupposes a belief in the field that instructional time in many ML classrooms involves copious amounts of English language use. The rationale for proposing this particular percentage of L2 use, incidentally, is not empirically substantiated. In a Center for Applied Linguistics survey of primary and secondary school teachers, 79% of high school teachers and 81% of middle school teachers reported using the target language for at least half of the time; only 58% of elementary school teachers reported using the target language half of the time (Pufahl & Rhodes, 2011). In a survey and classroom observation study conducted by Duff and Polio (1990) at one tertiary institution, a very wide range of target language use among instructors was found, ranging from 98% to only 10% of the instructional time. Levine (2011), aiming to create a model of the 'code choice status quo' of university-level classrooms, conducted a self-reported study of over 600 college students and 163 instructors and compared findings with the existing literature. He found that overall there is wide variability from instructor to instructor with regard to the quantity of L1 and L2 use, that instructors routinely use more L2 than students and that certain functions consistently align with either the L1 (discussion of classroom policies and assignments, grammar explanations) or the L2 (interpersonal exchange and communication). These findings would suggest that, at all educational levels, there is still a strong possibility that a great deal of English will be employed by teachers and learners in ML classrooms, which has implications for the kind of language exposure students receive and the extent to which they are actually engaged in interaction in the language they are studying. When we consider that, as early as the 1980s, researchers found that teachers speak for about two thirds of the total instructional time (Chaudron, 1988), there is really very little time and airspace available in general for student talk. From the perspective of student use of the language being learned, there is likely to be very little opportunity for productive use for individual students or the group as a whole in such classrooms, and a constrained set range of situations for use at that. Of course, certain approaches, such as communicative language teaching and task-based language teaching, expressly promote students' productive language use, and in those classrooms especially we might observe different patterns; but more traditional, teacher-fronted configurations in ML education are quite typical and yield far less opportunity for student language use. From both receptive and productive perspectives, ML classrooms are not always rich environments for promoting interaction in the ML being studied.

Beyond levels of target language use, we might also consider ML classroom discourse in terms of its content and focus. Casually, we might state broadly that language and culture make up the ML curriculum, but how these are conceived of more specifically, as we have already seen, is ideologically driven, and how these fundamental elements of ML curriculum are ultimately enacted in classroom discourse is a further question. The ML curriculum in many schools and universities is still organized in form-focused ways, if not explicitly through a syllabus organized around grammar points, then implicitly by structuring curriculum by topics that still are always accompanied by set vocabulary and particular grammatical forms (Long & Crookes, 1992). These construals and organizations of content impact the types of interactions that take place in the classroom. When the focus is on grammatical forms and/or sets of vocabulary items, interaction will often tend toward a rote, form-focused engagement with language. The results of this type of instruction and the interactions set up through such a pedagogical approach have admittedly not yielded an ability among learners to produce language forms in novel contexts as is hoped for in a communicative approach to language teaching. Larsen-Freeman (2003) calls this the 'inert knowledge problem'; teachers have 'taught' a form and students have ostensibly 'learnt' it as evidenced by their ability to reproduce it correctly in rote types of exercises or controlled communicative activities. However, when the very same learners find themselves in a situation of use that might call for that form later or in a slightly different context, the knowledge they have 'learnt' does not seem to activate in service of use. Larsen-Freeman takes as a lesson from this widespread problem that there is likely something lacking in instruction that leads to such a situation, and in addition to advocating abandoning an exclusively or heavily form-focused approach to grammar teaching, she also supports teachers seeking novel and more meaningful ways of engaging learners with grammar and how it operates, since lack of engagement constitutes another major obstacle in many approaches to grammar instruction. A preoccupation with form can also lead teachers to focus in interaction on the accuracy of forms and on practices based in prescriptivism, such as insisting on learners producing only complete sentences. Brooks (1993) summarizes well the way content is conceived of in ML education classrooms in the United States and the impact of these conceptions on language teaching and learning:

> Viewing the foreign language as an object 'out there' somewhere to be studied, looked at, corrected, conjugated, dissected, talked about, repeated, and hopefully mastered, decontextualizes it from the social and instructional conversations in which foreign language teaching and learning processes are inextricably embedded...The social and

linguistic context of the classroom conveys messages and information not only about what counts and what is acceptable as learning but also about the meanings of lessons and the goals of the foreign language classroom. These meanings are constructed as products of the learning opportunities and instructional conversations that transpire between and among the individuals [in the classroom].... What is neglected, unfortunately, is the underlying process of communication and social interaction through which teaching and learning goals are achieved in the classroom. (p. 234)

Given the nature of classroom discourse and interaction in many US ML classrooms, we might well ask what implications there are for intercultural learning. In many cases, instruction or discussion related to cultures occurs in English, and some theories of cultural learning (Byram, 1991) seem to encourage such breaks in target language use in order to engage students with cultures and interculturality. Importantly, the heavy focus on linguistic forms in many classrooms leaves little room for meaningful engagement with cultures, and even in those classrooms that adopt a more communicative approach, where students are involved in information exchange types of interactions, cultural meaning is rarely central to learning tasks. Finally, in more advanced levels of ML learning, where culture is seen to occupy a more rightful place in the curriculum, what counts as culture is often restricted to literary studies, and even when broader content is addressed, the ways in which teachers and learners engage with it are still quite constrained, as will become clear in the following section of the chapter.

At the same time, it is crucial to note that there are important exceptions to the norm when it comes to pedagogical approaches that could (and probably do) create more consciously meaning-oriented interactions in ML classrooms, which in turn create qualitatively different interactional and discursive spaces for intercultural learning. Notably, genre-based (e.g. Byrnes *et al.*, 2006; Byrnes *et al.*, 2010) and other literacy-based approaches to ML education (e.g. Allen & Paesani, 2010; Paesani & Allen, 2012; Swaffer & Arens, 2005; Warner, 2014) posit language form, propositional content and context (including cultural context) as constitutive of meaning and envision learners as becoming increasingly informed and agentive decision makers when it comes to language choices and language use in communicative situations and in relation to texts of all kinds. These curricular approaches represent openings for transforming the nature of culture pedagogy and intercultural learning in ML classrooms in the United States; however, empirical studies of classrooms are needed to specify how elements of the instructional environments and various interactional processes promote intercultural learning in novel ways. Such work would parallel and complement the building of curricular approaches and sequences.

Conceptions of Culture and Approaches to Culture in Modern Language Education in the United States

Turning from a consideration of classroom discourse and interaction in ML education in the United States to the specific area of culture-in-language-education, it is important to consider both the concepts of culture with which the profession operates and the practical manifestations of culture pedagogy that sometimes align closely with these conceptions and at others relate much less so. I translate these conceptions and common practices into a series of challenges facing culture-in-ML-education in the United States:

- the challenge of integrating language and culture;
- the challenge of defining culture;
- the challenge of undoing the treatment of culture in essentializing or reductionist ways;
- the challenge of getting beyond cultural 'facts' to acknowledge complexity and contradiction in cultural knowledge and experience;
- the challenge of moving away from conceptions of culture as procedural knowledge and imagining more dynamic roles for learners as language users;
- the challenge of specifying interpretive processes involved in intercultural learning;
- the challenge of connecting and also distinguishing the personal and individual from the cultural and shared;
- the challenge of overcoming surface comparison;
- the challenge of theorizing and implementing broader meaning-making approaches in ML education;
- the challenge of more deeply engaging subjectivities in culture-in-ML-education.

At other moments in this section, I point to alternative conceptions and possible practices in an effort to think forward and possibly envision things differently while also establishing a clear picture of the current landscape. The research reported later in this book provides clear evidence of an alternative approach to culture pedagogy.

One of the most pronounced characteristics of culture pedagogy in ML education in the United States has been that although language and culture are consistently claimed to be inextricably linked, in the curriculum, pedagogical practice and even some theoretical models of culture learning, the two remain starkly separated and compartmentalized in ways that avoid articulating how precisely language and culture function together (Magnan, 2008). In curriculum, the treatment of culture as a '5th skill' in ML education (Damen, 1987) definitely positions it as separate from the four traditionally acknowledged language skills (reading, writing, speaking and listening), which are themselves problematic in an intercultural literacy-based approach to ML education (Swaffar & Arens, 2005), and divorces linguistic and cultural forms and meanings in the process. Such moves render culture an add-on, peripheral to the 'real' business of ML education, which is a focus on language. Brody (2003) goes so far as to say

> From the perspective of a linguistic anthropologist considering the role of culture in second language education, it is apparent that although the concept of culture is drawn upon frequently in the second language teaching literature, it is often used in unconsidered, constrained and taken-for-granted fashion; the importance of culture is often recognized but seldom analyzed. (p. 37)

Instructional materials also tend to reveal the separation of language and culture in practice despite claims of their inextricability from all corners of the profession (e.g. Risager, 1991). This separation of language and culture can convincingly be argued to be artificial, as many have, on very sound logical and empirical grounds, explained the relationship between language and culture. In ML education specifically, Agar's (1994) concept of languaculture, for example, and Kramsch's (1993) writing about culture as a discursive and social phenomenon have both been routinely invoked to highlight the ways in which language and culture are reciprocally related. Yet, the curriculum, pedagogy and instructional materials do not yet adequately incorporate these insights. Articulating the particular ways in which language and culture relate at many levels of discursive and social interaction is a **challenge of integrating language and culture**.

Evidence of problematic divisions in culture pedagogy also appear in the way cultures are often stratified into 'high' and 'low' versions in ML education. Long before the communicative turn in language teaching, and before many learners actually used their additional languages for direct communication with speakers of those languages, language education still showed a concern for culture pedagogy, revolving primarily around an engagement with 'high' culture, mostly through the reading of great literary works. This particular orientation, based on the idea that the highest forms of language study involve interpretation and analysis of canonical literary texts, still prevails in some settings, such as many departments of MLs in US universities (Byrnes, 2002; Swaffar & Arens, 2005); however, as Byram (1994) describes, culture-in-language-teaching has over time grown to include the study of the experience of everyday life in addition to exalted arts and so-called 'high' culture:

> It has long been a commonplace among language teachers that their pedagogical aims include the encouragement in their learners of an interest in and opening towards a culture, people and country where the language in question is spoken. It is however in the interpretation of 'culture, people and country' that different periods and different forces have brought varying orthodoxies. 'Culture' has been variously interpreted as 'high' or 'classic' culture, in particular literature but also philosophy and fine art, or as the modes and conventions of social interaction in daily life and their reflection in literary and non-literary texts. Approaches to 'country' include study of its history, and of the contemporary affairs reflected in its media. 'Peoples' have been studied in terms of national characteristics or through descriptions of the mundane events of their daily lives. (p. 1)

The bifurcation of culture into the elite and the mundane has sometimes been referred to in ML education using the terms 'big C culture' and 'little c culture' (Brooks, 1960). The consequence of organizing culture in this dichotomous way is that a hierarchy is created, and potential valorization of one kind of culture over another in the curriculum and pedagogical practice is encouraged. This is a **challenge of defining culture** and of imbuing culture teaching and learning with rigid value systems such that the study of 'high' culture is perhaps viewed as more prestigious or elite, even as the study of 'low' culture may be seen as entirely practical and worthwhile. Categorizing culture along a high-low continuum also underscores a further major challenge in culture-in-ML-education – the **challenge of undoing the treatment of culture in essentializing or reductionist ways**.

In her work that traces the history of culture pedagogy in US and European language education contexts, Risager (2006, 2007) finds strong emphasis on nation-based views of culture, one of the most common lenses through which cultures are focalized (and reduced/essentialized) in ML classrooms. As Guest (2002) argues, it does in some cases make sense to consider cultures as national; however, he writes,

> our classrooms...are filled with individuals or small groups of real people who we come to interact with on a personal basis. So it is with almost all intercultural language encounters. Most linguistic interaction is not at the level of a monolithic, generalizable, culture, but rather with individuals or small groups...Culture, therefore, should be seen as an interplay between social and personal schemas...(p. 157)

Guest challenges the monolithic vision of cultures that a nation-based concept promotes above all others. Lo Bianco (2014) similarly questions the relevance of nation-based conceptions of cultures and the accompanying 'spatial distributions of languages' (p. 312) in ML education by advancing an argument rooted in the realities of globalization. Arguing for a transnational view of culture as an alternative, Risager (2008) describes a requisite 'recognition of linguistic and cultural complexity as a result of (local and) transnational flows' (p. 7). A transnational view in ML education, she claims, has implications for the ways we see language and linguaculture, the topics and discourses taken up in ML education, and the contexts and contacts that frame ML learning. An outgrowth of adherence to a nation-based view of culture in ML education is perhaps the belief that cultural learning only happens abroad or elsewhere, not in the classroom setting (Collings, 2007; Kearney, 2010; Kinginger, 2008).

A focus on countries and national contexts is often coupled with attention to culture as facts, a body of declarative knowledge that language learners can read about or absorb in other ways, commit to memory and then reproduce for evaluation purposes. Such an approach to culture pedagogy can amount to the collection of relatively useless trivia or, more productively, can contribute to at least a basic understanding of target-language cultures. Advocating a more process-oriented view of culture-in-ML-education, Damen (2003) writes, 'The *process* of culture learning as key to effective culture learning is often buried beneath a flood of cultural tidbits that may astound but seldom enlighten' (p. 74, emphasis in original). We need not completely dismiss definitions of culture as knowledge in ML education, however, since as Byram *et al.* (1994) caution,

> it would be misguided to assume that learners do not need some 'background information'. Indeed it is misguided to think that such information is mere 'background'. For the link between cultural learning and linguistic learning is indissoluble in principle, even if attempts have been made to reduce and diminish the link in practice. (p. 48)

Yet, Damen's reminder to attend to process remains important. When culture is treated merely as the objective and delimited content for language learning, and cultural learning as a process is only treated as entailing acquisition of 'facts', we cannot expect that learners' understandings will be very deep. Relatively fixed information can only be a starting point in addressing the **challenge of getting beyond cultural 'facts' to acknowledge complexity and contradiction in cultural knowledge and experience**.

In some cases, cultural knowledge in the ML classroom is not seen as just a body of declarative and objective knowledge; it can also be viewed as procedural knowledge, and culture learning, as a result, especially in some implementations of a communicative approach (Byram *et al.*, 1994), is interpreted as learning to apply this knowledge in appropriate ways in appropriate contexts. We might call this a view of culture as practices, where practices are concerned with knowing how to match language and culture in communicative situations of use. Approaches to culture pedagogy that focus on pragmatics and particular speech acts would also fall into a category of teaching culture as procedural knowledge. While many teachers may not describe their approach as having to do with pragmatics, discussion of politeness formula and levels of formality in language use are quite common in culture pedagogy, and many textbook materials are organized to offer up linguistic formulae that match particular social and cultural situations. In these cases, the potential prescriptiveness of attempting to pin down what is 'appropriate' in particular cultural contexts, for example, begins to restrict what such an approach to culture pedagogy can achieve. Furthermore, when culture learning is treated as the acquisition of procedural knowledge, the kinds of communicative situations that are taken up in the curriculum, and consequently the types of roles learners can occupy as they attempt to use language in culturally appropriate fashion, are circumscribed in limiting ways. Often, learners are limited to acting and speaking as consumers or polite tourists, when clearly there is a much fuller range of positions from which one can speak through a new language. Kramsch (2006) reminds us that 'not all communicative situations are amenable to straightforward talk in a brief, concise and sincere manner, and negotiation of meaning often flounders not because of a lack of linguistic comprehension, but because of a lack of understanding and trust of interlocutors' intentions' (p. 250). Conceiving of language-in-use as mere transaction and identifying sets of linguistic formulae to match dimensions of the social and cultural context fails to capture the true complexity of language use in interpersonal and intercultural contact. Pedagogical approaches that limit the situations of use learners encounter and that fail to imagine a broader range of roles that learners themselves are more actively involved with creating miss the fluidity, variation and agency of intercultural communication. Conceptions of culture as procedural knowledge do move from a view of culture as static content to culture as process to some degree, but clearly there are still limitations, and we are faced with the **challenge of moving away from conceptions of culture as a procedural knowledge and imagining more dynamic roles for learners as language users**.

A somewhat broader orientation to culture pedagogy is apparent in those approaches that adopt a 'culture-as-context' perspective and that view culture in terms of perspectives. These often anthropologically informed views of culture see social life as a set of multilayered and complex processes that have very much to do with the creation, interpretation and re-creation of meaningful contexts, often with heavy reliance on language. These notions of culture have led to formulations of what is considered good pedagogical practice, such as that reflected in the American Council on the Teaching of Foreign Languages (ACTFL)'s World Readiness Standards for Learning Languages (ACTFL, 2013). In these standards, culture is posited as a nexus of products, practices and perspectives, with perspectives serving as a driving force in and explanation for any manifestation of a cultural product or practice. Two of ACTFL's World Readiness Standards for Learning Languages (2013) that address culture read as follows:

Cultures: Interact with cultural competence and understanding

1. Relating Cultural Practices to Perspectives: Learners use the language to investigate, explain, and reflect on the relationship between the practices and perspectives of the cultures studied.
2. Relating Cultural Products to Perspectives: Learners use the language to investigate, explain, and reflect on the relationship between the products and perspectives of the cultures studied.

Comparisons: Develop insight into the nature of language and culture in order to interact with cultural competence

2. Learners use the language to investigate, explain, and reflect on the concept of culture through comparisons of the cultures studied and their own.

How products, practices and perspectives are linked with language is not made explicit in ACTFL's model since the standards refer to learners *using* 'the language to investigate, explain and reflect on' dimensions of culture. How they are to use it is unclear. Yet, viewing culture learning in ML education in this way does open up space for what can happen in classrooms, in that points of view and value systems become central when perspectives are put at the center of consideration. While ACTFL provides standards, Byrnes (2008) critiques that they 'remain largely silent on precisely how those learning goals are to be attained,' especially through curricular sequences. Furthermore, we know very little about how exactly teachers engage learners with perspectives in the context of their language teaching and about what understandings students develop through these experiences; that is, we know little about how perspectives are defined by teachers and learners, how they are made salient during classroom discourse and interaction, how they are discussed and interpreted, how they are understood and what, if anything, students end up taking away from classroom interactions and course assignments based on the exploration of perspectives. We might also wonder if viewing culture as the context for communication may position it as a mere backdrop, the stage upon which the real action of language use occurs. Similarly, positing 'perspectives' as the explanatory dimension that underlies cultural products and practices risks oversimplifying the reality that people's linguistic and other meaningful acts are not wholly explainable in cultural terms; that is, cultural perspectives risk being viewed in deterministic ways. In the way that many speak of culture as the context for language use, there is no clear sense of language and culture being intertwined, mutually informing discursive and social tools. We again see evidence of the challenge of integrating language and culture, but here, in a more precise manner, the question arises about whether culture explains language or if the two are more dynamically and reciprocally related. Dimensions of context and the means for interpreting products and practices as cultural or personal (or perhaps both) also are raised. Ultimately, these issues constitute **the challenge of specifying interpretive processes involved in intercultural learning** and, within these interpretive interactions in the classroom, **the challenge of connecting and also distinguishing the personal and individual from the cultural and shared**.

Alongside the many trends in culture pedagogy that have to do with the way culture itself is conceptualized (as knowledge, as practice, as process, as perspectives, etc.), theory and practice in the realm of culture-in-ML-education has also sometimes focused more squarely on students as actors in the teaching and learning process than on the content of that process. Culture pedagogy, therefore, is sometimes discussed as an occasion for learners' self-reflection or as an opportunity for the exploration of a broader range of subjectivities, although there are a number of distinctions that can be drawn between these two notions. In terms of encouraging self-reflection among students, culture pedagogy is sometimes seen as an exercise in comparing familiar and less familiar cultures, and through such comparison, the idea is that students will necessarily contemplate and potentially reconsider their own thoughts, lives and experiences. In fact, the fact that ACTFL's standards include 'Comparisons' may lead to teachers view this as the primary teaching and learning process through which reflection might occur in the ML classroom. The **challenge of surface comparison** raised earlier, however, again becomes apparent. Articulating similarities and differences does not necessarily prompt self-reflection. Going further, calls to refocus the field's attention on language learners' experience of language education and the rise of poststructuralist theories of identity have prompted theorists and practitioners of culture pedagogy to consider learners as cultural beings and language and culture learning as a potential site of identity development and for the exploration of various subjectivities. Moran (2001), for example, accords considerable weight to a 'knowing oneself' dimension of cultural learning when compared with 'knowing about,' 'knowing how' and 'knowing why'. In that culture can act as a mirror for language learners and prompt self-reflection, Moran argues that cultural learning in the language classroom is largely undergirded by comparative and reflective activity. The emphasis on comparison across cultures is heavy in ML teaching practice in the United States, perhaps in part because the ACTFL standards and many states' standards documents explicitly refer to comparison. Comparison and reflection can in practice remain at a surface level, however. Theoretically, Kramsch (2009) offers a deeper consideration of language learners' subjectivities in relation to language learning. She explains how ML learning can prompt exploration of new, unfamiliar, imagined subjectivities – this is a step beyond the norm but represents a new path for the curriculum and instruction in ML education. It is not yet commonly applied and represents **the challenge of more deeply engaging subjectivities in culture-in-ML-education**. It is precisely this type of substantive engagement that analysis and discussion later in this book, illustrated by examples from Emilie's classroom, will strongly endorse.

At present, the field of ML education in the United States has taken a turn toward meaning-based notions of language and culture learning. Culture viewed as a semiotic and symbolic system and cultural learning viewed as gaining facility with interpretation and generation of meaning around cultural texts is apparent in the Modern Language Association's (2007) report that cites translingual and transcultural competence as goals of language education; in Kramsch's (2006) theory of symbolic competence as an extension of the field's pursuit of communicative competence; and in multiliteracies-based conceptions of ML education like Swaffar and Arens' (2005) and Allen and Paesani's (2010). These theoretical and conceptual developments in the field ask us to deal in a more head-on way with the complexity and fluidity of languages and cultures, to involve learners in exploring texts and contexts with more depth, and to focus not on culture as content but on cultural learning as the development of interpretive and generative meaning-making abilities. These approaches point to the **challenge of theorizing and implementing broader meaning-making approaches in ML education**; they also suggest concrete means for facing this challenge.

In considering the ways culture has been treated in US ML education in recent decades, one can certainly discern that culture has been treated more as content and less as context or process, and in few instances has it been defined as a discursive partner with language. Although some theoretical models do indeed recognize this relationship, practice has been slower to evolve.

Juxtaposed with the great deal of theorizing and proliferation of models for how cultural teaching and learning take place are teachers' understandings of what culture-in-ML-education is. There is still a great deal of variety in what teachers think and actually do when it comes to their planning and instruction. In general, ML teachers do seem to prioritize culture pedagogy; language educators are routinely found to rank cultural learning among their top goals (e.g. Fox & Diaz-Greenberg, 2006; Sercu *et al.*, 2005). But how teachers interpret culture pedagogy and then actually implement it in their classrooms is largely unknown. We have very little knowledge about this, although anecdotal evidence and experience in observing many classrooms would lead one to believe that culture pedagogy is not terribly deep. Jernigan and Moore (1997) do present one classroom-based study that examined culture teaching in university-level Portuguese courses, using the ACTFL standards having to do with culture as a lens through which to interpret their data. They found that while some instruction focused on cultural products and practices, very little focused on perspectives; that much of the teachers' culture pedagogy was unplanned and only emerged spontaneously as classroom interaction unfolded; and that, while approaches varied widely from instructor to instructor, cultural teaching seemed to be filtered in all cases through the individual teacher's cultural lenses. Although much more empirical research in classrooms is needed, it does appear that overall, there is a jarring disjuncture between a stated priority – that culture teaching is important in ML education – and actual practice. A further disjuncture is between the field's and teachers' conceptions of what students need to know and do in terms of languaculture and what students may prioritize themselves in terms of culture learning. Mangan (2008) and Mangan *et al.* (2014) have shown that university-level students in the United States prioritize ACTFL's Communities Standard above all others, for example, whereas language educators tend to prioritize Communication and Cultures Standards. If we see culture pedagogy as having to do with promoting students' ability to understand, access and participate in other communities, then teachers' and students' priorities could possibly align, but at present, it appears that teachers and learners are not on the same page.

Rethinking Meaning-Making in Modern Language Classrooms

The challenges of addressing culture in ML education are many. They include dealing with the overarching ideological environment in which ML education occurs in the United States, strong monolingual ideologies as well as ideologies about language teaching and learning that touch attitudes, classroom behaviors and wider professional practices such as teacher education. The reach of ideologies that serve to undermine the development of high levels of competency (however defined) and deep and meaningful understandings in ML education cannot be understated. There are also challenges at the level of US universities, where ML education is structured in such a way that culture is only thought to be appropriately addressed in upper-level (usually literature-oriented) courses and only after learners have achieved a certain level of proficiency that will allow them, it is believed, to access cultural meaning through the medium of the language being studied.

Further challenges abound at the level of classroom discourse and interaction. In university-level ML classrooms as well as those in earlier grade levels across the United States, conventional discursive practices surrounding ML education – sometimes heavy use of English rather than the ML being learned, overreliance on decontextualized language instruction and overuse of rote grammar exercises, or on the other hand, implementation of 'communicative' approaches, but only ones that go as far as engaging students in transactional type exchanges of information or assigning roles in a rigid manner – also pose several challenges when it comes to addressing culture in meaningful ways. There is promise in the proposals that some theorists have made with regard to the ways we might reenvision language learning and the practice of ML education, specifically those models that focus attention on how we might foster more deeply engaging meaning-making processes in ML education (these will be discussed in more detail in the next chapter), but the challenge still remains in putting these theories into practice. Although the models may suggest the kinds of semiotic processes that would shift ML education and create opportunities for learners to engage with language and meaning in new ways, they do not identify specific interactional practices or pedagogical approaches and techniques that are likely to facilitate such engagement.

All of these issues add up to a two-part challenge facing ML education when it comes to addressing culture in language teaching and learning: one part of the challenge has to do with a broad reconceptualization of intercultural learning – its point, its substance, its process and its relationship to language learning – and the shifts in orientation in the field that need to accompany such a reconceptualization; a second part of the challenge then has to do with the substantial task of defining and experimenting with what a more semiotic approach to culture-in-language-education looks like in practice. That is, we need to generate a range of curricular models, pedagogical approaches and techniques that engage learners in deep meaning-making, processes of identifying meaningful symbols, interpreting semiotic resources and representations, negotiating symbolic meanings, imagining alternate form-meaning relationships and crucially, coming to an awareness that one has in languages a multitude of choices available and that selection of forms will shape meanings. It is the main aim of this book to address both of these challenges. It attempts to promote a rethinking of meaning-making in ML education and to encourage a move away from ML learning as acquisition of a new, compartmentalized linguistic system toward ML learning as an expansion of individual learners' singular meaning-making repertoires, which may include multiple 'languages' but also all the variations and alternatives that exist within what we refer to as particular linguistic codes, such as English, French or Mandarin, for example. This is ultimately a vision of ML education as potentially imbuing learners with what Kramsch (2006, 2009) calls 'symbolic power'. Scarino (2014) explains this emphasis on the development of learners as multilinguals in the following way:

> [L]anguage learning can no longer be conceived as a monolingual act of acquiring a particular 'target' language and treating learners' languages as parallel systems; rather, it needs to be understood as a process of 'moving between' the diverse linguistic and cultural systems in the mix with learners drawing upon their entire repertoire in order

to make meaning. As such, the process of learning languages is always interlinguistic and intercultural with the goal of language learning becoming the development of 'functional multilingualism' (Byrnes, 2006, p. 244). (p. 388)

By drawing on theories and research outlined more in the next chapter, I propose a re-thinking of meaning-making in ML education that entails delving more deeply into development of intercultural and symbolic competences.

Overview of Chapters in this Book

This introductory chapter opened with my own story of struggling with culture pedagogy in a university-level French class and then described the ideological environment in which ML education takes place in the United States and the classroom interactions that have come to typify ML instruction. It then discussed the way culture has been addressed in ML education in the United States. Having identified some challenges of addressing culture from a ML teacher's point of view and from the standpoint of the broader field of ML education in the United States, I finally advanced the claim that a rethinking of meaning-making in classroom-based ML education is needed if learners are to become more interculturally competent and agentive users of the MLs they study.

In the remainder of this book, I situate in more precise theoretical terms and explain the methodological details of the study I carried out to explore how meaningful intercultural learning can happen (Chapters 2 and 3). In Chapters 4 and 5, I share data and analysis that illustrate the fine detail of the engagements and interactions that led to meaningful intercultural learning in Emilie's classroom. The last chapter of the book takes a broader view, articulating what the example of Emilie's class can teach us in terms of pushing theory forward and in terms of improving the practice of ML education.

Notes

(1) All references to study participants in this book are pseudonyms.
(2) There is really not much sense in speaking of anything but the intercultural in ML education, since what we often refer to as cultural learning or culture pedagogy is, necessarily, always relational. Teachers' and learners' subject positions and cultural belongings are inescapably enmeshed with the exploration of other subject positions and unfamiliar cultural ways of being; indeed, their familiar frames intermingle with and mediate any understanding of culturally different ones.

2 The Culture Learning Target: Engagement with Meaning Potentials

> *[My goal] it is more, yes, a knowledge of oneself through the learning of the knowledge of the other. It's more that. It's also affirming oneself. In class we have seen with Sydney, who at the beginning, because she wasn't at ease speaking, finally she realized that French is just a vehicle. But that also gave her the chance to express herself. It's that too. It's finding a voice. It's finding a place in the class but equally to then realize that one has a place in society.*
>
> Emilie, 12/06

Speaking about her goals for students and of one student in particular who exemplified the kind of learning and development she aims for through her pedagogical approach, Emilie describes Sydney. Sydney had entered the class with the weakest overall language proficiency but nonetheless contributed regularly to class discussions and used written French through the class's main project to express herself, however maladroitly at times. Emilie explains that Sydney claimed the right to speak and ultimately came to fashion a voice. She developed an ability to express herself and in so doing to affirm herself, to understand her own potential through use of the new language she was learning. This is the most important way that we can think of modern language (ML) education leading to the expansion of students' meaning potentials. Through the learning of another semiotic and symbolic system, students can learn to understand new meanings but also how to mean for themselves in new ways. Of course, such a shift requires engagement with meaning potentials in a second way, that is perhaps the foundation upon which claiming one's right to mean in another language is based. Students must also develop a sense of the meaning potentials that already exist in the languages they study – what more or less socially and culturally plausible meanings reside in the linguistic and other symbolic forms they encounter.

In this chapter, I continue making an argument for a rethinking of meaning-making in ML education in the United States and begin to lay groundwork for conceptualizing the processes leading to the expansion of meaning potentials in Emilie's classroom and other ML classrooms, which will be the focus of the remainder of the book. To this end, I first discuss foundational theory and more recent conceptual developments around intercultural and symbolic competences. A small but growing body of empirical research that examines the development of these competences among language users is equally instructive as we chart new terrain for meaning-making approaches to curriculum and instruction in ML education. With the support of some anchoring theories in this chapter, I advance the argument that the meaning-making we need in ML education has to do with prioritizing form-meaning relationships and language-culture connections in teaching and learning activity. This entails a more expansive view and a deepening of our notions of what meanings are in play and are possible in language classrooms. That is, ML classrooms can be places where linguistic and other semiotic forms and representations are routinely treated not simply in terms of their referential meanings but also explored more deeply for their broader personal and symbolic meaning potentials. Building on the critical analysis of dominant models of culture pedagogy in ML education in the United States in the previous chapter, I begin by discussing theories of the competence that culture pedagogy could aim to foster through ML education. With these concepts laid out, I discuss a particularly useful perspective on the relationship of language and meaning and how it might figure in pushing forward our treatment of culture pedagogy in ML education. Ultimately, it is a social semiotic view of ML education that I advance in this chapter and which frames the entire book.

Models of Intercultural and Symbolic Competence Informing Culture Pedagogy

Two particular models of the kind of competence that can be developed in ML education contexts and that stretch far beyond the ability to use language in instrumental ways are discussed below, first by outlining the main principles of these theories of competence and then by explaining what processes these theories explicitly state or more subtly imply with regard to how individuals might develop such competence. Both the theorists responsible for these models, Michael Byram and Claire Kramsch, have long engaged with the idea that much more could be cultivated through ML education than linguistically proficient speakers, and both have critiqued communicative language teaching as an approach that does not go far enough in taking up issues of culture, interculturality and the subjective and relational dimensions of language learning and use. Byram proposes the theory of intercultural communicative competence (ICC) and Kramsch offers third places – an adaptation of Bhabha's (1994) concept – and, more recently, symbolic competence as models of an expanded vision of competence for the field of ML education. Both draw on a broad range of theories to construct their models of competence and to ground their stances on the nature of interculturality in ML learning[1]. These source theories are referenced and acknowledged throughout my discussion, although they are not laid out in all of their rich detail. A similar approach is taken in the last section of the this chapter, which presents an ecological, social semiotic view of ML learning by drawing heavily on Leo van Lier's scholarship; he too formulates a theory addressed specifically to the field of language education, namely in his 2004a book, but grounds this in a synthesis of wide-ranging theoretical work[2].

Intercultural communicative competence[3]

In earlier work, Byram (1997) writes that ML teaching is 'concerned with communication but this has to be understood as more than the exchange of information and sending of messages, which has dominated "communicative language teaching" in recent years' (p. 3). When communication is considered to be the transaction of information and as being limited to a narrow set of procedures and contexts, learner roles and actions are also constrained. Byram (1997) goes on to make the argument that learning a language is about more than grammar and vocabulary, or even the ability to perform in communicative situations or apply politeness formulae, which are typically the ways of addressing culture learning under a communicative approach – by treating cultural knowledge as declarative and procedural. In his view, culture learning in ML education does have to do with communicative exchange, but it also, and more centrally, concerns the ability to relate to others. He writes,

> successful 'communication' is not judged solely in terms of the efficiency of information exchange. It is focused on establishing and maintaining relationships...[E]fficacy of communication depends upon using language to demonstrate one's willingness to relate. (p. 3)

In relating to others, there is naturally an encounter with difference. Yet, with physical and cultural distance separating many ML learners and users of the language being studied, truly engaging students with otherness has sometimes been conceived of as a primary challenge in ML education. Byram et al. (2001), however, explain:

> In the foreign language classroom, what was often seen as a problem in teaching the cultural dimension, the lack of opportunity to travel to a foreign country and society, should not inhibit teachers and learners at all. This is not because new technology can 'replace' first-hand experience, but rather because the cultural dimension has become the intercultural dimension. In other words, it is recognised that it is not the teacher's task to provide comprehensive information and to try to bring the foreign society into the classroom for learners to observe and experience vicariously. The task is rather to facilitate learners' interaction with some small part of another society and its cultures, with the purpose of relativising learners' understanding of their own cultural values, beliefs and behaviours, and encouraging them to investigate for themselves the otherness around them, either in their immediate physical environment or in their engagement with otherness which internationalisation and globalisation have brought into their world. (p. 3)

Byram's theory of intercultural communicative competence is a componential model that involves knowledge, skills, attitudes and ultimately, action (see Figure 2.1 below).

The knowledge dimension of ICC, as Byram presents it, is construed in a much broader fashion than the way cultural knowledge is typically treated in the practice of ML education. Rather than a collection of trivia, 'food and facts' (Fox & Diaz-Greenberg, 2006: 406) and 'heros and holidays' (Nieto, 2002: 27), knowledge in Byram's (1997) model, or 'knowledge of social groups and their products and practices in one's own and in one's interlocutor's country, and of the general processes of societal and individual interactions' (p. 51), encompasses such areas as

	Skills interpret and relate (savoir comprendre)	
Knowledge of self and other; of interaction: individual and societal (savoirs)	Education political education critical cultural awareness (savoir s'engager)	Attitudes relativising self valuing other (savoir être)
	Skills discover and/or interact (savoir apprendre/faire)	

Figure 2.1 'Factors in intercultural communication' (Byram, 1997: 34)

- The national memory of one's own country and how its events are related to and seen from the perspective of one's interlocutor's country.
- Social distinctions and their principal markers, in one's own country and one's interlocutor's.
- Institutions, and perceptions of them, which impinge on daily life within one's own and one's interlocutor's country and which conduct and influence relationships between them. (p. 51)

The skills dimensions of the model are grounded in inquiry, interaction and interpretation, through which learners analyze the written, interactional and other texts they encounter and engage in producing; seek out information in order to interact with a text or interlocutor; and, in the process, reflect on their own and others' positioning, as represented in the attitudes dimension. Put differently, ICC involves a set of broadly defined 'knowledges', including the ability to interpret and relate in intercultural encounters (i.e. *savoir comprendre*), to manage in situations where existing knowledge is insufficient (i.e. to discover or *savoir apprendre*), and to 'recognise significant phenomena in a foreign environment and to elicit their meanings and connotations, and their relationship to other phenomena' (*savoir faire*) (p. 38). Knowledge and skills in Byram's model are all articulated around a core 'political education' or 'critical cultural awareness,' defined as 'an ability to evaluate critically and on the basis of explicit criteria, perspectives, practices and products in one's own and other cultures and countries' (Byram, 1997: 53). This capacity to engage goes beyond awareness, consideration or appreciation to suggest possible social action as well. Critical cultural awareness, then, is not merely a state of mind or a particular disposition; it is the capacity (and desire) for action and potentially for change. Overall, developing knowledge, skills, certain dispositions and awareness can promote, in Byram's mind, a kind of engaged citizenship (not limited to the nation-state, of course), an ability to be transformed and to be transformative in one's social and intercultural communities.

How ICC develops in the ML classroom, in Byram's (1991) view, is represented in Figure 2.2. He argues that all four of the processes included in the figure should be involved in ML education. There is at once a need for experience and reflection on that experience if learners are to gain intercultural competence and deeper understandings of themselves, and there is an alternating focus on language and culture. Specifically, Byram (1991) posits language learning, language awareness, cultural awareness and cultural experience as the essential elements of the language and culture teaching process, implying that these are also the building blocks

36 Intercultural Learning in Modern Language Education

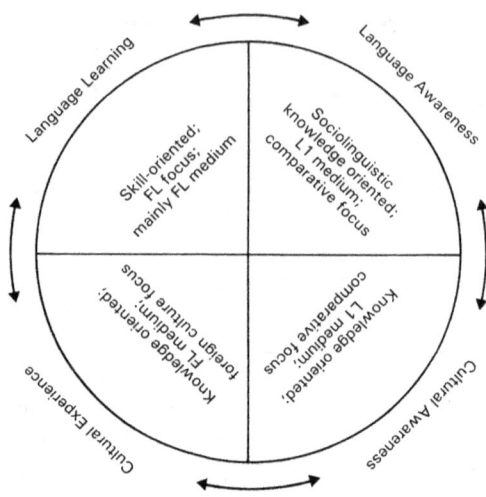

Figure 2.2 'The language and culture teaching process' (Byram, 1991: 20)

of intercultural learning among students. Language learning, as it exists in the British educational system that Byram writes about, in many ways resembles approaches to language learning that are prevalent in the United States. Beyond the marginal status that culture is accorded in textbooks and classroom instruction, Byram (1991) writes that deeper theoretical problems are evident in language pedagogy: 'Communicative competence is too frequently interpreted – especially in beginners and intermediate stages – as a capacity to fit appropriate language to specific transactions' (p. 18). This is a view of communicative competence that excludes social and cultural context in its diversity and complexity and that positions learners exclusively as consumers and tourists. While the communicative approach has made several worthy contributions to language pedagogy through its focus on authentic language and the encouragement of use of the language as a means of acquisition, it has failed to account for the social and cultural nature of language in any comprehensive way (Byram, 1991: 21). While this approach has managed to take 'some note of the social character of language embodied in the notion of a speech act,' an overwhelming concern for linguistic outcomes and proficiency persists (p. 21). In current practice, in both the British and the US contexts, such an approach to language instruction fails to adequately acknowledge the relationship between language and culture, and in so doing, greatly hinders the possibilities for intercultural learning and development in classrooms.

To remedy this issue, Byram (1991) proposes three other dimensions to accompany language learning, where all components work in concert to provide a more comprehensive experience and awareness for language learners. The language awareness component, in many ways, encourages learners to become sociolinguists, in that the goal is to 'arouse curiosity in their linguistic environment, to make them aware of their own linguistic competence,' in order to recognize the way that language and social life are intertwined and also to set the stage for comparison with a target language culture (p. 22). Part of this realization is that 'linguistic formulae are the surface indicators of native speakers' cultural knowledge, which is itself largely unconscious and difficult to articulate' (p. 23). Byram's model then begins to explicitly link language and culture in an attempt to understand both; this book offers a complementary conception of the language-culture relationship by way of meaning potentials, explaining more deeply how linguistic forms can function as surface markers of cultural insiders' shared knowledge but also showing how cultural forms are polysemous and cultural meanings are flexible and not only owned or produced by native speakers.

Similar to the language awareness component, the cultural awareness dimension serves to both support language learning and facilitate a 'general understanding of the nature of culture' (Byram, 1991: 23). This component is focused on 'the question of change from monocultural to intercultural competence' (p. 23–4), and in this phase, learners are likened to ethnographers who attempt to gain an insider's view of culture. However, Byram is careful to note that learners should not only be involved in explicating a foreign culture in the way that ethnographers are sometimes thought to do but should rather take on the role of both ethnographer and informant, allowing their own knowledge and experience to serve as the vantage point from which they can gain a new perspective; this is akin to Kramsch's third place discussed below, which is based in neither a native nor an 'other' culture entirely. Byram (1991) explains, 'In the process of comparison from two viewpoints there lies the possibility of attaining an Archimedean leverage on both cultures, thereby acquiring new schemata and an intercultural competence' (p. 24–5). Achieving such a position necessarily involves learner identities, and Byram addresses this by writing that culture learning is about seeing oneself more clearly. For the cultural awareness component, Byram suggests that only the learner's first language be used in discussing and debriefing after cultural experiences in order for there to be more ease and depth in reflection, and he argues that one of the reasons that the cultural awareness component is so essential is that during cultural experiences themselves, there is rarely the time to reflect while still trying to engage in interactions in real time. Reflection, though, depending on students' proficiency level and the nature of the pedagogical activity designed to facilitate reflection, could quite feasibly occur through the medium of the ML.

According to Byram (1991), cultural experience is 'not simply an opportunity to apply or put into practice the abstract cultural study and the rehearsal of linguistic skills' that learners may have been engaged in during their classroom-based learning but also 'another kind of learning, through direct experience, of the relationship between language and culture, of the way in which language is part of culture and also embodies the whole' (p. 26). The idea is not to transform learners into native speakers through their direct experience of the culture but to encourage a 'suspension of disbelief and judgment' that has been 'prepared for in the Cultural Awareness component' and that later will be analyzed there as well. The reciprocal relations among components is particularly salient here. While learners are encouraged to see culture from another perspective, it is not the aim of intercultural learning to force a categorical decision that abandons one cultural identity for another. Byram warns that the cultural experience component should not be seen as the final step toward intercultural competence. Instead, direct experience of the target culture is 'an integral contribution to the whole process which is prior to, simultaneous with, and subsequent to other components' (p. 27). Of course, what constitutes 'direct experience' is open to debate, and especially in the time that has elapsed since Byram wrote in 1991, access to new languacultures has greatly expanded as a result of technological development; however, social life in a globalized environment has also impacted when and where one might engage directly with a target-language culture and how one might even define what a target language culture is.

Byram's componential model of ICC has been very influential in the field, even if many ML education classrooms still do not specifically apply these notions. Yet, what specific processes of experience and awareness-raising support development of ICC and how exactly language professionals might facilitate interactions that foster these processes in the ML classroom remain to be elaborated. Upon doing so both theoretically and empirically, Byram's early model of the language and culture teaching process can be updated to more deeply address how the capacity for individual and social action and transformation might arise as a result of developing ICC in the ML classroom.

In recent years, Byram has explained the ways in which his model still calls for further development. This book focuses on processes for developing

ICC and speaks to the evaluation of ICC as well, especially with regard to critical cultural awareness/*savoir s'engager*, the core of Byram's model, which, he writes quite recently, is the place where most pushing forward of theory needs to happen. Specifically, Byram (2012) has called for more explicit linking of the development of language awareness and ICC on the one hand and the development of cultural awareness on the other. He posits that language awareness includes the levels of 'social analysis – the use of language in society – and self-analysis, analysis of the significance of language and culture for the self' (Byram, 2012: 8–9). Arguably, development of cultural awareness similarly occurs at both of these levels as well. I argue that studying specific interactions and patterns of teaching and learning activity over time, in which learners explore form-meaning relationships and deepen their engagements with meaning potentials (especially symbolic ones) can begin to clarify both practically and theoretically what development of this complex competence entails and can look like in real classrooms. The intention of presenting an analysis of teaching and learning activity from one classroom in detail, then, is not only to illustrate what the development of some of Byram's dimensions of ICC looks like in practice but also to push theory forward in the way he calls for.

Explicitly identifying what is still missing in the theorizing of ICC, Byram (2012) writes,

> It is noticeable that only a small minority of the models [of ICC] have explicit reference to language and language competence, and those that do, including mine, do not clarify the relationships between linguistic competences and cultural competences, the language-culture nexus, as realised in people's psychology. What we need is a model which represents language and culture competence holistically and shows the relationship between language competence – including language awareness – and intercultural competence, including cultural awareness. Such a model should be produced for pedagogical purposes, i.e. it should help teachers and learners to clarify what needs to be taught and learnt, and in such a model, the concept of awareness would be crucial. (p. 7)

In such a model, other types of relationships than just that between language and cultural awareness are likely necessary to be clarified. For example, bridging the individual and the social, connecting personal and cultural meanings or storylines and linking across scales of time and space are likely to be relevant. Once a model which elaborates these relationships more deeply is in place, a question still remains about how stakeholders in ML education classrooms might go about teaching and learning in such a way that interconnected awarenesses are developed and then put into action for various purposes and experienced in various ways. It is not just the *what* that needs to be clarified in a revised model of ICC but also the *how*.

Kramsch and symbolic competence

Another attractive model for thinking about the outcomes and potential target for culture pedagogy comes from Claire Kramsch's work in ML education. She has long been involved in shaping notions of how culture figures in the field and what processes underlie intercultural learning. Her early writing in this domain (Kramsch, 1993, 1998) connects language, culture and context and posits cultural meaning as relational, discursive and dialogic. Over time, she has continued to refine her model, and although still rooted in her foundational work on cultural meaning and intercultural learning, it has taken a decided turn in recent years toward the symbolic (Kramsch, 2006, 2009; Kramsch & Whiteside, 2008).

In her seminal work on culture learning, Kramsch (1993) first lays out how context, texts (conceived broadly), discourse and dialogism are relevant to the language learning enterprise, and then proposes a model of culture learning that is grounded in viewing culture as 'the product of self and other perceptions' (p. 205), a formulation that implies a reliance on interpretive practices in order to construct views of the world. In her discussion of the centrality of dialogism in ML and culture learning, Kramsch (1993) draws heavily on Bakhtin (1986) and asserts that dialogue across cultures 'is a "liminal" experience that creates a special place and time at the boundaries between two views of the world. It involves a sudden grasp of difference and an instantaneous understanding of the relationship between self and other' (p. 30). Kramsch (1993) claims that in language and culture teaching, moving beyond a 'single-voiced discourse' wherein learners attempt to approximate 'the ideal native speaker, speaking with one voice in all situations, through a universal linguistic code' (p. 27) toward dialogue opens a whole range of new possibilities for language learners. Elsewhere, Kramsch (1995) has also described this process of entering into dialogue with the din of voices present in another language by writing 'In order to teach a foreign language as oppositional practice, learners have to be addressed not as deficient monoglossic enunciators, but as potentially heteroglossic narrators' (p. 90). In addition to highlighting the dialogic approach to culture learning that might be adopted in the ML classroom, Kramsch here introduces the notion of narrative and the centrality of authoring and story in meaning-making, and the potential for language learners to draw on the many voices available to them in learning a new language to narrate the world from a different point of view, or at least to come to the awareness that other individuals and groups do so. Indeed, Kramsch (1993) recognizes that the language learner should be given the opportunity to develop as 'a social and an individual speaker' (p. 28). Notions of dialogue, voice and narrative, then, are central in Kramsch's theory of the culture learning process, as are imagination and perspective. These constructs all became quite central during the analysis of teaching and learning interactions in Emilie's classroom, as will become apparent in later chapters.

Recognizing a general shift toward viewing language learning as a social practice, Kramsch (1993) asserts that 'meaning is relational' (p. 205) and that culture learning necessarily entails a consideration of both familiar (what she calls C1) and target-language (C2) cultures. She also emphasizes that culture learning must be seen as a process and that this process 'applies itself to understanding foreignness and "otherness"' (p. 206). For Kramsch, this process necessarily involves conflict, something which may be uncomfortable for language teachers and learners alike. She writes that her approach

> is more interested in fault lines than in smooth landscapes, in the recognition of complexity and in the tolerance of ambiguity, not in the search for clear yardsticks of competence or insurances against pedagogical malpractice. It is convinced that understanding and shared meaning, when it occurs, is a small miracle, brought about by a leap of faith that we call 'communication across cultures'. (p. 2)

Part of dealing with complexity and ambiguity in teaching culture is going beyond just national categories, which are increasingly difficult to speak of anyway (as Risager, 2007 makes clear), to include dimensions such as age, class, gender, region and other markers of difference in social life and to more openly embrace the hybridities and fluidities of modern-day cultural identifications and belongings. In order to teach culture, Kramsch argues, instructors must be willing to abandon the view that culture is somehow uniquely embodied in literary works to include cultural accounts located in other disciplines, such as ethnography, sociolinguistics and other social sciences (p. 206). As a member of the Modern Language Association's Ad Hoc Committee on Foreign Languages, Kramsch was also involved in formulating the recommendation that 'cultural narratives that appear in every kind of expressive form' be analyzed more frequently in ML classrooms (Ad Hoc Committee, 2007: 238). Kramsch's approach then deals with culture learning by advocating a dialogic perspective inherited from Bakhtin (1986), who viewed all language as full of voices and hence full of various meanings, but she clearly views these voices as articulated at individual as well as cultural levels.

Another important concept for Kramsch, as she draws especially on Barthes' work on myth (1957), is 'cultural imagination', which forms from an accretion of historical events and literary and journalistic texts, as well as interpretations and public discourse surrounding all of these over long periods of time. There are cultural crystallizations that form the reference points and myths that characterize and serve as meaning-making material for any given society at any particular point in time. This cultural imagination, according to Kramsch, is just as real to people as actual events themselves. The idea of a cultural imagination points to the interpretive nature of this shaping of experience into myths, as Kramsch calls them. In her model of culture learning, where perception rather than any objective cultural 'truth' plays the central role, Kramsch (1993) enumerates a series of steps that constitute a path to 'cross-cultural understanding':

(1) Reconstruct the context of production and reception of the text within the foreign culture (C2, C2').
(2) Construct with the foreign learners their own context of reception, i.e. find an equivalent phenomenon in C1 and construct that C1 phenomenon with its own network of meanings (C1, C1').
(3) Examine the way in which C1' and C2' contexts in part determine C1" and C2", i.e. the way each culture views the other.
(4) Lay the ground for a dialogue that could lead to change. (p. 210)

The visual representation of cultures (which are themselves recognized as multifaceted aggregates) and perceptions of cultures that Kramsch discusses is reproduced in Figure 2.3.

Developing an 'intercultural stance' (Kramsch, 1999), according to this model, depends on building up understandings of both familiar and other cultures and the ways in which they interact and see each other. A teacher's first step, she suggests, when introducing any cultural text or phenomenon, is to help learners to reconstruct the context of production and of reception in the other culture (C2). C2 here refers to the context of production or the 'real' other culture, and C2' represents the context of reception or the environment in which a text would be encountered, interpreted and perceived by members of the other culture. In her example of an analysis of an American Coke commercial by Russian teachers of English, Kramsch (1993) explains that this first step toward intercultural understanding would involve identification and discussion of 'cultural codes' (p. 214) as well as 'generic codes' (p. 216). Cultural codes, as Kramsch describes them, are the myths and narratives that make up a cultural imagination. Generic codes have to do with the genre of a text (in this case an advertisement) and the conventions and symbols that are associated with it. Kramsch explains that this first step of specifying and reconstructing C2 contexts could also include the examination of other texts, resounding with other voices and perspectives on cultural codes, what we might qualify as counternarratives, or analysis of related genres.

In step two of the process of examining a text, focus shifts to the learner's native culture. Kramsch (1993) writes: 'Besides trying to understand the foreign culture on its own terms, learners have to be aware of their own cultural myths and realities that ease or impede their understanding of the foreign imagination' (p. 216). In the analysis of the Coke commercial, Kramsch asked the groups of teachers she was working with to create an equivalent commercial based on a Russian cultural context. One of the main results of this kind of creation is that learners must attempt to home in on the deeply held codes of their own cultures, a process which can lead to self-discovery.

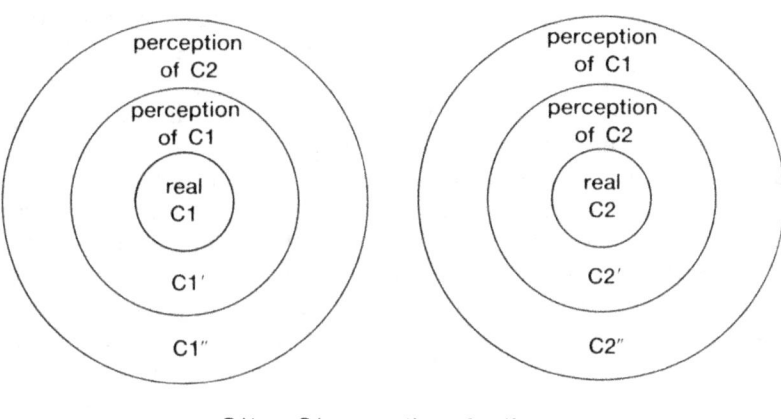

Figure 2.3 Path to cross-cultural understanding (Kramsch, 1993: 208)

As an illustration of the third step in developing intercultural understanding through analysis of cultural texts, Kramsch (1993) asked American teachers of German and a group of German visitors to the United States to recreate the same Coke ad for a German audience. What this exercise revealed was a certain level of projection of one's own cultural values onto another cultural context. The American group projected 'the degree of Americanization they perceived in German society and their own American underestimation of class consciousness' (p. 222) by including German soccer players and rock musicians drinking Coke. As Kramsch explains, 'in Germany, most soccer fans and fans of rock 'n' roll belong to a social class that draws its self-esteem from drinking beer, not wine or Coca-Cola' (p. 222). What this exercise makes clear is the degree to which our own self-perceptions contribute to our perceptions of others and the way that our perceptions of others can be, consequently, totally off the mark.

All of these steps, illustrated by the work that Kramsch has carried out with groups of teachers, are meant to create an environment in which intercultural dialogue can occur and are ostensibly exportable to classroom settings for use with language learners. Very little classroom-based empirical research, however, investigates processes of cultural learning in a way that uncovers the dialogic engagement learners have with cultures, particular cultural texts, cultural myths or cultural meaning, or the interculturality that might emerge through these processes. Kramsch does raise the question of whether analysis of other cultures and of one's own can fruitfully occur if one stays firmly planted in his or her own C1. This is where Kramsch (1993) introduces the notion of third places and the idea that language learning is, or at least can be, about personal and social change, a view that is increasingly prevalent in critical approaches to language learning (Graman, 1988; Kanpol, 1999; Osborn, 2006; Pennycook, 1990; Reagan & Osborn, 2002). The model necessitates 'a third perspective that would enable learners to take both an insider's and an outsider's view on C1 and C2. It is precisely that third place that cross-cultural education should seek to establish' (Kramsch, 1993: 210). Central to the accessing of third places and potential transformation is dialogue:

> Through dialogue and the search for each other's understanding, each person tries to see the world through the other's eyes without losing sight of him or herself. The goal is not a balance of opposites, or a moderate pluralism of opinions but a paradoxical, irreducible confrontation that may change one in the process. (p. 231)

What exactly the third place looks like, Kramsch (1993) explains, will vary for every individual:

> For some...it will be a small poem by Pushkin that will, twenty years later, help them make sense out of a senseless personal situation. For others...it will be a small untranslatable Japanese proverb that they will all of a sudden remember, thus enabling them for a moment to see the world from the point of view of their Japanese business partner and save a floundering business transaction. For most, it will be the stories they will tell of these cross-cultural encounters, the meanings they will give them through these tellings and the dialogues that they will have with people who had had similar experiences. (p. 257)

Kramsch offers illustrative examples of how the culture learning process could unfurl from her work with teachers and provides examples to illustrate the types of interaction that fit with her proposed model. Kramsch's work is notable since it both proposes a theory-based model of culture teaching and learning and suggests specific ways that it can be applied in real classrooms, yet research is needed that analyzes how actually occurring classroom interactions fit with her model. Moreover, much more classroom-based research focusing on the ways in which learners come to engage with a variety of cultural texts, identify narratives in their own and other cultures and construct meaning through their own narrative practices is sorely needed if we are to be more precise in defining intercultural learning processes, intercultural stances and thirdness in the ML context. In addition, more exploration of the ways that teachers can and perhaps already do attempt to guide their students toward a third place would be useful. While Kramsch's work provides examples of the way one might follow her proposed steps toward interculturality, more detailed analysis of classroom discourse and interaction, such as the analysis presented in the later chapters of this book, will extend Kramsch's research and theories.

Over time, Kramsch's original emphasis on creating third places in ML education has evolved into a more fully developed articulation of symbolic competence. Revisiting and refining the now very popular notion of third place, Kramsch (2011) writes, 'the notion of third culture must be seen less as a place than as a symbolic process of meaning-making that sees beyond the dualities of national languages (L1-L2) and national cultures (C1-C2)' (p. 355). Symbolic competence, still a movement beyond transactional and instrumental notions of communicative competence taken up in ML education and still based in many of the same foundational ideas as her work on third spaces, takes up some new dimensions of learners' communication and engagement with language and takes into account much more substantively the world of communication in which learners now live. That is, Kramsch (2006) stresses that the world language learners now inhabit does not always allow for the kind of 'straightforward talk in a brief, concise and sincere manner' (p. 250) that communicative approaches to language teaching have prepared them for; rather, in an environment of vast interconnectedness, the increased mobility of people, and accompanying shifts in notions of space, place, identity and cultural affiliation, learners need more fluid and symbolic competences; the ability to understand meaning-making practices, not just to make more or less conventionalized meanings; and the ability to turn meaning-making to their own purposes. Kramsch's reformulation is grounded in a specific view of language as symbolic. Referencing a classic tension between the orderliness and simultaneous flexibility and creative potential of language(s), she writes that

> Words uttered are symbols, whose meaning can be found in the textbook or the dictionary, and ciphers for other meanings: performatives, rituals, myths that index larger, factual or imagined realities and that are inserted into a social context in order to act upon that context by the sheer power of their enunciation. For foreign language learners, the symbolic nature of language is enhanced as connotations multiply across codes and additional meanings thrive in the interstices of different linguistic systems. (2009: 12–13)

She writes that learners face choices in learning and using new languages and that they are caught up in the conflict between two sources of symbolic power:

> As signs shared by a social community, symbols derive their meaning from the force of social convention. Learners of a foreign language have to adhere to the grammatical and lexical conventions of the symbolic systems they are learning and to the social conventions of its use. By conforming to these conventions they are given the symbolic power to enter a historical speech community and be accepted as members of that community. However, such membership has its price: grammaticality, social acceptability, and cultural appropriateness put limits on what an individual may say or write. On the other hand, the use of symbols triggers subjective resonances both in the users and in the receivers. It reproduces a speaker's sense of self and enables him or her to act upon the symbolic order of the speech community. (Kramsch, 2009: 6–7)

Furthermore, Kramsch's most recent work on culture-in-language-education reconceptualizes culture when compared with her earlier notions; today, culture is less readily identified as residing in stable institutions, practices or groups. Instead, culture is better seen as 'a mental toolkit of subjective metaphors, affectivities, historical memories, entextualizations and transcontextualizations of experience, with which we make meaning of the world around us and share that meaning with others' (Kramsch, 2011: 355). Her notion of cultures is still anchored in shared discourse, but rather than thinking of speech or discourse communities as having cultures and sharing meanings which 'both enabl[e] and limi[t] the range of possible meanings constructed by the individual' (Kramsch, 2011: 355), Kramsch's more recent conception of symbolic competence relates to discourse worlds that are more broadly conceived and that are more flexible. In this view of culture as discourse and as being anchored in meaning-making,

> the development of intercultural competence is not only a question of tolerance towards or empathy with others, of understanding them in their cultural context, or of understanding oneself and the other in terms of one another. It is also a matter of looking beyond words and actions and embracing multiple, changing and conflicting discourse worlds, in which 'the circulation of values and identities across cultures, the inversions, even inventions of meaning, [are] often hidden behind a common illusion of effective communication' (Kramsch, Zarate & Levy 2008: 15). While communicative competence was based on an assumption of understanding based on common goals and common interests, intercultural competence presupposes a lack of understanding due to divergent subjectivities and historicities. By defining culture as discourse, we are looking at the interculturally competent individual as a symbolic self that is constituted by symbolic systems like language, as well as by systems of thought and their symbolic power. (Kramsch, 2011: 356)

The symbolic competence learners need in the context of this type of cultural belonging, Kramsch (2011) asserts, requires attention to symbolic representation, symbolic action and symbolic power. Specifically,

> As a symbolic system, discourse is at once:
>
> - Symbolic Representation. It denotes and connotes a stable reality through lexical and grammatical structures (e.g. Saussure, 1916/1959; Benveniste, 1966). These structures are to be seen as conceptual

categories, idealized cognitive models of reality that correspond to prototypes and stereotypes through which we apprehend ourselves and others (e.g. Lakoff, 1987; Fauconnier & Turner, 2002). Discourse as symbolic representation focuses on what words say and what they reveal about the mind.
- Symbolic Action. Through its performatives, its speech acts, speech genres, facework strategies and symbolic interaction rituals (e.g. Austin, 1962; Goffman, 1967) discourse as symbolic action focuses on what words do and what they reveal about human intentions.
- Symbolic Power. Through the intertextual relations it establishes with other discourses, the moral values it expresses, the subjectivities and historical continuities (or discontinuities) it constructs, discourse as symbolic power (e.g. Weedon, 1987; Bourdieu, 1991; Butler, 1997) focuses on what words index and what they reveal about social identities, individual and collective memories, emotions and aspirations. (p. 357)

Symbolic competence, then, involves becoming adept at recognizing, analyzing, questioning and exploiting symbolic representations, actions and power, and it relies on such principles as production of complexity (the symbolic use of language as access to alternate possibilities and ways of being in and seeing the world), tolerance of ambiguity (or the inherent contradictions and tensions supported by language) and focus on form as meaning (rather than form simply naming a priori meanings). Taken together,

> These three components of a symbolic competence should lead teachers to view language and culture, that is, grammar and style, vocabulary and its cultural connotations, texts and their points of view, as inseparable. In turn, language learners should slowly understand that communicative competence does not derive from information alone, but from the symbolic power that comes with the interpretation of signs and their multiple relations to other signs. (Kramsch, 2006: 252)

Attention to subjectivity, historicity and performativity and the ability to reframe are also central to Kramsch's formulation of symbolic competence (Kramsch & Whiteside, 2008). Symbolic competence is 'a mindset that can create "relationships of possibility" or affordances, but only if the individual learns to see him/herself through his/her own embodied history and subjectivity and through the history and subjectivity of others' (Kramsch & Whiteside, 2008: 668). Development of symbolic competence, then, is about exploration of the self, the self in relation to others and the world, as well as a whole range of imagined and possible selves, and this involves reflection:

> The self that is engaged in intercultural communication is a symbolic self that is constituted by symbolic systems like language as well as by systems of thought and their symbolic power. This symbolic self is the most sacred part of our personal and social identity; it demands for its well-being careful positioning, delicate facework, and the ability to frame and re-frame events. (Kramsch, 2011: 354)

Decentering is a major element of this subjective and reflective dimension of cultivating symbolic competence. Yet, it remains to be seen on a practical level how instruction in ML classrooms especially will be able to engage learners in framing and reframing, positioning and repositioning as well as deep exploration of both familiar and unfamiliar subjectivities and historicities.

Development of symbolic competence is also necessarily a process that involves critical and ideological dimensions. Ultimately, symbolic competence relies on a concept of language and other semiotic systems as a repertoire of alternatives, from the level of particular forms to registers and entire linguistic codes (what we familiarly call 'languages'), and the idea that making choices from among these alternatives is not at all a neutral task. Development of symbolic competence would then have to do with cultivation of a 'variationist frame of mind adapted to our post-modern times' (Kramsch, 2008: 403), or a recognition that many alternatives exist in making meanings, but it also requires sensitivity to what impact choices among alternatives might have in particular interactions. This is a kind of critical awareness and critical action in language use that is largely unaddressed in current ML education.

What Kramsch's work in recent years illustrates is that approaches to the theorizing of intercultural learning in ML education have become increasingly complex and have attempted to take into account the experience of the learner and the complexity of culture and language in ways that previous models and approaches did not. Both Kramsch's and Byram's work advance our thinking about intercultural learning and development of symbolic competence precisely by focusing more intently on meaning-making as central to the enterprise. Kramsch's model of symbolic competence may address meaning-making more explicitly than Byram's; however, his recent scholarship clearly articulates the need to build stronger connections in our theory building between forms and meanings, awareness and experiences, and individual and collective levels of all of these. While both models have much to offer as we think about intercultural learning in ML classrooms as the potential growth of learners' meaning-making potentials and expansion of their meaning-making repertoires, especially with regard to the learning processes they suggest might underlie development of these competences, neither get at the specific interactional or instructional processes that are thought to facilitate this kind of learning.

Theories of what processes are involved in intercultural learning and what it means to be interculturally or symbolically competent continue to be developed; however, the realm of theory is now put aside in order to focus on the actual lives of those who participate in ML education. While both Byram's and Kramsch's models are based on a consideration of the classroom environment, looking to real teaching and learning sites offers a wholly different perspective on culture teaching and learning than does theory. The studies reviewed in the following section help to situate the study reported in the rest of this book.

Empirical Studies of the Development of Intercultural and Symbolic Competences in Modern Language Education

Intercultural and symbolic competences as goals of ML education have to some degree marked professional dialogue and impacted teaching practices. Yet, ML education could be positioned even more clearly as a site for working with meaning potentials and expanding meaning-making repertoires. In order to do this, a great deal more empirical research needs to be conducted that will clarify the processes that can occur in a range of possible teaching and learning interactions and the various pedagogical or curricular approaches that will facilitate growth of personal meaning-making potentials among learners as they tap into the shared, although dynamic, meaning-making potentials of the languages they are studying. Research will also need to apply rigorous methods and standards for making claims about what constitutes adequate evidence that the development of intercultural competence, and symbolic competence specifically, has taken place for individuals or groups of learners.

It is notable that there has been far more theorizing about culture pedagogy than empirical study of what transpires in classrooms that would allow us to gauge the ways that culture teaching and learning in ML education actually occur (Byram & Feng, 2004). There are, however, a few classroom-based studies that offer some initial insight into what interactional processes might be at the core of developing symbolic and intercultural competences in ML education. In one case, a study focuses on how a classroom environment fails to foster meaningful engagement with intercultural learning; a handful of other studies offer a contrasting view in laying out the way learners access and make meaning as they engage with cultural representations and texts and in intercultural dialogue.

Collings' (2007) study of a university-level Russian classroom advances the claim that regardless of a teacher's efforts to incorporate culture, students resisted and rejected her pedagogical agenda in favor of a focus on linguistic form. The researcher explains this apparent rejection of culture in the Russian classroom in terms of students' expectations for classroom discourse patterns. That is, when the teacher tried to engage students in 'authentic conversation' about a particular Russian poet and the importance of poetry in Russian culture, for example, she suggests that students likely experienced this as a radical departure from the initiation-response-evaluation structure more typical in most classroom discourse. Collings argues that departures from ML classroom discourse norms were therefore rejected and resisted by students, and in the end, they saw their Russian classroom as a place for focusing on linguistic forms and developing accuracy, whereas study abroad in Russia was viewed as the appropriate site for engaging with culture. However, it should be noted that based on Collings' descriptions, the teacher's attempts to inject culture into her classroom seemed largely unplanned and not embedded into the curriculum in any significant way. Furthermore, it does not appear that students' cultural learning was assessed in any way in this course. Given these factors, it is perhaps understandable that students did not have reason to view culture as central to the content or discourse of their Russian class. While Collings' work importantly points out that students are likely to arrive in ML classes with certain expectations – perhaps based on previous language learning experiences – of what content will figure as central in the class's activity and of what shape classroom discourse will take, it is also necessary to look critically to the curricular and pedagogical environments for evidence of what kinds of interactions and learning they actually afford. In this case, it does not appear that the classroom environment itself was designed to promote intercultural learning, and as a result, the teacher's efforts to add culture in on occasion were not taken up by students.

In some of my own previous work on cultural learning in ML classrooms, I have examined the identification of cultural reference points and interpretive activity surrounding classroom participants' engagement with cultural texts (Kearney, 2008, 2009, 2012). From that work, I have hypothesized several processes that are part of intercultural learning in ML classrooms. These processes include:

(1) gaining access to the frames of reference that others use in interpreting and shaping their individual and collective experience of the world;
(2) coming to an awareness of what a point of view is—a kind of cultural tool that mediates our experience of the world;
(3) taking on unfamiliar perspectives and attempting to view the world, at least temporarily, through these new lenses;
(4) in a reflective movement, denaturalizing one's own familiar cultural perspective and potentially seeing oneself as others do. (Kearney, 2010: 334)

These processes share much with Kramsch's (2006, 2011) postulation of what is involved in development of symbolic competence. Specifically, Kearney (2009) looks closely at how a teacher supports students in interpreting a visual text and how engagement in interpretation of cultural texts can lead to 'perspective-taking,' which is defined elsewhere (Kearney, 2012) as:

> a shift of point of view at various levels of language and meaning, through which [ML learners] can gain awareness of the existence of different meaning-making resources and become more adept in interpretation of language-, culture-, and context-specific meanings. Through perspective-taking, though, they can also generate meanings while leveraging the resources of a new languaculture (Agar 1994) and also forging meanings between semiotic systems (intercultural meanings). (p. 61)

Drawing on Kress and van Leeuwen's (1999) theory of visual interaction, which focuses on the way that the visual mode is in fact interactive, and documenting the ways a teacher and learners read the symbols and meanings of a particular visual text, this work begins to develop the range of interpretive and semiotic processes that are likely involved in meaningful intercultural learning and that are explored further in this book.

In a different setting and with a focus on different kinds of learners, Palpacuer-Lee (2010) also investigates the processes of identifying meaningful signs and of engaging with interpretation of these. Her participants were US-born teachers of French who participated in an innovative study abroad program that took them to Paris for two weeks. During that time, the teachers made regular visits to the Louvre and viewed the art on display there. But they also had sessions with a docent at the museum who engaged them in discussions about learning how to look at particular pieces of art. In the interactions between the teachers and the docent that Palpacuer-Lee analyzes, negotiations of linguistic meanings, visual symbols and the learners' interpretations of a painting are all apparent, highlighting the necessarily multimodal nature of meaning-making around cultural texts and the centrality of symbolic meaning. More specifically, when the learners in this setting hypothesize about what various visual elements of the painting might mean symbolically, divergent interpretations arise regarding the meaning of a bare breast represented in a painting of a woman. Rather than some resolution of which interpretation is more credible or the forging of a middle-ground interpretation, Palpacuer-Lee argues that the emergence of symbolic competence among interlocutors in the interaction has more to do with the 'participants' apprenticeship of difference [through which] they are exposed to new discursive possibilities' (p. 318). Further, the author lays out the ways in which the learners' interactions in the museum that day show their negotiation of an unfamiliar symbolic performance – participating in museum discourse to comment on art. They initially take up discourse patterns more fitting to a ML classroom and as a result position themselves and the docent they interacted with in particular ways (as language learners versus a language expert, as language teachers attempting to learn something about French art versus a knowledgeable professional of the art world). Discursive performances, Palpacuer-Lee illustrates, are closely related to symbolic power in these interactions, with the docent occupying a more powerful position in this space; but as the learners continued their visits to the museum and their interactions with the docent, they did begin to practice performances of museum discourse – a description-analysis-interpretation pattern in particular – and in doing so carved out and enacted new symbolic selves. Importantly, Palpacuer-Lee addresses the question of how such experiences among ML teachers who participate as learners in such a program abroad might translate to their professional practice back in their ML classrooms. Integration of some of the pieces of art the teachers encountered and analyzed while at the Louvre did not seem possible to some of the teachers on the grounds that the art was perhaps not appropriate for or relevant to the students and the curriculum they taught. However, the awareness raised among the teachers and the broader processes of engaging in interpretation and meaning-making around artistic texts may offer a great deal to the teachers' overall approach to addressing culture and meaning in their classes. Palpacuer-Lee summarizes:

> Approaching intercultural competence as a discursive and symbolic competence does not circumvent ambiguities or discomfort. On the contrary, intercultural competence capitalizes on ambivalences to pave the way towards learning. In some instances, cultural and intercultural

mediation are quite precarious, and the participants who experienced moments of discomfort resorted to alternative discursive strategies, such as humor or even silence. Adopting a view of intercultural competence as symbolic competence, however, opens up possibilities for understanding and investigating cultural and intercultural encounters. In this view, culture is fluid and multi-faceted, anchored in context and language use. (p. 326)

Although not always expressly focused on the examination of the development of intercultural or symbolic competence, classroom-based studies of language play and humor nonetheless highlight the opening of spaces for ML learners' discovery of subjectivities and exercise of new voices, the subversion of traditional notions of linguistic and communicative competence and generation of new and personal meanings among learners, all of which are central to such competences. Belz (2002), for example, shows how multilingual language play around language names and syntax in an L2 German class impacted students' identities, which were increasingly multicompetent, or more than simply the sum of two grammars (Cook 1991, 1992). She writes, 'These frequently creative uses of language may be iconic and indexic signs of the destabilization and subsequent reconceptualization of the learner's subjective sense of person and his or her relations to the world' (p. 21). Novelty and neologism as sources of creativity and as generating meanings for learners are one rich possibility in ML learning that aims at intercultural and symbolic competences, but Pennycook (2007) also argues for a 'parallel philosophy of creativity' (p. 581) that is anchored in sameness and the ways that repetition or mimicry represent a 'same-but-different space' that recontextualizes similar forms and expressions in order to forge new meanings (p. 580). Such recontextualization of forms is highly evident in some of the student work that is analyzed in a later chapter of this book and that also points to learners' expanded meaning-making abilities. Pomerantz and Bell's (2007) research, which takes up humor and language play in a university-level Spanish course and which does focus explicitly on development of symbolic competence, looks at how students 'jointly manipulate[d] linguistic forms, semantic units, and discourse elements for the amusement of themselves and others' and how such 'unscripted language play can destabilize institutionally-sanctioned assumptions about what counts as a meaningful or legitimate act of language use, momentarily reconfiguring the definition of linguistic expertise and broadening the possibilities for acceptable language use' (p. 556). Analyses of interactions among students in the Spanish class as well as of the writing students did in the German class Belz (2002) studied demonstrate how, in encountering new languages, learners often explore and create a range of meaning potentials around new linguistic forms, even if such exploration is not officially part of the curriculum or the teacher's agenda. Indeed, Kramsch (2009) warns us that we are fooling ourselves if we think that learners only or even primarily attend to language as taught. Instead, they engage on multiple levels and come to know language through engagement that has cognitive, social, affective and material dimensions. These studies on language play and humor further underscore that ML learning, even in classrooms far from so-called target cultures, can be a rich site for stretching communicative repertoires and exploring new subjectivities and new modes of articulating the world precisely because this kind of language use encourages expansion of meaning potentials, both when it comes to language forms themselves and language users' own repertoires. What these studies make clear is that such play is rarely planned for or viewed as official classroom activity, and there is therefore a need to consciously make space for these potentially rich engagements with language in ML curricula and classrooms.

Investigations of technology-mediated, intercultural encounters among ML learners and speakers of those languages offer still further empirical evidence into processes in developing intercultural competence and symbolic competence and teachers' complicated roles in facilitating such learning. Specifically, they highlight how differences (personal and cultural) are negotiated, how intercultural stances and open and curious attitudes toward other cultures are taken up or not and linguistically achieved in discourse, and the ways that internet-mediated communication and telecollaborative tools represent their own 'cultures-of-use' (Thorne, 2003), which language teachers also must contend with. As Belz and Thorne (2006) assert, although technology receives a great deal of attention in research on ML education and has occupied a more prominent role in its practice over the years, Internet-mediated exchanges between learners and users of the languages they are studying are of interest primarily on the grounds that they are intercultural, that they might 'serve as a site for the complexification of the self on linguistic, social, cultural, and ethical planes through lived experiences of communicative interaction with persons from other cultures in both additional and native languages' (ix). Belz's (2003) study of e-mail exchanges between two German university students and a student in the United States, which investigates how intercultural attitudes are linguistically indexed and negotiated across a series of exchanges, shows that such exploration of subjectivities does not necessarily or naturally take place just because students are put into contact with each other. In this case, the students' lack of awareness of culturally-specific discourse patterns and linguistic means in their own and the other's language for indexing affective and epistemic stances are major stumbling blocks in their establishing more deeply intercultural communication. Based on her careful analysis that draws on appraisal theory in linguistics and the specific intercultural learning objectives articulated by Byram (1997), Belz ultimately returns to the role of the teacher in such computer-mediated communication: '[T]he teacher in telecollaboration must be educated to discern, identify, explain and model culturally-contingent patterns of interaction in the absence of paralinguistic meaning signals..., otherwise it maybe the case that civilizations ultimately do clash – in the empirical details of their computer-mediated talk' (p. 92–3). In a similar vein, Ware and Kramsch's (2005) analysis of an instance of misunderstanding that emerged between US and German students involved in intercultural telecollaboration provides a basis for the argument that teachers must be flexible enough to adapt pedagogically, to harness the potential of intercultural miscommunications and to propel productive negotiations of meaning (on a semiotic level) rather than to allow communication to stall completely in the wake of students' or their own discomfort. In describing the *Cultura* project, which puts university students from the United States and France into telecollaborative exchange around parallel topics and materials in order to enhance 'cultural literacy,' Furstenberg *et al.* (2001) provide specific examples from student work that begin to reveal the range of interactions students engage in to express and explore culturally familiar and unfamiliar perspectives. Certain processes of inquiry, dialogue and analysis (such as exploration of semantic networks and cultural connotations, hypothesis building, etc.) are clear in the description of the project. Yet, no systematic analysis of the intercultural interactions students' engage in is presented, nor are teachers' instructional moves presented in detail, such that one might gain a sense of how teaching and learning interactions function within the curricular project to produce engagement with a range of subjectivities and symbolic meanings that are central to intercultural and symbolic competences. Overall, research in this area has demonstrated that especially because computer-mediated communications shift genres, semiotic practices and assumptions about language users and possible subjectivities, they present a complex environment in which interculturality and symbolic competence can be developed and exercised. Flowing from this, consequently, a consistent finding of such work is that language teachers' roles require serious re-consideration in online environments. Research to date, however, has not investigated how exactly teachers can productively model or enact intercultural stances in computer-mediated communicative settings and provide the kind of instruction that prepares for, debriefs and reflects on intercultural interactions, nor has it yielded detailed, rigorous analyses of instances in which students' effectively establish interculturality in collaboration with peers who speak other languages and belong to different cultures. Furthermore, the symbolic dimensions of intercultural, computer-mediated exchange have yet to figure in the empirical literature. Such studies would not only be of great interest to practitioners seeking to foster intercultural dialogue and understandings through online tools, but also to theorists, since they would offer further insight into the media and processes through which learners can effectively engage with symbolic meaning and potentially forge novel symbolic meanings of their own.

In sum, there is very little classroom-based empirical research that attempts to analyze teaching and learning interactions for the ways that these might facilitate (or hinder) development of symbolic competence. Those that do exist, however, underscore the need to focus on the ways learners enter into dialogue with language and a fuller range of semiotic resources and representations, the ways they participate in a range of dialogic and discursive practices that may stretch their existing repertoires, and the ways these experiences and engagements during ML instruction have impact on students' meaning-making practices (as evidenced in interaction itself but also on other types of assignments and projects) as well as their own self-concepts.

An Ecological, Social Semiotic View of Modern Language Learning

Scholarship in the fields of language education and applied linguistics has found ecologies (e.g. Kramsch, 2003; van Lier, 2004a) and dynamic systems (e.g. de Bot *et al.*, 2007; Larsen-Freeman, 2012, 2014; Larsen-Freeman & Cameron, 2008; Waninge *et al.*, 2014), to be attractive metaphors for capturing the complex, fluid and emergent nature of languages, language learning and language use and for the endless, creative potential afforded in such environments. If we view a ML classroom as an ecology, a system of relationships among numerous resources and processes that create affordances or 'relationships of possibility that allow the learner to act and interact with growing effectiveness in the linguistic environment' (van Lier, 2004b), we depart radically from the dominant but limited and limiting views of language that currently drive the practice of ML education. Adopting an ecological perspective on language phenomena of all kinds, including ML learning and education, productively prompts a rethinking of what people do with languages and does so by requiring a deep consideration of what is meant by context and by focusing our attention squarely on the dialogic relations and actions that connect language and other semiotic resources, subjectivities and identities, and meaning-making processes in context. Van Lier (2004c) writes that 'both language and the self are dialogical by their very nature. Not only that, perception is also dialogical, so that our dealings with the world, our meaning making (semiosis) are essentially dialogical and interactional in nature' (p. 94). The dialogism and complex ecological nature of the 'real' world is not something that ML education need shy away from or attempt to reduce and simplify in order to make language and language use accessible to learners in classroom environments. Quite the opposite; the ecological and social semiotic view of language education I adopt, described in more detail below, invites complexity, dynamism and interconnectedness (as well as disjunctures) as conditions that are actually ideal for intercultural learning and the development of symbolic competence in ML classrooms.

Van Lier's ecological perspective includes a strong emphasis on semiosis, which is clearly traceable to Halliday (1978), who popularized a functional, semiotic view of language in the fields of linguistics and applied linguistics. The study of semantics has to do with signs and their referents; this is a structuralist or formalist pursuit that has had some bearing on applied linguistics and, more specifically, the way language is treated in the practice of ML education (Kramsch, 2002). But a more functional, socially-anchored view of language focuses instead on *semiosis,* or meaning-making processes. Such a linguistics studies signification and interpretation processes that are necessarily embedded in and motivated by social purposes. Halliday (1978) writes:

> We have to proceed from the outside inward, interpreting language by reference to its place in the social process. This is not the same thing as taking an isolated sentence and planting it out in some hothouse that we call a social context. It involves the difficult task of focusing attention simultaneously on the actual and the potential, interpreting both discourse and the linguistic system that lies behind it in terms of the infinitely complex network of meaning potential that is what we call the culture. (p. 4–5)

Given this anchoring of language in social and cultural life, theorizing and study of semiosis is particularly conscious of issues of power, agency and constraint in language use, and both the affordances and limitations of particular semiotic environments and relationships become of central concern in understanding how language choices and the deployment of other semiotic resources make meanings. How exactly individuals and groups come to mean in particular ways and by drawing on semiotic resources is explained in more detail in the next section by focusing on the key construct of meaning potentials. Before turning to this discussion, however, it is worth deepening the discussion of a social semiotic view of ML education and commenting on what exactly it affords us as we attempt to understand and enhance intercultural learning and the development of symbolic competence, particularly in ML classrooms.

As was noted above, a social semiotic view of ML education prioritizes and prompts a deeper consideration of context. Van Lier (2004c) explains that '[a] semiotic and ecological view of language and of learning entails that the context – physical, social and symbolic – is a central element in teaching and learning, and that issues such as embodiment of language and spatiotemporal structures are instrumental in the creation of learning opportunities' (p. 79). Context is therefore a multidimensional and multimodal network in which action emerges from the possibilities created by the relationships among resources in that environment. From these affordances, learning, which essentially involves adaptation, can occur: 'From an ecological perspective, all learning is the ability to adapt to one's environment in increasingly effective and successful ways' (van Lier, 2004b: 97). The interaction between a person and his/her existing resources and the elements of a new environment especially, one rich in its own material, social and semiotic resources, requires from the outset the development of that person's perceptual processes. That is, in order to potentially adapt and become increasingly adept with and able to make agentive choices about use of resources in new contexts, a learner needs first to be able to become aware of, notice and perceive from unfamiliar perspectives.

Opportunities to develop and to adapt in order to function agentively in new contexts in this way often come about as a result of affordances made possible by the teacher in classroom interaction, complemented largely by the nature of the semiotic environment that is established through curriculum and materials. This is not to underestimate students' roles and contributions in their own learning[4]; a teacher's instructional moves, curriculum and materials, however, tend to be more planned and therefore provide potentially more structured affordances from which learning can arise. Van Lier and others who adopt a social semiotic view of language education are extremely careful to point out that learning is not about learning the semantic code of another language and culture. This would be a one-way, transmission-like type of learning and development. A dialogic, reciprocally transformative kind of learning is more in line with a social semiotic perspective, and the process of learning is seen as necessarily involving exploration and possible transformation of subjectivities and identities as well as always involving issues of power. Van Lier (2004c) writes that 'development of ideological and political perspective is part and parcel of the language learning process, in the same way that ideological and political stances and power relations are deeply embedded in language itself' (p. 97).

Further specifying the ways that selves and identities are implicated in meaning-making in ML education and with the goal of proposing arguments 'for a move away from safe, tried-and tested language classrooms into more critical, challenging democratic directions,' van Lier (2004b: 83) writes that for language learners,

> The development of proficiency in a language depends on the development of a dually compatible identity, that is, compatible with the self, and compatible with the life space of the new semiotic reality, in essence, an identity that can provide a solid link between the *self* and the *new reality*. This in turn requires having a *voice* in that language, and having both the right to speak and the right to be heard, as well as having something of consequence to say. (p. 82)

As analysis in this book will demonstrate, this link between a learner's familiar self and the 'life space of the new semiotic reality' need not involve fashioning his or her personal and authentic 'voice' in the new language; shaping and using a voice can also involve exploration of subjectivities in other ways, such as through narrative but fictive writing. Overall, van Lier (2004c) summarizes learners' engagement in ML learning in the following way:

> New modes of semiosis need to be established, with iconic, indexical and symbolic sign processes freely developing so that a person's actions, thoughts and meaning can establish connections between the self and the environment, i.e. Can develop new identities (without necessarily giving up old ones, of course)...Negotiating new identities, creating new semiotic networks, and language learning are intimately connected in a language learner's world. Since these are dialogic pursuits, the host environment must be amenable to this development, rather than curtail, block or force it in self-threatening directions. In this perspective then, a democratizing education for a language learner will encourage the free flow of semiosis in a rich social life space. In such a context,

multidimensional perception and contingent action are crucial elements of an ecology of learning. (p. 96–7)

Kramsch, also viewing ML learning as an enterprise whose stakes are high because it involves negotiation of the symbolic self, explains that a social semiotic view of language education throws into question several key constructs, starting with language itself: 'A social semiotic perspective on language rehabilitates looking at language as a problematic medium,' not just something that reflects and records a static, objective reality, 'something our students are well prepared to do and will increasingly need to do in the future' (Kramsch, 2002: 12).

This social semiotic view of language represents a broader alternative to the form-focused conception of language that was discussed in Chapter 1 as being central to the current practice of ML education; it assumes language to have much broader meaning-making functions in personal and social life and, by extension, posits ML learning as a potentially much deeper engagement than the acquisition of linguistic forms. Questioning the commonly held view that language learning is a staged process, Kramsch (2002) writes

> Growing into bilingualism and bicultural sensitivity is not like learning math from a more knowledgeable adult. It is not a matter of growing from baby French (French 1) to adolescent French (French 3) to full adult French (French 5), where an adult native speaker yardstick of competence is used at all stages. All stages present opportunities for various discoveries of self and of one's multiple signifying resources, including one's other languages and language varieties. (Kramsch, 2002: n.p.)

She goes on to write that a social semiotic view of language education also requires a reinterpretation of interlanguage, an often invoked construct in research on second language acquisition and in ML teaching; this expands from an exclusive focus on the evolution of mental representations of linguistic (mostly grammatical) forms in individual learners' minds, a process impacted by native language knowledge and including approximations of L2 forms, to a concept that is more inclusive of semiotic elements: 'Interlanguage...as not only a psycho- or sociolinguistic phenomenon but also as...a composite of multiple emotional memories, sensibilities, and potential identifications...a social semiotic construct in which style, genre, and textuality all play a role in defining the mediating process of the acquisition of another semiotic code' (Kramsch, 2002: n.p.).

This transformed view of interlanguage also then has implications for the way we see input and communicative competence, as she writes:

> Input has been up to now only the linguistic forms to which the learner is exposed, made comprehensible by skillful teacher talk and interactive classroom practices. In a social semiotic perspective, input is both the form and the content, indeed the form *as* semiotic content...it is not enough to teach what the interlocutors say and hear. One has to factor into the meaning of a scene how the protagonists stand in relation to one another; how their behavior enacts their attitudes and feelings; how their words match the context in which they are uttered, their past history, and their prospects for the future. In order to understand the context, students must textualize the scene, that is, remove it from its context, objectify it, and reflect on it with the social semiotic tools acquired in academia. (n.p.)

Kramsch's description here of what a ML pedagogy could look like – one that fosters the development of interlanguage broadly conceived, that provides input that extends far beyond current conceptualizations of linguistic forms and meanings, and that ultimately makes possible the cultivation of a competence that is symbolic in nature and facilitative of growing learners' capacity for symbolic action – is borne out in the empirical research presented in later chapters. In that analysis, we will see that processes of noticing and accessing semiotic content and of 'textualizing' – analyzing and reflecting on particular acts of meaning (what Kramsch calls 'scenes' here) – are the foundations upon which students are ultimately able to quite actively engage in producing novel meanings and shaping voices with the semiotic resources they are becoming more and more familiar with.

As some of the teaching and learning processes that might be involved in a social semiotic approach to ML education are becoming clear, we might well ask in addition how we as teachers and students will be able to tell that symbolic competence is in fact growing. In a social semiotic view of language education, the means by which we can assess success are cast by van Lier (2004c) not at all in terms of measurable outcomes but on quality of experience, which suggests that we need to look to meaning-making processes and practices themselves for indications of developing symbolic competence. The goal (van Lier, 2004b) can be summarized as follows:

> The quality of educational experience is that which the learner remembers long after the test scores are forgotten. It cannot be

measured in test scores, but it can be evidenced objectively in terms of diversified perception and action, the ability to cope under stress, increasing control of one's own physical, social and symbolic environment, the establishment of mutually rewarding relationships, and the development of one's talents and interests in a supportive environment. (n.p.)

The notion of looking to learners' meaning-making activities and practices (in class, through assignments, etc.) in order to discern evidence of 'increasing control of...[the] symbolic environment' is of particular interest in gauging the development of symbolic competence. Of course, it is very likely that the development of symbolic competence that is sparked in a classroom setting will continue to evolve long after the class has ended and in many other settings, especially if the class was successful in instilling 'the social semiotic tools acquired in academia' that Kramsch (2002) writes about. However, even in the more immediate-term context of a particular class, growth of symbolic competence, viewed as increasingly diversified abilities to perceive and act in a semiotic environment and increased control over semiotic resources, is certainly observable. Part of this assessment can focus on the way learners engage in interpretation of signs and meanings over time – the types of interpretive processes they are apprenticed into and that they then apply more and more independently when encountering symbolic texts and representations. Another indication of learners' developing symbolic competence is when the signs that students encounter in texts and analyze and negotiate in interactions around these texts then resurface (in original or adapted and novel form) in their own productions. In cases like these, such as the extended writing project discussed later in this book, there is clear evidence that engagement with acts of meaning leave traces in learners' own meaning-making repertoires and that these traces are then available for deployment in learners' meaning-making acts. This process is described in more depth below, along with a discussion of meaning potentials. The quality of learners' experiences in ML classrooms is also, finally, analyzable through the learners' own reflections on their learning processes. Their characterizations of the engagement they experience in their ML classrooms can offer insight into the broader impact that ML learning and the growth of one's meaning-making abilities through language study might have on conceptions of the self and of one's place in the world. This kind of reflective commentary can offer a more retrospective angle on students' learning to complement evaluations and characterizations of learners' development of symbolic competence based on analysis of classroom interactions and student language use.

A social semiotic view of language and of ML education are extremely useful in framing our thinking about the development of symbolic competence in ML classrooms and the study reported in this book. This perspective focuses our attention on language and meaning in context, on language users' agency and decision-making as a result of being situated in a semiotic landscape, and discovering meaning-making affordances that arise from the synergy between themselves and their existing resources and the new semiotic and other material available to them in the new environment. This is a complex view of what is inherently a complex facet of human activity and experience, yet it brings order to our thinking about individual and collective meaning-making while also maintaining complexity, dynamism and flexibility. The following section provides even further detail on the ways we come to make meanings as individuals and as groups, and how these levels of meaning-making relate.

From meanings to meaning-making potentials

While the meanings of language (words, phrases, whole texts) have been treated in somewhat narrow ways in much ML education in the United States to date, shifting to focus on more complex *meaning potential*, through a social semiotic view of language, opens up new possibilities for teaching and learning. Our tendency has been to treat meaning in purely referential ways. Vocabulary lists that associate words with a particular referent, usually a translation in the learners' first language or sometimes more simply an image, are a common example. We also sometimes refer to learners making meaning through their interactional negotiations related to a communicative task (such as an information gap task where pieces of information are distributed across learners and they must use the ML to transact information and 'negotiate meaning' in the service of some goal). In these cases, the meanings learners make and negotiate are limited. The parameters of the interaction are predefined, as is oftentimes the language to be used, and many of the scenarios are highly transactional in nature. But perhaps most importantly, meanings in these scenarios are assumed to be relatively predetermined. These ways of treating meaning in ML education construe language as a much more static system than it is and present meanings as largely fixed (e.g. word A in language 1 = word B in language 2, or communicative chunk A fits situation A).

What is most often lost in ML classrooms today is any engagement with language forms as richly variable in their meanings and with meaning as being symbolic as well as referential. As outlined above, Kramsch (2011) advocates going beyond the basic referents that linguistic and other semiotic forms denote to access and explore what forms represent more broadly and symbolically, what particular points of view and positions they represent and allow, and what they make people think and feel:

> While symbolic representation has usually been interpreted by language teachers as the referential function of language, it has usually been taught as dictionary meanings applied to an outside world. It has not been taught as a way of making and organizing meaning through signs, symbolic and conceptual metaphors that not only refer to the outside world but shape the minds of their users and receivers as well. In particular, it has not shown students how the choice of one word over another sets a frame for all the others…and can thereby change the tenor of the discourse…While symbolic action has been seen in CLT as the pragmatic or interpersonal function of language, it has usually been taught in the US as interaction rituals of a predictable kind, the good manners and etiquette of everyday life. It has not been taught as the construction of social reality through performative speech acts and the emotional and ideological impact of words. (p. 364–5)

An engagement with meaning more in line with what Kramsch describes does not just envision language learners' learning the fixed meanings of others, just on a larger scale than currently is common ML classrooms; rather, an expanded view of the meaning at the heart of ML education pushes engagement to the realm of meaning potentials, potentials that learners need not just absorb and reproduce, but potentials they can shape through their own use of the ML. Kramsch's work speaks to engagement with and expansion of meaning potentials as a priority in ML learning and the norm among multilingual, intercultural people. Indeed, she regularly advances the notion that it is the meaning-making that occurs when linguistic difference comes to learners' attention, when they gain ability to apprehend and perceive and resignify from new vantage points that are neither wholly foreign nor familiar that subjectivization occurs, personal meanings are made and personal fulfillment possibly gained. It is in these moments and subjective spaces that we can better grasp the meaning of ML learning. An additional body of theory, however, will complete the framing through which it makes most sense to view the detailed study of Emilie's classroom that begins in the next chapter. This is a linguistic theory that speaks quite directly to what meaning potentials are when we talk about the more or less shared, conventional meanings of language forms while also taking up the issue of language learners' meaning potentials.

Systemic functional linguistics (SFL), developed originally by Halliday and therefore very much representing a social semiotic perspective, lends support to our understanding of meaning and meaning potentials. As Matthiessen (2009) explains, language, through the lens of SFL theory, is a 'complex adaptive system' (p. 206) through which language is not only a vehicle 'for carrying meaning, the central property of semiotic systems, but also for creating meaning' (p. 207). Not only does he explain that our 'personalized meaning potentials' develop through meaning-making acts and our experiences with these instances over time, but he also points out that these individual processes connect to collective development of meaning potentials over broader social scopes and longer timescales. Meaning-making occurs, then, in various timeframes, the 'logogenetic – the creation of meaning in text; ontogenetic – the learning of a personalized meaning potential; and phylogenetic – the evolution of a collective meaning potential' (p. 206).

In the following excerpt, Matthiessen explains the reciprocal relationship between particular instances of meaning-making (language in use) and broader meaning potentials and further asserts how this relationship connects to learning:

> Because the central characteristic of language is that it is a resource for making meaning, we can say that the *acts of meaning* that make up a text unfolding in time instantiate a meaning potential, noting that these are simply different phases of language as a meaning-making resource: acts instantiate potential, and potential emerges from acts. This is where we can locate *learning*: Learning takes place when instances are distilled into potential higher up along the cline of instantiation. (p. 207, emphasis in original)

The mutually dependent and flexible nature of the relationship between utterances and meaning potential in broader scale language use, potential that might be shared by social groups, becomes clear here. Through instances of use, speakers index or instantiate a broader meaning potential; yet, through their single uses, speakers also have the ability to possibly reshape that larger meaning potential. For language learners, as Matthiessen points out, experience with particular instances will over time create a store of occasions from which a broader meaning potential can be synthesized. He writes, 'a person learns through text in interaction with others, distilling meaning potential from acts of meaning and constantly revising their own personalized meaning potential, both qualitatively and quantitatively. This learning involves both learning language and learning "content" through language, locally within a single text or cumulatively over many texts' (p. 206). Specifically, learning 'takes place if instances leave a trace in the learner's systems (personalized meaning potential); a systemic memory. Learning language means learning how to mean by learning a complex, adaptive, inherently variable system' (p. 214). This explanation recalls quite vividly Kramsch's notion of learners developing a 'variationist frame of mind' and learning about alternative forms available and possible in languages for making various meanings.

How learners make sense of meaning within and across instances of language use likely occurs differently in first as opposed to additional languages, as those learning a new language already possess a store of meaning potentials related to their first language. The process of relating instances of meaning-making to meaning potentials while learning a new language deserves our attention because, in contrast to those growing their understandings of meaning potential in a first language, ML learners may be tempted to draw on translation to a linguistic code they are familiar with (their L1s) as a meaning-making strategy (in fact they may be encouraged to do so in some instructional environments), rather than attempting to make sense of a form on its own terms, as it appears in a particular text and context and in the L2 system and context. Matthiesson assures us, though, that

> Whether people learn how to mean in their mother tongue or in a second/foreign language, their most important material for building up their own personal meaning potentials is text in context: Learning means distilling meaning potential from the acts of meaning that make up text. (p. 214)

The consequence of this for ML education is clearly that we need to pay close attention to and exercise particular care in establishing textually rich classroom environments and then in engaging learners in ways that help them understand contexts of use more deeply. These are questions of curricular content but also of creating a discourse environment and interactional architecture in ML classrooms that attends to levels of meaning in a way that has perhaps been uncommon to date.

Theory and research must interrogate the degree to which such environments are actually created in ML classrooms at present and the extent to which formal ML education expands learners' meaning-making repertoires or, put differently, their personalized meaning-making potentials. Answers to these questions are likely to depend greatly on the kinds of texts (in context) learners encounter and engage in interpreting and creating and the sort of interactions that surround acts of meaning in the ML classroom. Attention to these issues is not merely a matter of understanding how ML education might grow students' abilities to communicate. As Matthiesson writes:

> When people learn languages, they build up their own personalized meaning potentials as part of the collective meaning potential that constitutes the languages, and they build up these personal potentials by gradually expanding their own registerial repertoires - their own shares in the collective meaning potential. As they expand their own registerial repertoires, they can take on roles in a growing range of contexts, becoming semiotically more empowered and versatile. (p. 223)

Learning to mean in a new language increases students' stake in shared meanings and allows them to take on new roles, to grow their agentive potential alongside their meaning potential and ultimately to gain possible leverage on language and communication in a way that allows them to shift meanings and transform contexts. Herein lies the power and promise of a social semiotic view of ML education that focuses intently on expanding learners' meaning potentials.

The analysis of classroom interactions and students' written work later in this book is presented precisely with the desire to illustrate how growth in students' personalized meaning potentials can be facilitated by creating particular curricular and discursive environments, by fostering particular classroom interactions and then by making space for students in their own independent work and assignments to exercise and stretch their meaning-making abilities. Through this explanation and analysis, it is clear that students become more agentive (i.e. conscious and deliberate) in their use of language to carry out a range of social actions and purposes. They draw on knowledge and awareness of meaningful forms and are able to perform acts of meaning in understandable and plausible ways, making informed choices about using forms to craft meanings, sometimes by indexing shared understandings of the meaning potential of a form and at others by stretching the meaning potential of a form in ways that are novel and creative.

Notes

(1) Kramsch's scholarship, especially, has the weight behind it of insights gained from a far-reaching synthesis of critical and poststucturalist feminist theory (e.g. Kristeva, 1980), sociology (e.g. Bourdieu, 1991), social interactionism (e.g. Goffman, 1981; Gumperz, 1996), philosophy of language (e.g. Butler, 1997; Derrida, 1971;

1972) semiotics (e.g. Bakhtin, 1981, 1986; Barthes, 1957), cognitive linguistics (e.g. Fauconnier & Turner, 2002; Lakoff, 1987) and neurological somatic theory (e.g. Damasio, 1994, 1999, 2003; Schumann, 1997).

(2) Van Lier's (2004) synthesis ranges from Broffenbrenner (1979, 1993) on ecological theories and Vygotsky (1962, 1978, 1986, 1987) on sociocultural theories of human development, to Bruner (1986) on cognitive psychology, to Hallidaysian (1975, 1978, 1993, 2001) systemic functional linguistics, philosophy of language (Peirce, 1992, 1998; Wittgenstein, 1974, 1980) and to Saussure's structuralist linguistics (1907/1983) and Chomsky's transformational grammar (1986) to cite some of the major strands contributing to his work.

(3) Several paragraphs in this section have been only minorly adapted from text appearing in Kearney (2008). Similarly, a few paragraphs in the following section on Kramsch's theoretical contributions to the theorizing of intercultural learning in ML education are slightly revised versions of text appearing in Kearney (2008).

(4) Indeed, those who adopt ecological and complex dynamic systems views of language learning and use argue that a shift in our thinking about language learners must occur alongside such shifts in orientations about the process and experience of language learning. Learners are, consequently, not just multicompetent (or something other than deficient native speakers) and they are not just efficient communicators of relatively fixed messages and routines; language learners are meaning makers, language users with potentials for turning conventionalized forms and functions (i.e. resources) to their own purposes and meaningful pursuits.

3 Creating and Investigating Intercultural Worlds in a Modern Language Classroom

> *The 'simulation globale' is the story of an Emilie who was asked to teach a content-based intermediate French class for the first time three days before the start of classes, who looked at the reading pack full of documents and explanations of the French experience of World War II and thought it was not bad, who proceeded to use it. Then, during a mid-semester oral exam, a student made the statement that 'Tous les Français étaient collabos' (all the French were collaborators) during the Second World War. When I asked why he thought that, he said 'It's just a gut feeling.' The 'simulation globale' then is a way of bridging the distance between students and the material they were studying when only using the reading pack and listening to my mini-lectures. Students' engagement during the 'simulation globale' is an emotional one.*
> Emilie (Interview 19 December 2006)

Explaining the genesis of a pedagogical innovation called global simulation in her class, Emilie, a university-level instructor of French in the United States, also provides insight into the type of understandings she hopes students to gain from her class. Beyond learning particular content (events and experiences of World War II in France in this case), acquiring linguistic forms and features, or even developing communicative abilities across modes, functions and situations, Emilie above all hopes to foster a deep engagement in her classroom, one that can go so deep as to reach students' emotional core. Emilie's concern after teaching her content-based course for the first time was that students, like the one whose response she describes at the one-on-one oral exam, came away with all or nothing, black or white, right or wrong judgments of history and of historical actors. This kind of sweeping generalization baffled Emilie, given the six weeks she had spent providing rich detail in her mini-lectures about the range of experiences French people had during the war and the diverse stances they took up toward wartime events. She surmised that even in those cases where students did register and appreciate the nuance in her presentation of events and perspectives in class and in the materials they read and studied, they were unlikely to be connecting emotionally or personally to what they were studying. Ultimately, this raised questions about the sense students made of the content Emilie was attempting to relate in her class. With the aim of creating deeper connections, Emilie set out to transform her pedagogy and to make cultural learning in her French class more meaningful.

This chapter sets the stage for an in-depth discussion of meaning-making practices in Chapters 4 and 5 by describing environments conducive to symbolic meaning-making and intercultural learning. It first presents Emilie's classroom and describes in detail the narrative nature of the classroom environment and the global simulation project that organized the class's activity for the first half of the semester. I share Emilie's characterization of her overall goals for the course before outlining the content of her class (French experiences of World War II) and her main pedagogical approach (global simulation) and providing examples that show how content and teaching approach were situated in a textual environment rich in narratives. These examples highlight the broad range of texts that were accessible in Emilie's class, the variety of modes through which they were expressed, and the array of voices, perspectives and narratives these texts brought into dialogue. The chapter then explains the ethnographic and discourse-analytic research methods used to document and rigorously analyze interaction in Emilie's classroom, methods which were parallel in many ways to the interpretive and meaning-making activity the class participants also undertook. I attend in this presentation of methods to enumerating the goals of my analysis, which had to do with generating detailed descriptions of the curricular and pedagogical environment of Emilie's classroom and illuminating the meaning-making processes that were highlighted and afforded in such a setting. The chapter closes with clarification of the analytic means for connecting individuals' everyday stories with larger cultural narratives, and it explains why this was essential to creating opportunities for intercultural learning in Emilie's class and to my own analysis of the class's activity.

Establishing the Global Simulation in Emilie's Class

Emilie began teaching the intermediate-level, content-based 'bridge' course that would come to include a global simulation approach in 2003. When I asked her to describe how she came to teach this course using a global simulation approach, Emilie told me that in her first attempt at teaching the course, she tried a lecture style, which students did not seem prepared for, and used the materials that had already been assembled by a previous instructor. At the time, she went through the texts with students, supplementing them with some of her own materials, but looking back, she qualified this approach as 'too robotic' and as not delving deeply enough into the real complexity of the material. During that first semester of teaching the course, a moment came, though, that would shock her into changing her approach. When the mid-term oral exam arrived, Emilie began to gauge what students had taken away from the class's six weeks of work. In administering an oral exam, one student told Emilie, *'Tous les Français étaient collabos'* (All the French were collaborators). When Emilie asked what made this student think this, he said that it was 'just a gut feeling'. At this point, Emilie said she became aware that students were not making a real connection to the material and were not considering the great variety of responses to the Occupation that existed at the time of the Occupation and ever since. Students, she said, were going through an intellectual exercise, not engaging in a 'human activity'. In an attempt to engage students more deeply in a process of examining how individuals may have reacted to the war and to encourage them to 'project themselves' into this history, Emilie introduced the global simulation as part of the course, and since then she has been very satisfied with the different kind of engagement with the complexity of culture and history that students experience. Introducing the global simulation was a way to establish 'continuity' in the students' work, and Emilie felt that the project functions as the 'cement' of the course, not only in terms of bringing new meaning and coherence to the content and learning activity but also in solidifying the students' engagement in the class and the development of their relationships with her and each other. Before delving more deeply into the pedagogical principles behind a global simulation approach and explaining how it was taken up in Emilie's course, it is useful to know more about the class and the students Emilie was teaching.

Emilie's class

The course in which Emilie developed a global simulation project was a fifth-semester, intermediate class at her university, which was intended to link the introductory level courses (i.e. the four-semester sequence of courses that correlated with the university's ML requirement) with upper-level courses in the department that included study of literature and cultural studies. As a result, students in Emilie's course were there more by choice than by requirement (as is the case in other earlier courses), and many were undergraduate students majoring or minoring in French. The course was organized around two 'dossiers', one called *'la France sous l'Occupation'* (France under the Occupation) that focused on the World War II era as experienced from French perspectives and another called *'les Jeunes'* (Youth) that focused specifically on youth culture in Paris and its surrounding areas. Each curricular unit lasted about six weeks with some transition time in between. The global simulation approach was implemented only for the first 'dossier'.

During the six-week period that the class studied France under the Occupation and World War II from French perspectives (meeting four days a week for 50 minutes each time), they encountered a wide variety of texts having to do with this period of history. These ranged from primary source documents like speeches, policy documents and news reels to first-person retrospective accounts like memoirs of Jewish children who were adopted by Catholic families during the war to historical fictions such as films and a novel. There was also a collection of short readings and images and reproductions of historical documents that served as a kind of informational base from which all other class discussion and activity was built. Students would read a few pages in this packet as homework, for example, before class the next day, during which they would clarify their understanding and then extend it through other types of analytic activities. It is important to note that the texts in Emilie's class represented many different genres, perspectives and voices; some could be easily classified as primary source, nonfiction texts, while others were very clearly fiction. Texts also spanned modes from written to spoken to visual, often combining modes. It is worth noting the role that Emilie's personal stories played in the curriculum as well; students' personal accounts also played a part, albeit to a lesser degree or at least in a less public and overt fashion than Emilie's stories. Emilie regularly told stories of her family's experiences of World War II, specifically events from her grandparents' lives. Emilie's family lived in the countryside on a farm, and her grandfather had participated in combat early in the war. Emilie was still in close contact with her family in France, although at the time of the study she had been living in the United States for many years with her American husband and the family they had started together. All but one of the students in Emilie's class were born and raised in the United States; however, a few students spoke in interviews of living with parents who had immigrated to the United States. Regardless of their origins and family histories, students' educational and social backgrounds were diverse. Some had gone to private or boarding schools, while others had attended public schools. Some had travelled the world extensively while others were planning their first trips abroad at the time of the study. The precise details of their language learning histories did not figure explicitly in interview questions, yet many talked about having had access to French outside of school environments in addition to their regular classroom instruction. What all of the students in Emilie's class shared was that they had been accepted to an elite academic institution and were in their first or second year of undergraduate study. Students' contributions to the rich textual environment of the classroom were made predominantly through the extended writing project at the core of the global simulation approach; however, on rare occasions, they did cite personal connections to the World War II era or to a France touched by the war. Never did they tell stories of their own family's involvement in World War II, if they had those connections.

Global simulation

Global simulation is 'simultaneously an approach, a set of classroom techniques, and the conceptual framework for a syllabus' (Levine, 2004: 27). The approach naturally integrates assessment as well since learners are generally focused on producing a written document, a performance or some other tangible or observable project that is the culmination of all of the other activities that make up the global simulation. A global simulation project involves the (re)-creation of a context, setting or phenomenon in which learners can design and play out an activity, storyline or phenomenon over an extended period of instructional time. For example, global simulation projects have been built around such settings as the building, the island, the business and the village (Caré, 1992, 1993). These settings are 'fictive yet culturally grounded world[s], [in which] students assume the role of a self-developed character and collaborate with other members of their community as creators and inventors of their own world' (Mills & Peron, 2008: 2). These elements promote a highly experiential mode of learning, require collaborative work among students, productively mix reality and creative invention and, because of the extended timeframe for such projects, encourage deep engagement (Dupuy, 2006; Mills, 2011).

The particular global simulation Emilie created for her class was inspired by Debyser's (1980, 1996) original global simulation project, called *L'Immeuble* (the Building). Like the original project, Emilie's global simulation prompted learners to imagine that they were all inhabitants of the same apartment buildings in a Parisian neighborhood. In Emilie's project, she even selected an actual location for the students' two apartment buildings (Nos. 5 and 7 rue de la Convention), real street addresses for which she could show pictures of the still existent buildings through Google Maps images.

These addresses played a major role in the novel *La Cliente* that students also read during the curricular unit. The students' global simulation would take place assuming this real-world physical setting but would be projected into the past to include the immediate pre-war period, the war years themselves and then a stretch of time just beyond the end of the war. In specifying the setting for the global simulation in this way, Emilie established a very particular physical environment in which the students' fictional characters would live and interact; her students had a clear image of the buildings' exteriors but still had space to imagine the interior decor of the structure. In doing so, she also set the stage for students to imagine the workings of the lives of the buildings' inhabitants, to explore the relationship between social status and physical space in the building and to populate the building with not only students' characters but a whole cast of other personalities taken from the texts and films the class was analyzing. A balance of real-world anchoring and student-invented details about life in the building was greatly facilitated by establishing these pillars of context. Anchoring decor in this way is a hallmark of the global simulation approach and an initial instructional step.

Indeed, one of the first activities that Emilie engaged students in, shortly after having them write a first draft of who their imagined character for the project would be, was to negotiate with other students in class where in the apartment building everyone's characters lived. This discussion was aided by a handout students received that had a picture of the buildings on it as well as a listing of two or three apartment numbers per floor so that students could situate their characters in the buildings. Some of the apartments were already noted as having particular occupants, including characters from the films the class would watch and from the novel they would read. Before students broke into their two groups to introduce themselves as their characters and to reach consensus on the living arrangements in the buildings, Emilie provided some clarification to the class about the criteria they should use in making these decisions. She reminded them as well not forget certain inhabitants, such as the concierge who would have lived on the first floor of the building, the Fechners (a family from the novel they had started reading) and Monsieur Klein as well as Marion Steiner (main characters from two films the class would watch). In mentioning these last two, Emilie said that on one hand, these were people with money, and she added that on the other hand, if you were a student, you would not have lived in a large apartment in the building unless your parents had a lot of money too. Over the course of the following 20 minutes, as students worked on situating their own characters in the building, Emilie continued to provide details about how '*ce sont des indications culturelles et sociales*' (these are cultural and social indications), including mention of the bare-bones *chambres de bonnes* (maid's quarters) that were located on the top floors of Parisian apartment buildings and that were inhabited mostly by students or those just arriving in Paris from the countryside (Observation 09/13/06). At one point, Emilie says that she wants to direct them toward *'précision encore une fois culturelle, sociologique et historique'* (simultaneously cultural, sociological and historic precision) and makes the direct statement that *'plus vous êtes en bas et moins votre statut social est haut...et c'est à vous de voir où votre situation sociale va vous placer'* (the lower you are in the building the lower your social status is ...and it's up to you to see where your social situation places you [in the building]).

The global simulation in Emilie's class was enacted through a range of activities, the most central of which was the individual writing that students did for the *Mémoires* project. In-class, interactive activities not only served to engage students with historical content in a variety of ways but also played a role in providing them with materials, ideas, perspectives and relevant language they could use in their writing. This extended writing project asked students to tell the story of the character they created, who lived in one of the apartment buildings Emilie had designated and who interacted with the characters other students had created as well as ones that came from other texts and films the class was reading and viewing. In addition, Emilie planned a weekly *Café de retrouvailles* (Reunion Café) exercise, during which each building's inhabitants got together to discuss their pasts 60 years after the fact. In these 'meetings', students spoke through the first-person voice of their characters, but now in retrospect and with recourse to more past-tense and hindsight perspective than was characteristic in their *Mémoires* compositions, which tended to recount events and states of affairs in a past-tense form but with more present tense mixed in to achieve immediacy in the writing. Finally, the global simulation project called on students to attend a one-time *Confessional*, during which they also spoke through the first-person voice of their invented character. This was an exercise that students completed individually outside of class in a recording room on campus, and it took place toward the end of their study of the Occupation, so the students were focused on reflecting, as their characters, on their overall experiences during the war period.

In order to achieve these main 'products' of the global simulation, the students of course needed to have a strong foundational understanding of the events of the war period and important and more mundane historical actors, as well as a sense of dispositions, perspectives and ideologies driving various events, phenomena and sentiments. Consequently, the class was engaged in regular activities which formed this base of understanding the Occupation era, all of which served as the source material from which students drew in creating their fictive, but historically rooted worlds in the global simulation. On a daily basis, students prepared for class by reading from a collection of texts that presented short descriptions of phases of the war or particular figures and also included images, excerpts from speeches or posters making legal proclamations, for example. On some occasions, students were asked to prepare responses to discussion questions related to these readings before class; on others, they were asked to analyze a particular image or text, an analysis that would then be taken up, clarified and extended in class. Outside of class, students were also routinely asked to prepare by viewing a film that related to the week's theme or range of years, or by reading some chapters from the novel *La Cliente*. In the case of both of these kinds of preparation activities, students were given viewing and reading guides with a series of questions on them to help them think about the material they were encountering and to document their initial interpretations before arriving in class.

As might be expected, Emilie's treatment of the curricular content through a global simulation approach and all of the supporting assignments and engagements necessarily created a rich textual environment and conditions for complex analytic, interpretive and semiotic activity in the group. The nature of this text-rich environment is detailed further below, but first I discuss Emilie's culture learning objectives and how they were well matched with the global simulation approach she employed.

Emilie's objectives

While the global simulation certainly figured prominently in Emilie's approach to teaching this course, introducing the project was rooted in her objectives for culture teaching and her concept of intercultural learning. Emilie expressed her objectives to me in interviews, and these were confirmed by the pedagogical and curricular decisions I observed her make. When I first asked Emilie what goals she had related to culture in the teaching of this course, she said, 'I don't have any goals in themselves. Well, I can't define it in a tangible way like that. It isn't that I want them to know how to take the metro in Paris. It's not that.' Despite Emilie's claim that her goals resisted clear articulation, further discussion did seem to uncover Emilie's thinking about the teaching and learning of culture, if she did not have 'tangible' objectives. Throughout our ensuing discussions, Emilie's responses reflected three major objectives: supporting students' ability to 'decode' a culture, encouraging students to reflect and gain self-knowledge and guiding students to make connections between familiar and unfamiliar cultural contexts.

Although Emilie initially found it challenging to explicitly articulate her goals for learners in the class and even defined her objectives first in terms of what she was not aiming for with her pedagogical approach, further on in our interview she did offer one way that she might characterize her approach to teaching the class:

> My objectives [for students] are a lot more, how can I say this, more objectives related to metacognition, to knowing who they are, to learn who they are through the learning of a foreign language, precisely through the encounter with a culture that is different um... it's more to let them decode a world that isn't theirs, that seems completely strange to them, that seems bizarre to them, but after, so familiarizing them with that world. It's more, so giving them the tools to decode...tools that will serve them in other situations. (19 December 2006)

Emilie's comments here recall Moran's (2001) insistence that *knowing oneself* is the major organizing dimension of culture learning and several other theorists' convictions that culture learning is primarily about relating to others, reflecting and growth of the self (Byram, 1997; van Lier, 2004b), and her mention of metacognitive development seems to be in line with arguments that raising awareness and development of perceptual abilities are also central to intercultural learning (van Lier, 2004b), alongside the development of particular knowledge and a set of interpretive, relational and reflective skills (Byram, 1997).

During a teacher meeting I observed, Emilie reiterated her belief that learning in this class involved developing decoding abilities: 'One of my objectives is to try to allow students to decipher. That is, not only that they be able to express themselves and function with the language, but... to decode a culture' (Observation, 26 September 2006). A bit further on in the conversation, she added: 'One of my objectives is to furnish them with a whole reference network'. In my interview with her, Emilie described learning in this class as a process of 'cultural discovery' rather than the learning of any particular facts, and through her description of her objectives it becomes clear that decoding necessarily referred to both information (parts of the 'code' and their relationship to each other in the 'reference network') and processes (skills of decoding, which might include developing skills for perceiving signs and for making sense of them).

A first observation about Emilie's expressed objectives is that ML learning for her is not just about her students developing the ability to express their own intended meanings; in more complex ways, she also wants them to be able to express meanings from a range of subjectivities (including their own) while also gaining facility with interpretation of others' meanings. Intercultural learning is posited as an interpretive and analytic activity in Emilie's remarks; she uses language that revolves around the concept of 'code' (such as 'decipher,' 'decode' and 'reference network'). While in ML education 'code' very often refers to a particular language system (e.g. French, Spanish, English), Emilie extends the notion to culture learning, which involves deciphering a 'code' as well. The idea of culture as codified suggests that there are conventionalized meanings to be unlocked and revealed if learners can find a way to break the code, and it is in this respect that Emilie's assertion that she wants to provide students not only with knowledge of cultural references but also the tools necessary for decoding makes sense as a starting point in her instructional approach (the process of decoding and of aiding students to develop decoding skills is discussed in detail in Chapter 4). Emilie's approach, then, not only includes exposing students to a variety of reference points and stories of the war from French perspectives (what she calls providing 'cultural references') and helping them to identify the common and contrasting symbols and themes in and across them, but it also involves arming students with the analytic skills necessary for analyzing texts for the narratives they relate and the points of view they represent.

Emilie's goals for students to expand their meaning-making repertoires through actual use of these 'codes' and 'reference networks' was never as explicitly articulated in interviews; however, when she described in the teacher meeting I observed a moment that encapsulates how she knows when the global simulation has 'worked,' we get a sense both of her underlying (if unexpressed) goal that students exercise their meaning-making potentials, as well as the deeply social semiotic character of her goals, even if, again, she never stated them in exactly these terms. She explained that often students' lexical choices come from a particular text the class reads, *Paroles d'Etoiles*, and that

> *c'est souvent qu'ils reprennent le vocabulaire et moi je suis heureuse de le retrouver dans une des des compos et c'est là en général que je vois que c'a marché quand ils ont repris* (it is often that they take up the vocabulary and I am happy to find it in one of the compositions and it's then in general that I see that it has worked when they have taken up).

When students come to integrate others' words and symbols into their own production of meaningful texts, Emilie considers her approach to have worked. In explaining the *Mémoires* project to her students, Emilie did underscore more explicitly what the exercise was intended to encourage.

On 14 September 2006, after students had submitted their first *Mémoires* chapter, Emilie took a few minutes at the start of class to remind them of the goals of the writing assignment: *'L'intérêt c'est oui que vous racontiez une histoire culturellement et historiquement précise, mais c'est également un exercice de style'* (The idea is yes that you tell a culturally and historically accurate story, but it is also an exercise in style). She then gave an example of the repetition and flat language she can sometimes encounter in reading 15 chapters each week, all on the same general topic and phase of the Occupation. She encouraged the students, as a result, *'soyez un peu passionnants'* (be a little bit passionate) and encouraged them to take risks in their drafts. In any case, she explained, she doesn't grade these facets of the first draft. She said *'vous êtes écrivains...vous voulez communiquer avec vos lecteurs'* (you are writers...you want to communicate with your readers) and asked them to push themselves in order to forge this connection. On this occasion and others, when Emilie refocused students on the goals of the extended writing project, she often highlighted these aspects of making meaning, crafting a voice and entering into dialogue with an audience, and achieving style as opposed to getting the facts right, so to speak.

Emilie's goals were well served by a global simulation approach since global simulation invites a network of interdependent stories, collaboration among learners to make meanings, occasions for reflection and many opportunities to exploit the affordances of the rich semiotic ecology that was set up through the global simulation. In the next section, the richness of this semiotic environment is described in terms of the 'web of texts' which is expressed in many modes and brings into dialogue a wide array of voices and perspectives in Emilie's classroom.

A 'web of texts'

Apparent in Emilie's approach is a view of intercultural learning as a process of becoming familiar with the cultural narratives that shape a worldview. Part of a broader cultural view are many smaller, more particular views, or many stories, that are shared by members of a cultural group. Some of these stories are told over and over again and take on particular significances. Learning what these stories are and what they mean, then, is part of the culture learning process for language learners, and any student of culture really. At an even more particular level are individual or personal stories that might correspond to a greater or lesser degree to larger cultural narratives but that, in all cases, have unique characteristics. Learning how cultural narratives are constructed from semiotic materials and how they shape the way individuals and members of a group see the world is one part of cultural learning, and relating individual voices to larger cultural narratives is another. Culture, though, is not a static system, so it is not sufficient to 'acquire' some fixed filter, a repertoire of cultural narratives, through which to view the world differently. This would suggest a passive kind of learning process and that narratives, even when they are shared, do not change. On the contrary, culture learning is very much active, with those seeking entrée into a cultural world, to whatever extent that might be, needing to engage in a process of active making-meaning in addition to the interpretation of meaning. In the narrative approach Emilie employed, the writing portion of the global simulation project was the most important way for students to move from identification and analysis of the important symbolic touchstones (words, images, other iconic symbols) and stories of the war to a restorying of this experience from the perspective of someone who they imagined to have lived it. Both acts involve a repositioning, and preceding either act is the coming to awareness that a web of meanings, or what we might call a complex of cultural references and narratives, different from one's own even exists.

In Emilie's class, an incredibly rich textual environment was created. Emilie spoke in one of our interviews of catching students in a 'web of texts' wherein narratives echoed and entered into dialogue with each other. As the semester went by, I could not help but notice the ways she made moves in classroom interaction to position students over and over again as imagined subjects, and it occurred to me that she was also modeling how students could reposition themselves, particularly for the writing of the *Mémoires* project, in which they wrote from an imagined subject position. In Emilie's approach to culture teaching, repositioning seemed to be a way of engaging students in viewing cultural narratives and personal stories from an unfamiliar point of view. In their written work, however, students were asked to generate stories that drew on cultural narratives and that presented one personal story that was situated within a broader cultural context.

Encouraging familiarity with a range of voices and stories in the classroom was effected through the creation of a 'web of texts,' as Emilie said. To more clearly convey how Emilie's classroom was a learning environment rich in narratives, I have identified the variety of narratives that were present during an early class period I observed and have organized them in Table 3.1. The main 'stories' that were present that day were apparent to me because they were often marked by a shift from Emilie's 'teacher voice,' a shift in the positioning of the students (Emilie repositioned them) or a framing that explicitly asked students to 'imagine'. While I did not orient

Table 3.1 Narratives apparent on one day of class (11 September 2006), from Kearney (2012)

The French on bikes seeing the sea for the first time, a story associated with the socialist Front populaire government of Léon Blum and the summer of 1936, which takes on new meaning during the war period. (A photograph from this time, also shown here, was included at the top of the students' weekly schedule.)	

The drôle de guerre narrative explains how the French gave a name to this phase of the war, having heard "funny" when encountering English accounts of the war, which characterized it as a "phony" war. In telling this story, Emilie asks students to "Imaginez que vous avez une oreille français."

The guerre éclair (lightening war) narrative, emphasizing intimidation tactics used by the German forces. Emilie asks students to "Imaginez que vous êtes la population française."

Story about Emilie's grandfather, who, at the start of the war, came out of a stupor after a German bombing of his military unit's camp, only to realize that he and another soldier were the only survivors.

Discussion of various stories the students read for homework from a collection of memoirs written by those who experienced the war in France as children, called Paroles d'Etoiles. These excerpts centered on the experience of the mass exodus from Paris when German troops advanced toward the city.

Another narrative related to the mass exodus in which Emilie asks students to "Imaginez que vous êtes juin 1940...vous participez à l'exode...qu'est-ce que vous faites?" This is a story co-constructed with students. Emilie guides their responses with her questions and leads them to focus on what modes of transportation they used and what they brought with them.

Story about Emilie's grandmother, who left behind her farm at the start of the war. A joke about leaving behind all her animals but not her mother-in-law brings some levity to the story. (Linked briefly to another narrative, that of Claudine in Paroles d'Etoiles).

A visual narrative in the form of a clip from the film Jeux Interdits, which portrays the mass exodus from Paris. Before showing the clip, Emilie says "Absorbez les images pour créer vos personnages, vous plonger dans l'époque."

to the notion of a multiplicity of narratives operating on both collective and individual levels while I was in the classroom, I did write in my field notes after just the first day of observation that 'Emilie really gives them several ways to relate to the "content" – through discussion of readings, through her own personal stories and with the film clip.' Already in initial stages of spending time in her class, the various 'stories' that were recounted in Emilie's class were of analytic interest.

In the 50-minute class period, at least nine narratives were in play. The first three narratives occurred as the class discussed the *Identifications* activity that on this particular day centered on the political climate in France before the war, the initial phases of the war and how the population reacted to the German invasion. So beyond simply discussing the who, what, when and where of history, these 'facts' are supplemented with stories and imaginations of the effects these conditions and events might have had on particular people. In examining the various narratives that were present in this class period, a movement between individual and broader cultural narratives is apparent. At times, Emilie evokes particular images that would have meanings for particular social and cultural groups (like the 'French on bikes' image as representing a particular storyline of peace and happiness related to the prewar period), and at others, she recounts the stories of individuals, like her grandparents, that relate to the larger cultural narratives but that have their own unique trajectories and defining characteristics as well. That Emilie tells the students at the end of the class, right before they watch the video clip from *Jeux Interdits*, to 'absorb the images' as a way of forming ideas for the stories they will write in the *Mémoires* project is particularly important, since it makes clear the connections that Emilie hopes her students will make across large (cultural) and small (personal, individual) stories. Her approach then encourages intertextuality as the class goes about making sense and meaning around culture. Indeed, her vision of the web of texts lends itself well to this practice of weaving stories and meanings together.

As I typed up my field notes after observing on this day, I described students' reactions to the film clip they saw at the end of class, which focused on a particular family whose car breaks down and whose daughter is nearly shot as German planes rain bullets down on the convoy of fleeing Parisians. Several students reacted, and one student remarked that an 'every man for himself kind of atmosphere' was illustrated by a group of people who push the family's car over an embankment to get it out of their way. In my bracketed notes, I wrote, 'This is a great example of students entering into dialogue with particular texts and with the subject more generally.' Making connections across texts, identifying recurring storylines and individual voices and experiences within these larger cultural templates, then, was in play in this class right from the beginning.

The global simulation

While it was clear to students from the first day of class that they would be engaged in the study of World War II from a range of French perspectives, it wasn't until the end of the first week of classes that Emilie introduced the overarching project that would organize their activity. She distributed a description of the overall project to them (see Figure 3.1) that laid out the basic parameters of the assignment and that began to immerse them in the narrative world that they would work together to develop. The handout that Emilie gave to students described the project in the following way:

In translation, this document reads:

> Imagine that you all lived in the same apartment building in Paris, on Convention Street, before the war broke out. Everyone knew each other more or less well. Everyone had a particular role in this Parisian microcosm. There were, among others, the chatty concierge; the Fechner

---

Mémoires de Guerre

Imaginez que vous habitiez tous dans le même immeuble à Paris, rue Convention, avant que la guerre n'éclate. Tout le monde se connaissait plus ou moins bien. Chacun avait un rôle bien particulier dans ce microcosme parisien. Il y avait, entre autres, la concierge piplette; la famille Fechner, qui possédait une boutique de fourrure dans la même rue; la magnifique Marion Steiner et son mari, propriétaires du Théâtre Montmartre; l'énigmatique Monsieur Klein; Mme Armand la fleuriste; et bien entendu, vous.

La guerre a éclaté et tout a changé. Pas toujours en mal, heureusement.

Vous allez créer un personnage qui consignera, dans ses Mémoires, ses souvenirs de ce troublant épisode de sa vie. A travers ses mots et son histoire, c'est toute l'Histoire du pays qui sera reflétée. Chaque semaine, il nous fera le récit de ce dont il a été témoin et de ce qu'il a subi pendant l'Occupation.

Ainsi, 50 ans après les événements pourrons-nous identifier les différents acteurs de la plus sombre période de l'histoire de France et tenter de « comprendre » ce qui s'est passé.

A vos plumes...

Figure 3.1 Description of the global simulation project

family that owned a fur store on the same street; the magnificent Marion Steiner and her husband, owners of the Montmartre Theater; the enigmatic Monsieur Klein; Madame Armand, the florist; and of course, you.

The war broke out and everything changed. Not always for the worse, luckily.

You are going to create a character who will record, in his memoirs, his memories of this troubling episode of his life. Through his words and his stories, it is all the history of the country that will be reflected. Each week, he will tell us the story of what he witnessed and what he underwent during the Occupation.

In this way, 50 years after the events, we can identify the various actors of the most somber period of French history and attempt to 'understand' what happened.

Take up your pens…

In the description of the project, several important dimensions emerge. The first and second short paragraphs serve to initiate the students into a rich narrative world. The first paragraph introduces a setting and a cast of characters among whom students (addressed as 'you' here) would 'live'. The characters that are listed are all figures that the class would encounter in the films they saw and the novel they read. Monsieur Klein and Marion Steiner, for example, were characters in two films the class watched, and the Fechner family was the main focus of the novel the class read. Emilie included a concierge in this cast of characters as well, since a concierge was present in nearly all Parisian apartment buildings during this era, and she wanted to be sure that students would include one. The imaginative exercise is clear from the beginning since it is after all introduced with the imperative form 'Imagine'. As will become apparent in later chapters, the directive to 'imagine' was also pervasive during classroom interactions when Emilie introduced particular narratives and asked students to project themselves into these situations. A storyline also begins to emerge in these first two paragraphs. The baseline plot from which all of the students would create their characters and stories was that they all lived in the same building, knew each other pretty well and shared good and bad times during the war.

There are certain elements of these first two paragraphs that also start to communicate the objectives of the project. The first paragraph announces that 'Everyone had a particular role in this Parisian microcosm'.

One goal of the project, then, was to create a group of characters that were in some ways representative of the larger Parisian population. In order to do so, students would need to understand what this larger population was like and then would need to be able to credibly reconstruct the context in which the population lived. The third paragraph offers even more detail about what the students would actually do to complete the project. That is, they would create a character and write his or her memoirs. There is particular emphasis in this paragraph on relating the 'words and stories' of the character that connect to larger history, an explicit invitation to connect an individual's voice to larger cultural narratives and a broader context. The fourth paragraph also reveals what the larger goals of the project are – to identify relevant historical actors and to try to 'understand' what happened. Identifying the 'various actors' again seems to suggest that the ability to discern and reconstruct both individual and more collective social voices was a goal of the project. That the word 'understand' is in quotation marks is also noteworthy, as if to suggest that truly understanding this historical era might not be so straightforward.

In total, students wrote seven compositions, including six chapters of the memoirs and a preface, which was written instead from an editor's point of view rather than the character's, and was composed after all of the other chapters were completed. For each chapter, students were provided with a prompt, all of which appear in translated and summarized form below (Table 3.2). As the weeks progressed, the characters' stories unfolded temporally as well. Emilie gave the students loose guidelines so that they could situate their characters' stories such that the first three compositions recounted events occurring between 1939 and 1941, the fourth and the fifth related the years between 1942 and 1944, and the sixth focused on 1945. The preface was to be written from the point of view of an editor collecting and introducing the memoirs in 2006. For each chapter, except the preface, of which there was only one version, students turned in a first draft, received comments and feedback from Emilie (pertaining to content, style and linguistic form), and then resubmitted their draft as a final version. At the end of the project, students turned in to Emilie all of the revised chapters, the preface and a cover that included an image of some sort. In the end, then, a considerable and tangible final product was produced.

It is noteworthy that even in the prompts, Emilie addressed the students as their characters. This is the case for all the chapters except for the preface, where the voice of an editor, really meant to represent the students' own voices, is introduced. Beyond the voices explicitly identified in Emilie's written directions to students, the incorporation of other characters and

Table 3.2 Summary of prompts for *mémoires* chapters

Chapter	Prompt summary
Chapter 1	Introduce yourself and briefly describe your life before the war. Communicate whether you were a supporter of Pétain or de Gaulle in June 1940 and why.
Chapter 2	Explain your life under the German occupation. Describe how the National Revolution affected your life (or not). Tell us whether your life in the 'French House' was good.
Chapter 3	Life in the building was no longer the same. The walls seemed to have ears and prying eyes were everywhere. Life became particularly difficult for certain people. Tell a story that illustrates the tragic absurdity of the times.
Chapter 4	You were the victim or author of an act of betrayal that you can't forgive (or can't forgive yourself for). Entrust it to your readers.
Chapter 5	One day the Fechners disappeared. At the time, you thought that they were victims of a denunciation and that the guilty party lived with you in the building. Whom did you suspect and why?
Chapter 6	The war was officially over. But was it really finished? Some people never came back to the building. Henri Fechner came back but never spoke about what happened to his family. He continued his life and reopened the family's boutique. Describe Parisian life in this time of refound 'peace' and tell how your life got back to normal.
Preface	The editor of your memoirs is the author of the preface. In this preface, he or she explains the interest of such an account for the generations who didn't live through the war. [Through the words of the editor it is <u>your own voice</u> that we should hear.]

perspectives was in store, not only by way of including central and well-known historical actors and fictive characters from the texts the class studied that Emilie did not make reference to, but also through the cast of characters the students would all create. Since the students' characters would inhabit the same buildings, their paths were sure to cross; indeed, Emilie encouraged the interweaving of plotlines among students once they had firmly established their own character in early chapters. In these rapidly populated narrative worlds, a heteroglossia quickly became audible, with singular and social voices all telling the stories of the Occupation era, filtered through the mind and understandings of each student.

When Emilie described the *Mémoires* project to the class, she often said that the work needed to have *'points d'ancrage historiques'* (historical anchoring points) and that through the stories (*histoires*) of their characters, history

(*Histoire*) itself would be revealed. (The word for 'story' and 'history' are the same in French, only distinguished on occasion by writing 'history' with a capital 'h'. This lexical feature became a rich point for communicating the message that students' stories were meant to capture both a story and history writ large.) When Emilie spoke of historical anchoring points, she was not simply asking students to include references to names, dates and events that the class was learning about (although that was important too), but also themes cutting across these basic 'facts' (as the prompts for each chapter suggest) and stances toward various historical actors, moments and happenings. In order to raise students' awareness about integrating historical detail in the early stages of the project, Emilie carried out one short exercise with students in which they had to identify anachronisms and other inaccuracies in sentences that were taken from previous students' compositions. By asking students to identify what did not fit in each sentence (see Figure 3.2), Emilie helped the class come to the awareness that while including certain details would render their accounts more authentic, knowledge of what not to include would also be helpful.

Emilie's decision to design a short pedagogical exercise such as this one at the start of the class's work on the *Mémoires* project reveals her

---

Qu'est-ce qui cloche?

1. Le jour où les Allemands ont envahi Paris je regardais mon programme préféré à la télévision. (*The day that the Germans invaded Paris I was watching my favorite show on television.*)
2. Ma mère était concierge. Tous les samedis, je faisais du shopping sur les Champs-Élysées. (*My mother was a concierge. Every Saturday, I went shopping on the Champs-Élysées.*)
3. Mon père était directeur de banque et nous habitions une chambre de bonne. (*My father was a boss at a bank and we lived in a maid's room.*)
4. Bonjour, je m'appelle Soleil. (*Hello, my name is Sun.*)
5. Mon amie Clara et moi, nous passions des heures au téléphone. (*My best friend Clara and I, we spent hours on the telephone.*)
6. Déjà avant la guerre le général de Gaulle était mon héros. (*Already before the war, General de Gaulle was my hero.*)
7. En juin 40 je soutenais de Gaulle car je détestais les idées nazies de Pétain. (*In June of 1940 I supported de Gaulle because I hated the Nazi ideas of Pétain.*)
8. Ma chambre était typique d'une adolescente très cool. (*My room was typical of a cool teenager.*)

Figure 3.2 Qu'est-ce qui cloche? (*What doesn't fit?*) with translations of the anachronistic sentences provided

concern that the students pay attention to getting historical and cultural details right, but in the following excerpt, it is clear that key to accurately or plausibly portraying a historical context are the linguistic choices and symbolic choices students make. As Emilie reads the sample sentences aloud and invites students to explain why the sentences do not work, she stresses certain words; the students, too, focus on these and other word choices as they search the sentences for inaccuracies. When the interaction first begins, it is notable that the first student contribution focuses on grammatical rather than historical or cultural inaccuracy (line 7), but students very quickly move on to offering hypotheses related to the substance of the example sentence rather than its linguistic correctness. Language choices then become a question of symbolic or stylistic appropriateness rather than grammatical correctness.

Excerpt 1 *Qu'est-ce qui cloche?* (What doesn't fit?)

01 **Emilie**: Je vais juste vous distribuer ça c'est des choses que j'ai trouvées dans um des
02   compositions les semestres précédents (9) et vous allez me dire d'après vous pourquoi
03   alors qu'est-ce qui cloche dans ces phrases ça veut dire qu'est-ce qui ne marche pas
04   qu'est-ce qui est bizarre merci première phrase le jour <u>où</u> les Allemands ont envahi
05   Paris je regardais mon programme préféré à la télévision pourquoi est-ce que moi mes
06   cheveux font ça (holding up her hair in the air) quand je lis ça
07 **S1**:   Où
08 **S3**:   Il n'y a pas de télévision
09 **S4**:   Non
10 **Emilie**: Oui (1) fin il y a la télévision mais vous pensez qu'en 1939 en 1940 vous regardez la
11   télévision pendant (2) trois heures (2) vous pensez que vous regardez uh (2) Desperate
12   Housewives
13 **Ss**:   Haha
14 **Emilie**: Et c'est en France ça maintenant avec ce titre Desperate Housewives vous pensez que
15   vous regardez ça pendant trois heures en 1940 (students shake head 'no') essayez de
16   penser aussi à ça
17 **S5**:   Anachronisme
18 **Emilie**: Comment
19 **S5**:   Est-ce que ça c'est un anachronisme
20 **Emilie**: Ouais ouais attention aux anachronismes (1) maintenant ma mère était concierge tous
21   les samedis je faisais du <u>shopping</u> sur les <u>Champs-Élysées</u> (rolls eyes)
22 **S3**:   Shopping
23 **Emilie**: Anachronisme linguistique du shopping et puis quoi d'autre oui
24 **S6**:   Que autre um si sa mère était uh concierge elle uh ne peut pas faire du shopping sur les
25   Champs-Élysées

26	**Emilie**:	Ouais vous pensez que votre mère est concierge vous allez sur la cinquième avenue à
27		New York (Ss laugh) d'accord donc ça aussi d'accord je sais que vous n'êtes pas vous
28		n'êtes pas supposés tout savoir déjà d'accord ça c'est aussi un objectif de l'exercice
29		moi je ne vais pas vous pénaliser pour ce genre de chose c'est pour ça que ça soit la
30		<u>première</u> version je vous indiquerai mais réfléchissez quand-même un petit peu
31		demandez-moi mon père était directeur de banque et nous habitions dans une chambre
32		de bonne
33	**S7**:	(unintelligible)
34	**Emilie**:	Oui voilà votre père est complètement fou et c'est une expérience que vous faites je ne
35		sais pas alors bonjour je m'appelle soleil (Ss laugh)
36	**S8**:	Il n'y a pas de noms comme ça dans les années 40
37	**Emilie**:	Ouais alors les noms un peu bizarre soleil pomme prune (Ss laugh) ça c'est (Ss laugh)
38		mais ça c'est très très c'est récent jusque jusqu'aux années 80 85 d'accord 1980 1985
39		vous ne pouviez pas appeler votre enfant comme vous le vouliez il fallait que le
40		prénom soit sur le calendrier chrétien (3) d'accord donc soleil tout ça non il fallait que
41		vous alliez au tribunal et très compliqué d'accord donc ça impossible mon amie Clara
42		et moi nous passions des <u>heures</u> au téléphone
43	**S3**:	(unintelligible)
44	**Emilie**:	Voilà téléphone télé uh non (1) déjà avant la guerre le général de Gaulle était mon
45		héros
46	**S8**:	Non
47	**Emilie**:	Pourquoi
48	**S7**:	Il est inconnu
49	**S8**:	Parce qu'il n'était pas un général avant la guerre je pense
50	**Emilie**:	Comment
51	**S8**:	Il n'était pas un général avant la guerre
52	**S3**:	C'est le général Pétain que c'est un héros
53	**Emilie**:	Alors le maréchal Pétain et tout d'abord de Gaulle n'était pas général avant la guerre
54		mais aussi personne ne le connaissait à moins que ça soit votre c'était peut-être votre
55		voisin et que vous jouiez avec quand vous étiez petit en juin 40 je soutenais de Gaulle
56		car je détestais les idées nazies de Pétain
57	**S9**:	Il n'avait pas des idées nazies avant avant (unintelligible)
58	**Emilie**:	exactement d'accord on ne parle pas de nazis encore on parle d'armistice avec les
59		ennemis mais l'idéologie c'est après et enfin ma chambre était typique d'une
60		adolescente très cool
61	**S10**:	Cool
62	**Emilie**:	Là cool en 1940 fin même si c'est un adjectif maintenant une dame de 80 ans ne va pas
63		dire oh ma chambre était cool voilà

01	**Emilie**:	*I am just going to hand this out to you; these are things that I found in um compositions*
02		*from previous semesters (9) and you are going to tell me why in your opinion so what*
03		*is wrong in these sentences, that means what does not work what is strange. thank you*
04		*first sentence the day the Germans invaded Paris I was watching my favorite show on*
05		*television why does my hair do this (holding up her hair in the air) when I read that*
06	**S1**:	*Where/when*
07	**S3**:	*There isn't television*
08	**S4**:	*No*
09	**Emilie**:	*Yes (1) so there is television but do you think that in 1939 in 1940 you watch television*
10		*for (2) three hours (2) do you think that you watch uh (2) Desperate Housewives*
11	**Ss**:	*Haha*
13	**Emilie**:	*And that's in France now with that title, Desperate Housewives, do you think you watch*
14		*that for three hours in 1940 (students shake head "no") try to think about that as well*
15	**S5**:	*Anachronism*
17	**Emilie**:	*What*
18	**S5**:	*Is that an anachronism*
19	**Emilie**:	*Yeah yeah be careful of anachronisms (1) now my mother was a concierge every*
20		*Saturday I went <u>shopping</u> on the <u>Champs-Élysées</u> (rolls eyes)*
21	**S3**:	*Shopping*
22	**Emilie**:	*A linguistic anachronism shopping and then what else*
23	**S6**:	*What else um if her mother was uh a concierge she uh cannot go shopping on the*
24		*Champs-Élysées*
25	**Emilie**:	*Yeah do you think that if your mother is a concierge you go to 5th Avenue in New York*
26		*(Ss laugh) ok so that too ok I know you are not you are not expected to know*
27		*everything already ok that is a goal of the exercise too I'm not going to penalize you*
28		*for this type of thing that's why it's a <u>first</u> draft I will tell you but still think about it a*
29		*little bit ask me my father was a boss at the bank and we lived in a maid's quarters*
30	**S7**:	*(unintelligible)*
32	**Emilie**:	*Yes exactly your father is completely crazy and it is an experiment you are doing I*
33		*don't know so Hi my name is Sun*
34	**S8**:	*There aren't names like that in the 1940s*
35	**Emilie**:	*Yeah so names that are a little strange Sun Apple Prune (Ss laugh) that's (Ss laugh) but*
36		*that is very very it's recent up until up until the 1980s 1985 ok 1980 1985 you could not*
37		*name your child what you wanted the name had to be on the christian calendar (3) ok*
38		*so Sun all of that no you had to go to the courthouse and very complicated ok so that*
39		*impossible my friend Clara and I we spent <u>hours</u> on the phone*
40	**S3**:	*(unintelligible)*
42	**Emilie**:	*Exactly telephone TV uh no (1) already before the war General de Gaulle was my hero*
43	**S8**:	*no*

44	**Emilie**:	*Why*
45	**S7**:	*He is unknown*
46	**S8**:	*Because he isn't a general before the war I think*
47	**Emilie**:	*What*
48	**S8**:	*He wasn't a general before the war*
49	**S3**:	*It was General Pétain that was a hero*
50	**Emilie**:	*So Maréchal Pétain and then first of all de Gaulle was not a general before the war*
51		*but also no one knew him unless it was your he was your neighbor and that you played*
52		*with him when you were little in June 1940 I supported de Gaulle because I hated the*
53		<u>*Nazi*</u> *ideas*
54	**S9**:	*Of Pétain there were not Nazi ideas before before (unintelligible)*
55	**Emilie**:	*Exactly ok no one talks about Nazis yet they talk about the armistice with the enemies*
56		*but the ideology that's after and finally my room was typical of a very cool teenager*
57	**S10**:	*Cool*
58	**Emilie**:	*That cool in 1940 even if it is an adjective now a lady of 80 years of age is not going to*
59		*say oh my room was cool there it is*

(Observation from 13 September 2006)

To underscore the reactions produced in readers by the inclusion of cultural and historical inaccuracies and in order to draw the students' attention to particular forms and notions represented in the sample sentences, Emilie relies on more than just stress of certain words, although this is an effective attention-getting technique (lines 20, 39 and 53).[1] She also on two occasions likens the content of a sample sentence to something students are more prone to be familiar with, in effect recontextualizing the anachronistic or ridiculous act in a more understandable frame of reference. She does this in emphasizing the unlikelihood of watching television for three hours in 1940 by adding the detail in her direct questions to students (lines 9–10 and 13–14) about whether they think they would have watched *Desperate Housewives* for three hours if they lived in 1940. Emilie again employs this strategy when the class reads a sentence about a character who asserts that her mother is a concierge but that she likes to shop on the Champs-Élysées every weekend (lines 25–26). In this case, Emilie likens the Champs-Élysées to Fifth Avenue in New York and again directly asks students if they think that they would be shopping on Fifth Avenue if their mother held such a station in life. In both cases, students react with laughter and seem to clearly receive Emilie's messages about the dissonance that these propositions would present to a reader.

While making the point that students should pay attention to the inclusion and exclusion of certain details in their *Mémoires* writing, Emilie does communicate to her students that she does not expect that they will have all of the information they need to successfully craft the contexts they are creating for their characters (lines 26–29); her goal appears more to be that students begin thinking about these details more deeply as they write and that they carry out at least some of their own research to render even their first drafts more believable. At this early point in the semester, Emilie is encouraging students to draw on the resources available to them (class texts and materials, herself as the teacher) to achieve more plausible texts, and she regularly advised students during class interactions to draw on particular texts, images and film clips as they composed their weekly chapters. Throughout this excerpt, the example sentences are often analyzed with reference to imprecision in language choices, as in the example about naming of a character (lines 33–39), the use of the term 'nazies' in the early stages of the Occupation (lines 52–56) or the use of the term 'cool' by a narrator who was 80 years old (lines 56–59) illustrate.

Preparing students to integrate themes and stances toward events in their compositions was effected by creating an environment where first, relevant (and irrelevant) reference points (dates, names, events, symbols) were identified and then thematic connections could be made; and where a variety of positions on the same events were also available for consideration. Alongside the *Mémoires* writing project, a second major aspect of the global simulation was the *Café de retrouvailles* (Reunion Café) activity, which was a weekly event during which students took on the voice and persona they had created in order to interact with other students' characters. The group of 15 students was divided into two apartment buildings so that they could more easily converse with each other and so that they had a more manageable amount of reading to do before class. (In preparation for the *Café de retrouvailles* activities, students were asked to read the first version of their classmates' work that was posted on a website the class used.) Just as students were provided with prompts for the writing of their characters' memoirs, they were also provided with a theme and sometimes a few questions to help them to get conversation started among their 'former neighbors'. These prompts were closely related on most occasions to the prompts that students consulted before writing their chapters. On the first day that the class engaged in the *Café de retrouvailles* activity, Emilie explained, '*Je vais vous demander un gros exercice d'imagination*' (I am going to ask an enormous imaginative exercise of you) (Observation from 13 September 2006). She explained that over the course of the following seven weeks, this activity would be an interactive as well as imaginative exercise.

Methods for Investigating Meaning-Making in a Modern Language Classroom

As I thought about studying Emilie's approach to intercultural pedagogy and the implementation of the global simulation in her class, I focused on designing data collection and analysis that would allow me to gain an overall sense of the curriculum, the typical features of the classroom discourse environment and Emilie's general instructional procedures and style, while also capturing the very fine details of interactions in the classroom and of engagements students had with the course through their assignments, especially the extended writing project. As a result, I decided to study the class for an entire semester and to visit on a regular basis with my video recording equipment (about two times a week on average while the class met four times a week). This plan translated to a total of 28 classroom visits over the course of the 13-week semester. Immediately after all visits, field notes were composed. Seventeen class sessions were video-recorded, totaling approximately 14 hours of video; 13 of these recorded sessions were just during the Occupation dossier and totaled approximately 11.5 hours of video. I also collected 2 hours and 15 minutes of students' *Confessional* recordings as assignments students completed outside of normal class time, for which they prepared some notes and then went to a small audio recording studio on campus to speak through the voice of the character they had created for the global simulation project. The written products of the global simulation – *Mémoires* projects from 13 of the 14 students in the class – were also collected (one student enrolled in the class did not participate in the research). These written assignments were the final versions that students submitted to Emilie. I conducted two recorded interviews with Emilie and, near the end of the semester, I conducted interviews with 10 students. These were the primary data that I drew on to investigate meaning-making and the global simulation project in Emilie's class. As is common in classroom ethnographies of this type, outside of observing her classes, I spent time at the university where Emilie taught to get a slightly broader understanding of the environment in which she worked; through these observations, I composed a set of informal notes and made recordings from related events at the university such as a meeting of teachers who all taught the same content-based course as Emilie and a teaching assistants' training day that took place in August, before the start of classes and of observation in Emilie's class.

My goal in analysis was to identify the ways that interactional moments and recurring episodes constructed larger social processes – in this case, intercultural learning and the development of symbolic competence in a particular classroom. Between particular interactional moments and broader, ongoing processes such as intercultural learning and development of symbolic competence, there are clearly going to be mediating activities and processes, and this is the level of activity that I was keen on identifying and analyzing for structure and substance. This is where I thought I would find semiosis potentially occurring in patterned ways (rather than in one-off instances), and I wanted to know in what ways it was occurring and what interactional forms it took. This level of interaction in the classroom might be thought of as the ways that Emilie and her students engaged with cultural texts and representations and made meaning around them. I do, however, make claims about broader learning and development processes eventually, such as the way that meaning-making practices in Emilie's classroom interactions supported broader intercultural learning and development of symbolic competence with regard to the ability to understand and potentially shift one's perspectives. But the initial work of my analysis was to look closely into interactional moments and episodes.

Even as I was still visiting Emilie's class and collecting data, I began to organize and analyze video recordings and field notes. I first turned to the video records of classroom sessions and began by making video logs of major activity types, noting time codes in those places where discernable boundaries between activities occurred. In general, when social actors change topic of conversation, shift gaze or physical position, mark discourse verbally in particular ways or usually make some combination of these changes, it signals that some new social activity is occurring (Erickson, 2006). In Emilie's class, there were clear discourse markers as well as paralinguistic markers of shifts in phases of activity during each class period, which aided in breaking up each classroom meeting into smaller phases of activity that were relevant to the participants themselves. Once these basic records of activity in the class were established, it was possible to begin classifying activity types and generating analytic memos about the kinds of processes that might underlie these activities. For example, *identifications* activities (discussed in depth in Chapter 4) were a recurring and highly structured type of activity that always occurred in the beginning phases of class sessions. By focusing in on all *identifications* activities, it became possible to then analyze for typical and atypical content, patterns in interactional structure and the sorts of affordances this particular routine produced in terms of meaning-making. Textual analysis was also rapidly apparent as a major activity type in Emilie's classroom, and identifying instances in the video logs allowed for deeper investigation, again, of the affordances such activities created in terms of semiosis. In addition to identifying activity types, analysis throughout the data collection and beyond was supported by the drafting of analytic memos about processes that seemed to cut across activity types in Emilie's class. An example of this is the notion of narrative and narration, which became a major focus even in the early weeks of data collection and analysis. Meaning-making in Emilie's class seemed to be facilitated by the preponderance of narratives and narrative practices in the classroom ecology. The notion of narrative practices is an analytic concept that I adopt from the field of linguistic anthropology:

> a discipline in which storytelling practices are viewed as culturally-shaped and culture-shaping participation structures that privilege certain narrative content, who is seen as a legitimate teller and/or recipient of a story, and sequential or formal structures. All of these conventions tend to produce or favor certain social identities, socialization processes, and other social phenomena (e.g. Ochs & Taylor, 2009). (Kearney, 2012: 64)

While marked by conventions and permeated by norms, power and ideology, narrative practices are also highly practical and local; that is, they serve everyday sense-making purposes as people attempt to bring order and ascribe meaning to their experiences of the world, and they are a site of learning and development. This dimension of narrative is discussed in more detail below; however, this sense-making function of narrative practices was essential in analyzing classroom interactions recorded in Emilie's class and in analyzing students' writing, since engagement with narrative practice could be investigated from the point of view of both semiotic processes on their own terms as well as semiotic processes as intercultural learning and development of symbolic competence in the context of ML education. In analyzing the students' narrative writing specifically, my process was to make summaries of each student's collection of chapters, documenting the main elements of plot and the main reference points and symbols students integrated into their work. In relation to the anchoring reference points students included in their *Mémoires*, I attempted to list possible intertexts from the class's broader work these might relate to (e.g. speeches the class analyzed, texts they read, films they viewed and discussed, images they encountered and analyzed). I then analyzed students' writing for the narrative devices they employed, especially voicing and intertextuality, as a means of more deeply understanding the way reference points and symbols were contextualized and how particular meanings were generated around these.

Everyday Narrative Sense-Making and Storying to Make Meaning at Grander Scale

The global simulation in place in Emilie's class and global simulation projects in general lend themselves to narrative sense-making. They are designed to rely on the advancement of a plotline through students' individual and collaborative efforts and, therefore, create a narrative product. But a global simulation approach also naturally fosters narrative sense-making processes as students and a teacher work together to make a narrative product possible.

Narrative has many functions in social life (Mishler, 1995), but one of these is a broad sense-making function. Especially the stories we tell in everyday life are opportunities to negotiate the meanings of happenings and our own and others' roles in them, and to piece together perspectives on events, ourselves, others and the world. As Ochs and Capps (2001) make very clear, narratives produced in everyday sense-making are distinct from the kinds of narratives we encounter in books and more canonical, planned and polished genres (such as speeches, songs, short stories, etc.). Everyday narrative practices produce stories that are messy, unfinalized, potentially nonlinear and often co-constructed with other interlocutors. These are stories that are being developed as they are told, as are the perspectives, stances and points they may ultimately make. Sometimes, they are contradictory in the perspectives they construct in contrast with more literary narratives that generally have decided morals, for example. In Emilie's class, such an orientation to narrative practices as sense-making is quite helpful, since the interactional environment of the classroom especially was a place where Emilie and her students could engage in narrative practice as a way of building meanings around texts and representations (which themselves also presented individual stories or indexed cultural narratives). As I have pointed out elsewhere, 'Because narrative is one of the primary sense-making resources humans have at their disposal, narratives of all kinds are not only abundant but replete with referential and symbolic networks of meaning, including the range of plausible storylines, symbols and social types that become conventionalized through shared narratives' (Kearney, 2010: 334).

That narrative practice and narrative sense-making occur at multiple levels is also important to note. Individual accounts of personal or shared, real or imagined experience are narrative instances that are inevitably linked to broader, shared narratives. This relationship between particular stories and broader cultural narratives aligns exactly with the theory of meaning potentials described in Chapter 2; in order for particular acts of meaning (particular stories) to make sense, they must instantiate to some degree broader, shared meaning potentials. In the same way, individual stories serve to potentially reshape shared notions of meaning potential. In the field of ML education, the term 'cultural narratives' has been used to refer to the 'multiple (sometimes competing), conventionalized storylines that cultural groups produce and use to make sense of and attribute meaning to their shared experience' (Kearney, 2012: 59). The MLA report (2007) asserts that cultural narratives are evident in 'every kind of expressive form' (p. 238) and are rich sites for engaging learners in meaningful development of 'translingual and transcultural competence'. Insights from Bakhtinian (1981, 1993) theory are also useful in connecting individual stories and broader cultural narratives, especially his proposition that all language resounds with many voices (heteroglossia) and that any seemingly singular voice actually relates to larger social voices, previous language uses, registers and styles of language, etc. From this point of view, all narrative productions (Bakhtin wrote about the novel in particular) necessarily intertwine individual utterances and storied instances with voices of different social types and of different social scales. In the students' written work for Emilie's class, such intermingling of voices in order to make meanings was clearly apparent. Of course, students were individually crafting narratives and as a group weaving coherent narrative environments for the global simulation project, but these stories were also the means through which students gained access to larger cultural narratives that circulate in the L2 society. Chapter 5 takes up a more detailed discussion of the way students achieved heteroglossia and a diversity of voices in their own writing as well as the specific textual practices they employed in order to connect one character's story with cultural narratives.

Taken together, the types of classroom experiences Emilie designed and the students' narrative writing assignment created space for multiple forms and levels of narrative sense-making, in addition to exposing students to a vast array of narrative texts and representations. In ecological terms, the curricular content Emilie prepared, the global simulation approach she adopted and the instructional activities she established as routine created affordances for deep engagement with meaning and meaning-making among students, as the next two chapters demonstrate in different ways. It is important to note that although the rich network of resources Emilie brought together in her course were a precondition for student learning and development, including diverse, compelling texts in the curriculum and planning a range of activity types for the classroom will not alone lead to deep and meaningful intercultural learning. In

Chapter 4, I will lay out precisely the in-the-moment, interactional-level elements of culture pedagogy that leverage the planned textual resources and instructional activity types in contingent ways; that is, patterns in Emilie's instructional moves, as she dealt with students' emerging understandings and unexpected contributions to classroom discourse, are presented and analyzed. Chapter 5 then takes up the possible impacts of Emilie's instructional work by looking to students' writing for the global simulation project. In these chapters, I explore in great detail the kinds of intercultural learning that was made possible as a result of the conditions Emilie established in her class – the rich textual environment resounding with narratives – and highlight especially the way that form-meaning connections were formed and meaning potentials developed as Emilie and her students compared, reflected, interpreted and took on various voices and perspectives. Through their joint activity, orchestrated masterfully by Emilie, a deep and collaborative kind of engagement flourished and students' meaning-making repertoires were expanded in multiple ways. Chapter 4 specifically focuses on the interactional processes that allowed students to develop their abilities to perceive culturally relevant signs and symbols and to expand their understanding of the meaning potentials of various symbolic forms by engaging in a range of interpretive and narrative practices that were designed and scaffolded by Emilie. Chapter 5, meanwhile, turns to students' written work for the class, the *Mémoires* accounts, as an illustration of the ways students called into action and even further stretched the meaning-making repertoires they were developing in the class. Excerpts from interviews with students are also woven into Chapter 5 in order to support the claims I advance about the impact of this pedagogical experience on students' language and culture learning in Emilie's class.

Note

(1) All in-text references to line numbers correspond to the English translations of participants' original spoken or written language.

4 Understanding Signification and Interpretive Acts Through Engagement with Cultural Representations

> [Emilie] is good at explaining things on multiple levels...Most teachers would only go into about half of that detail. - A student, Susan, describing the 15-minute interactive analysis that Emilie led in relation to a poster produced by the Vichy government in 1940. (Interview, 4 November 2006)

> As the class compared historical figures that were drawn on as symbols under the Republic and then the National Revolution, Emilie says that Joan of Arc will be a touchstone for Petain's government. She goes on to say that even today, Joan of Arc is a symbol that political figures take up and that 'si vous allez en France, dans une famille, et qu'ils vous disent qu'ils adorent Jeanne d'Arc et qu'ils vont à la célébration de Jeanne d'Arc, vous savez qu'ils votent à droite, extrême droite. D'accord. Il faut savoir décoder les petits signes de la culture comme ça' (If you go to France, in a family, and they tell you that they love Joan of Arc and that they go to the Joan of Arc celebration, you know that they vote on the right, extreme right. Ok. You have to know how to decode the little signs of culture like that. (Observation, 14 November 2006).

> [T]o me it kind of was like a history course and I really liked that. I learned a lot about things I had already learned but from a totally different perspective and I think that's really important... Jeannette then talks about an African history class, a film class and political sciences classes that all seemed to resonate with her French class. She describes her current class, 'it's so content-based you know and there is constant dialogue and I just think that it's, it's more intense in terms of letting you think critically in French as opposed to just learning what is you kind of have to contemplate like what's happening in history and how that intermingles with culture and have debate so it's a lot more intensive.' – A student, Jeannette, explaining how this course problematizes perspective. (Interview, 8 December 2006)

Two students' and Emilie's remarks begin to characterize the kinds of interactions Emilie's pedagogical approach allowed for. Susan's comments speak to Emilie's ability to introduce content, to highlight the layered complexity of form-meaning connections and to provide students with assistance in learning how to identify forms (symbols, reference points) and explore their meanings. Emilie herself advises students, once she has explained the indexical meaning of a family claiming deep admiration of Joan of Arc, of the need to be able to interpret signs such as this. This ability, she suggests, could be quite useful in their futures, and she even paints them a picture of a hypothetical situation to illustrate how knowledge of symbolic language use might help them to read a situation. Jeannette begins to suggest how Emilie's approach fostered deep engagement with meaning and problematized perspective by making apparent the multiple viewpoints and stances one might identify in relation to the same event or text. These comments raise the question of *how* exactly Emilie did all of this and how other language teachers might do the same. How can language teachers help learners understand cultural texts that contain forms and meanings they do not readily recognize and that may represent unfamiliar points of view? How do they facilitate shifts in perspective, both in interactional moments and in more enduring ways as part of this process of developing understanding of others' symbolic meaning-making systems?

Gaining awareness of symbolic forms and their meaning potentials and exploring perspectives and points of view are facilitated by a narrative-rich classroom environment like Emilie's (described in detail in the previous chapter). When individual and cultural narratives are unfamiliar, a language teacher's work involves not only an invitation to students to share their interpretations but also, and firstly, to provide the foundational reference points needed to recognize culturally relevant symbolic forms (words, expressions, images, etc.) and to support exploration of the meanings of those forms. Some of that exploration may be quite explicit, with a teacher offering direct explanations. But, it also can be more implicit through scaffolded interpretive activities or through connections made to other cultural texts or, in still other instances, it can take a more experiential shape, with a teacher animating cultural narratives through voicing and embodiment and making moves to reposition students and herself in time, place and discourse. All of these configurations within classroom discourse and interaction were apparent in Emilie's teaching and aim to facilitate the identification of reference points and the inhabiting of a range of perspectives. Ultimately, her planful, regular and interactive use of these routines, I argue, promoted students' access to the culturally shared meaning potentials of the linguistic and other symbolic forms they were encountering as well as the expansion of learners' personal meaning potentials.

Describing and analyzing the ways in which engagement with cultural texts and exploration of the forms and meanings in these was facilitated in Emilie's classroom form the core of this chapter. How interpretation of cultural texts was instructionally and interactionally achieved is presented through several examples that illustrate the diverse means through which interpretive and meaning-making processes were fostered by Emilie's instructional approach. These particular examples are meant to illustrate general processes and the kinds of instructional moves that would work in other classroom contexts and with other content. I begin by explaining how Emilie aided her students in identifying forms as culturally significant or symbolic in some manner and then discuss several ways in which Emilie supported students in exploring the meaning potentials of those forms. In social semiotic terms for construing learning, the processes described in this chapter supported learners' ability to achieve 'diversified perception and [semiotic] action' (van Lier, n.d.) and represent, for the most part, Emilie's work to make ways of perceiving and acting from French perspectives more accessible to students.

Identifying Cultural Reference Points and Symbolic Forms

Culturally symbolic forms are semiotic resources based in language, images, objects and other representational matter that, over time and through shared experiences, come to signal particular meaning potentials for certain groups of people. Of course, not all symbols are interpreted or deployed in the same way among individuals within cultural groups who otherwise share a broad orientation, worldview or experience. What anchors symbolic forms as having cultural meaning is that they are points of reference that groups share and with which they tend to make particular meanings. Very often, these are the symbols around which cultural narratives and a range of counternarratives coalesce. In a ML classroom, building a store of reference points and a repertoire of form-meaning connections available for interpretation and performance in the L2 is like building a cultural vocabulary or a semiotic navigation system of sorts. This does not imply an agentless language learner, who learns a set code of form-meaning associations and then reproduces them in appropriate contexts; on the contrary, an agentive language user, one who is symbolically competent, as Kramsch (2006) argues, is adept in the manipulation of symbolic systems and turns culturally symbolic forms to his/her needs and advantage when necessary. Emilie, in attending to provision of a 'network of reference points' in French (Interview 1), was offering students the basis upon which they could interpret cultural texts from the point of view of their original contexts of production (Kramsch, 1993) but also with which they could make their own meaning-making decisions. Agentive use of this semiotic navigation system is clearly apparent in the students' writing projects, explored in more detail in the next chapter, but we see the beginnings of this meaning-making ability being built in the classroom interactions described and analyzed below, most basically in the evidence that students were becoming more aware of the semiotic network available in French and having to do with the Occupation era but also in their participation in interpretive activities in class.

Across the Occupation dossier, Emilie established a routine for instruction and interaction that very much supported the identification and exploration of culturally symbolic forms. Emilie's classes were organized such that the first 10 minutes or so of nearly every class meeting were devoted to an activity that she called *Identifications*. The interactions students had with each other and with Emilie to start off each class served as the most consistent means through which students gained awareness of and began to initially explore the meaning potentials of culturally salient referents, particular words, images, phrases and other symbolic forms. Of course, there were other moments of classroom activity during which identification of culturally symbolic forms occurred, and some of the examples below review these less routinized yet still meaningful interactions. The highly planned nature of the *Identifications* activities translated into a consistent structure in the class's interactions around symbolic forms. Other instances of identifying symbolic forms, however, were present and took different interactional shape. These were mostly what we could call text analysis activities, during which the class's attention turned from explicit focus on particular terms and referents to the consideration of forms and meanings in the context of various texts (images; video clips; transcripts of speeches; excerpts from novels, films and first-person memoirs; legal texts, etc.). Through these interpretive activities, the class gained awareness of and proficiency with interpreting these forms in specific contexts.

Identifications

When students arrived in class, they typically encountered before them on the blackboard an *Identifications* list like the one shown in Figure 4.1.

At left, Emilie outlined dimensions along which students should discuss Pétain and de Gaulle during a comparative activity. At right, she

Figure 4.1 Screen grab of identifications activity (09/11/06)

listed four terms and two dates (*la drôle de guerre, la guerre éclair, la débâcle, 17/6/40, 18/6/40, l'armistice*) that students were expected to discuss and identify.

Across the 11 class sessions I observed during the 7-week Occupation dossier, five included a formal *Identifications* activity[1] with three including particular dates, two including names or references to groups of people (e.g. *le Front Populaire, Maréchal Pétain*), one including quoted material from a speech and one including reference to new sets of laws passed by the Vichy government (e.g. *le Statut des Juifs*). This range of symbolic forms present during *Identifications* activities created particular affordances for exploring meaning potentials. Including quoted material, for example, might promote a focus on the individual and social voices relevant in considering the forms that were grouped together in a set of *Identifications* terms. Dates and names of places were anchoring points in time and space for meaning-making. These formal *Identifications* activities occurred more regularly at the start of the dossier than at the end and were intended in this sense to initially focus students' attention and awareness. *Identifications* activities were central in orienting students to relevant reference points (dates, names, phrases and terms) and setting the stage for deeper interpretation and analysis of forms and meanings. The terms that figured in the lists Emilie wrote on the blackboard offered a range of entry points in engaging with the meaning potentials of symbolic forms.

At the start of the semester, Emilie provided both explicit guidance and more implicit modeling of how she intended students to carry out *Identifications* activities. She particularly endorsed a 'who, what, when, where, how' routine that students could take up in their discussions. In Excerpts 2 and 3 below from class sessions early in the semester, Emilie provides explicit guidance to students about how to approach their *Identifications* discussion and models the sorts of questions that could support their exploration of the meanings of these reference points:

Excerpt 2 Identifications directions

```
01 Emilie:  Ce que j'aimerais que vous fassiez c'est vous mettre en groupes de deux ou
02          trois on est combien (counts students) mettez-vous par deux d'accord et
03          j'aimerais que vous identifiez ce que j'ai mis au tableau c'est-à-dire que vous
04          me disiez qu'est-ce que c'est qu'est-ce qui s'est passé qui est-ce d'accord
05          qu'est-ce qu'il a fait donc premièrement le Front Populaire d'accord
06          deuxième c'est quoi ça comme date (4) c'est quelle date ça oui
06 S1:      Uh la France est entrée [(inaudible)
07 Emilie:                          [Oh non non non (waving both hands to halt the
08          student's response) ne répondez pas ça c'est quelle date c'est quoi trois
09          neuf trente-neuf
10 S1:      Oh
10 S2:      Trois septembre
11 Emilie:  Trois septembre d'accord ne faites pas l'inversion c'est pas le neuf mars
12          trois septembre trente-neuf dix mai quarante quatorze juin quarante
13          qu'est-ce qui s'est passé à ces dates-là la drôle de guerre qu'est-ce que c'est
14          la guerre éclair définition et le maréchal Pétain qui est-ce alors vous vous
15          mettez par deux d'accord vous parlez vous n'écrivez rien d'accord c'est pas
16          la peine d'écrire tout est dans votre bulkpack là vous allez parler je vous
17          donne environ dix minutes pour identifier ce que j'ai mis au tableau
18          d'accord c'est parti allez par deux

01 Emilie:  *What I would like you to do is to get in groups of two or three how many are*
02          *we (counts students) get in pairs ok and I would like you to identify what I*
03          *have put on the board that is to say that you tell me what it is who it is what*
04          *happened who is it ok what did he do so first the Front Populaire ok second*
05          *what date is that (4) what date is that there yes*
06 S1:      *Uh France entered [(inaudible)*
07 Emilie:                     *[Oh no no no (waving both hands to halt the student's*
08          *response) don't answer what date is that what is it three nine thirty-nine*
09 S1:      *Oh*
```

10 **S2**:   *September third*
11 **Emilie**:   *September third ok don't invert the date it isn't March ninth September third*
12   *thirty-nine May 10th 40 June 14th 40 what happened on these*
13   *dates the phony war what is it the lightening war definition and Maréchal*
14   *Pétain who is it so you get in pairs ok you talk you don't write anything it's not*
15   *worth writing anything everything is in your bulkpack there you are going to*
16   *talk I'll give you about ten minutes to identify what I've put on the board ok*
17   *it's started go ahead in pairs*

(Observation from 11 September 2006)

The very next day Emilie gave similar instructions at the start of a new *Identifications* activity:

Excerpt 3 What was it, what happened, when, where, why, how

01 **Emilie**:   Pour commencer avant de sauter au 17 et 18 juin 40 à l'armistice j'aimerais
02   qu'on se remémore ça d'accord que des choses soient bien claires ce que je
03   vais vous demander de faire c'est de vous mettre par deux et de retracer les
04   évènements depuis la drôle de guerre à l'armistice d'accord donc qu'est-ce
05   que c'est qu'est-ce qui s'est passé quand où pourquoi comment tout ce que
06   vous savez vous me le dites d'accord encore une fois vous n'écrivez rien du
07   tout vous parlez d'accord c'est bon

01 **Emilie**:   *To start before jumping to the 17th and 18th of June 1940 to the armistice I would*
02   *like us to remember this ok so that things are very clear what I will ask you to*
03   *do is to put yourselves in pairs and to retrace the events from the phony war*
04   *period to the armistice ok so what was it what happened when where why*
05   *how all that you can tell me ok once again you don't write anything at all you*
06   *talk ok is that good*

(Observation from 12 September 2006)

Emilie emphasized, especially at the start of the semester when students were just settling into the routines of her class, that she wanted them only to talk with each other as they considered the items in her *Identifications* lists. She routinely reminded them that they should write nothing so that they could use these activities as an exercise in information recall (as students were to have read as homework the night before content related to the terms on the board) as well as an opportunity to draw on their classmates as resources in clarifying any information they had missed or misunderstood during their own individual reading of the assigned texts. Discussions among students during the *Identifications* activities almost always followed in exact order the list Emilie had written on the blackboard and were almost always cut off by Emilie after about 5 or 10 minutes. During this time, students had an opportunity to begin using the terms Emilie had designated as relevant and to work with other students to start figuring out the range of referential and more symbolic meanings associated with these terms, although clearly, at this early stage, referential meanings were paramount. When Emilie called the students' attention back together, further opportunity for clarifying their understanding and for narrowing their focus on the particular forms that Emilie had selected was possible. Emilie often invited students to share what they had discussed, moving term by term down the list. On some occasions, she skipped a term or asked questions that related all at once to multiple items from the *Identifications* list.

In the following examples, which represent typical class discussions that followed the small-group phase of *Identifications* activities, how exactly the class came to 'identify' culturally relevant reference points and how students were encouraged to initially explore these forms' meaning potentials becomes more clear.

Prior to the interaction represented in Excerpt 4, the class had been studying the rise of the Vichy government, and the focus of this class session, Emilie announced, would be the 'fameuse Révolution Nationale' (*the famous National Revolution*). Before engaging students in identifying the terms written on the board, Emilie explains that the class will enrich their study of this phase of the war by watching several clips from a documentary film called *L'Oeil de Vichy* (the Eye of Vichy). She distributes a packet of information and discussion questions related to the film and asks them to bring it with them to class every day. The terms that are the focus of the *Identifications* activity in Excerpt 4 are explored even further immediately following the class's initial discussion of them, as Emilie shows the students a speech by Pétain and some other propaganda videos produced by the Vichy government in support of the National Revolution.

Of note in Excerpt 4 is the way in which forms Emilie has designated as culturally or symbolically relevant in some way are related to each other in the course of the class's interaction, ultimately building a network of form-meaning associations. The way she scaffolds students' process of establishing some basic referential meanings around these particular forms also becomes apparent.

Excerpt 4 *L'état français* (the French state)

```
01 Emilie:  On y va alors dites-moi l'état français qu'est-ce que c'est (4) ça remplace
02          quoi ouais S1
03 S1:      La république
04 Emilie:  La république d'accord donc la république a été abolie par qui
05 S1:      Par par qui ?
06 Emilie:  Mmhm
07 S2:      Pétain
08 Emilie:  Qui était qui à ce moment-là quel [statut est-ce qu'il avait
09 S3:                                        [le chef de Paris (unintelligible)
10 S4:                                        [le chef du gouvernement
11 Emilie:  Pas de Par- oui mais quel titre est-ce qu'il se donne chef
12 S5:      D'état
13 Emilie:  De l'état d'accord il est le chef de l'état et qu'est qu'il a qu'est-ce qui lui
14          permet de faire tous les changements qu'il veut
15 S6:      L'assemblée nationale
16 Emilie:  Qu'est-ce qu'elle lui a donné (1) qu'est-ce qu'il a reçu
17 S7:      Le pouvoir
18 Emilie:  Quel pouvoir
19 S8:      Le président le président Lebrun lui a donné um la la position
20 Emilie:  Ça c'était en juin 40 d'accord en juin 40 on l'a appelé le président l'a appelé
21          pour venir aider ensuite le président a démissionné d'accord donc on a
22          désigné le Maréchal Pétain comme successeur mais surtout qu'est-ce qu'on
23          lui a donné qui l'a transformé en superman oui
24 S9:      Um président Lebrun?
25 Emilie:  Ça c'est le président Lebrun qui lui l'avait donné d'accord mais qu'est-ce
26          qu'il a reçu si vous voulez quelqu'un m'a dit des pouvoirs d'accord il y aussi
27          des pouvoirs mais quels pouvoirs
28 S10:     Les pleins pouvoirs
29 Emilie:  Merci les pleins pouvoirs (6) (writes term on chalkboard) si vous deviez
30          paraphraser qu'est-ce que ça veut dire recevoir les pleins pouvoirs
31 S11:     Tous les pouvoirs
32 Emilie:  Tous les pouvoirs il a tous les pouvoirs il est le maître (2) d'accord il est le
33          maître du pays donc le 10 juillet 1940 le Conseil lui donne les pleins
34          pouvoirs et alors là il fait la fête imaginez il dit ok super maintenant c'est
35          moi alors plus de république on abolit la république la France devient l'état
36          français s'il n'y a pas de république il n'y a pas de président je suis le chef de
37          l'état français et là on arrive à toute une rhétorique militaire d'accord
38          qu'est-ce qu'il fait d'autre il abolit la troisième république quoi d'autre
39          qu'est-ce qu'il fait
```

01 **Emilie**: *Let's go tell me the French state what is it (4) what does it replace yeah S1*
02 **S1**: *The Republic*
03 **Emilie**: *The Republic ok so the Republic was abolished by whom*
04 **S1**: *By by whom ?*
05 **Emilie**: *Mmhm*
06 **S2**: *Pétain*
07 **Emilie**: *Who was who at this particular moment what [status did he have*
08 **S3**: *[leader of Paris (unintelligible)*
09 **S4**: *[Leader of the government*
10 **Emilie**: *Not of Par – yes but what title did he give himself head*
11 **S5**: *Of state*
12 **Emilie**: *Of the state ok he is head of state and what does he have what allowed him to*
13 *make any changes he wanted*
14 **S6**: *The national assembly*
15 **Emilie**: *What did it (the assembly) give him (1) what did he receive*
16 **S7**: *Power*
17 **Emilie**: *What power*
18 **S8**: *The president the president Lebrun gave hum um the the position*
19 **Emilie**: *That that was in June of 40 ok in June of 40 they called him the president called*
20 *him to come help then the president stepped down ok then they designated*
21 *Maréchal Pétain successor but above all what did what was he given that*
22 *transformed him into superman yes*
23 **S9**: *Um president Lebrun?*
24 **Emilie**: *That it's President Lebrun ok that gave it to him ok but what did he receive if*
25 *you like someone told me powers ok there are powers but what powers*
26 **S10**: *Full powers/absolute power*
27 **Emilie**: *Thank you <u>full</u> power (6) (writes term on chalkboard) if you had to*
28 *paraphrase what does that mean to receive absolute power*
29 **S11**: *All the powers*
30 **Emilie**: *All the powers he has all the powers he is the master (2) ok he is the master of*
31 *the country so on July 10th the council gave him absolute power and so there*
32 *he celebrates imagine he says ok super now it's me so no more republic we*
33 *abolish the republic France becomes the French state there is no republic*
34 *there is no president I am the head of the French state and there we arrive at*
35 *a whole military rhetoric ok what else does he do he abolishes the third*
36 *republic what else what does he do*

(Observation from 14 September 2006)

Following almost exactly five minutes of students' small-group discussion of the terms, Emilie calls the students' attention back together and immediately engages them in discussion of the first term on the

Identifications list, *'l'état français'* (line 1). In the nearly three-minute-long sequence that the transcript in Excerpt 4 represents, the class moves from the original term to take up a series of related references and forms (*la république, chef de l'état, le président, l'assemblée nationale, les pleins pouvoirs, le Conseil, Lebrun*). Already in line 1, Emilie associates 'the French state' with what it replaced (the republic), which a student is able to readily identify by name in line 2. Emilie quickly moves to another association in line 3, by asking who abolished the republic. This question sets in motion a much lengthier and deeper discussion of Pétain, how he came to power and how shifts in naming practice (for himself and the French government/political system) were symbolic acts with real-world effect (lines 6–34). What becomes apparent is that in a short timeframe of interaction, Emilie and her students begin to weave a web of meanings by bringing the set of forms in relation to each other.

Analytically, what we can say about this interaction is that in the class's joint work to identify culturally and symbolically salient forms, Emilie was intent on ensuring referential and linguistic precision, and she also quite consistently drew attention to the way forms referenced and related to each other. In addition to the fact that Emilie helped students create these networks of associated forms and establish some basic referential meanings and relationships among forms, we can also look to the way that Emilie facilitated the interaction itself. That is, we can focus on her means for guiding the interaction so that students were involved in pinpointing relevant forms and beginning to explore their meanings.

The sequences from lines 7 to 12 and then from lines 15 to 31 both illustrate well how Emilie insisted on students arriving at precise terms. In the first sequence, after two students offer their ideas of who Pétain is at this moment of the war (they say 'leader of Paris' and 'leader of the government'), Emilie uses the word 'title' to try to elicit further responses and gives the students half of the title *'chef...'* before trailing off (line 10). A student, in line 11, offers the term *'l'état,'* Emilie reinforces it (while also linguistically correcting it to *'de l'état'*) and immediately asks two more questions about what allows Pétain to make any changes he likes in France. We see a similar sequence between lines 15 and 33 as students attempt to respond to Emilie's questions. She repeatedly questions and prompts them so that finally in line 26, a student comes out with the specific term *'les pleins pouvoirs'* that Emilie was driving at (her 'thank you' in line 27 is prime evidence that this is exactly the term she was waiting for students to land on). As Emilie prompts students continually and as they offer their responses, a rich set of associations and details emerge regarding Pétain, the kind of power he gained, and how he gained it. The '*pleins pouvoirs*' in this excerpt are associated with 'being transformed into a superman', 'all the power' and Pétain becoming the 'master of the country'. In line 27–28, Emilie even asks students to paraphrase what is meant by the term '*les pleins pouvoirs*,' solidifying that this particular term is culturally and symbolically very important while also allowing students to explore its meaning by attaching definitions to it in their own words, in addition to the explanations and associations she herself has offered. Finally, at the end of the excerpt, Emilie expands the discussion of what '*les pleins pouvoirs*' means by asking students to 'imagine,' a very common marker in Emilie's class for students to envision another reality, and she proceeds to speak as Pétain at the moment he received absolute authority (lines 32–34). In so doing, she brings a speaking voice to the idea of '*les pleins pouvoirs*' and characterizes Pétain as receiving these powers in a particular way, saying '*super*' and adding her own commentary that he '*fait la fête*' (celebrated).

In this *Identifications* activity and so many more like it, it was clear that Emilie narrowed the field of symbolic forms students would engage with by preparing a limited set of terms she deemed most central to the day's content. She then made interactional space for them to begin exploring the meaning potentials of these forms. They did so first in small groups by collaborating with each other to draw associations in a relatively routine fashion (i.e. by focusing on who, what, when, where and how questions). Those initial discussions prepared students to engage in dialogue with Emilie and other classmates when the class came back together to further their exploration of the terms. It is at this point that Emilie's instructional moves to support and extend students' burgeoning understandings of the meaning potentials of symbolic forms becomes apparent. She pushed for linguistic accuracy and referential precision in identifying forms and involved students actively in constructing networks of meaningful associations around the day's set of terms. Emilie's pedagogical approach in the early phases of working with symbolic forms and their meanings did involve treating forms as referential; indeed, the students' small group work; her advice that they focus on anchoring discussion of terms with regard to referential questions like who, what, when, where and how; and the nature of Emilie's questions during whole-class discussion of terms all substantiate the claim that bringing students to understand forms as having meaning potentials, both referential and symbolic, began with firm establishment of the more basic and probably more conventionalized meanings associated with these terms. However, even in *Identifications* activities, movement into deeper exploration of form-meaning relationships – into the realm of the symbolic – was already emerging, as can be seen, for example, when Emilie engaged in voicing and animating moves (illustrated with more examples below).

Embedded in *Identifications* activities, there were often instances of the exploration of terms not appearing in the set list Emilie presented to students for initial discussion. The surfacing of the very important term *'les pleins pouvoirs'* in Excerpt 4 is a primary example. Another example, early in the class's study of World War II experiences in France, arose when Emilie initiated discussion of the phrase and notion of 'été 36' (summer '36), explicitly identifying the form and glossing its meaning, *'les Français à vélo'* (the French on bikes), as illustrated in the excerpt below. The interaction, like the one presented above in Excerpt 4, revolved around referential and more symbolic meanings, precision in reference and elaboration of multiple meaningful associations. As the class discussed the *Front Populaire*, one of the terms on the day's *Identifications* list, the following interaction unfolded:

Excerpt 5 *Eté 36* (Summer of '36)

01	**Emilie**:	Donc c'était un parti politique d'accord qui a remporté les élections en quelle année
02		(2) les élections de quelle année (3)
03	**S1**:	Trente-trois
04	**S2**:	Trente-huit
05	**Emilie**:	Trente-trois trente-huit
06	**S3**:	Trente-sept
07	**Emilie**:	@Trente-sept@
08	**S4**:	Trente trente-six
09	**Emilie**:	Trente-six d'accord souvenez-vous trente-six (unintelligible) vous en souvenir
10		pensez à l'été trente-six d'accord si vous dites l'été trente-six les Français savent de
11		quoi vous parlez ils vont dire Front Populaire et surtout qu'est-ce qui s'est passé en
12		été mille neuf cent trente-six qu'est-ce que beaucoup de Français ont fait pour la
13		première fois
14	**S5**:	Les congés payés
15	**Emilie**:	Les congés payés et donc qu'est-ce qu'ils ont fait comme ils avaient des vacances
16		payées (2)
17	**S6**:	Ils ont vu la mer
16	**Emilie**:	Ouais ils ont vu la mer comment ils sont allés voir la mer (2)
17	**S6**:	En bicyclette
18	**Emilie**:	En bicyclette vous connaissez la chanson à bicyclette (students shake head no) non
19		parce que vous avez à cette époque il y a beaucoup de chansons avec le thème
20		justement des vacances de la bicyclette qui sont sortis uh donc été trente-six pensez

21   les Français à vélo parce que pour la première fois ils ont des congés payés et ils
22   vont aller voir la mer bien sur tous les Français ne sont pas partis à la mer
23   malheureusement uh mais là on parle surtout des Parisiens parce que la Normandie
24   n'est pas très loin finalement

01 **Emilie**: *So it was a political party ok that won the elections in which year (2) the*
02 *elections in which year*
03 **S1**: *Thirty-three*
04 **S2**: *Thirty-eight*
05 **Emilie**: *Thirty-three thirty-eight*
06 **S3**: *Thirty-seven*
07 **Emilie**: *@Thirty-seven@*
08 **S4**: *Thirty thirty-six*
09 **Emilie**: *Thirty-six ok remember thirty-six (unintelligible) in your memory think about*
10 *summer of thirty-six ok if you say the summer of thirty-six the French know*
11 *what you are talking about they are going to say Front Populaire and above*
12 *all what happened in nineteen thirty-six what did a lot of French people do for*
13 *the first time*
14 **S5**: *Paid leave*
15 **Emilie**: *Paid leave and so what did they do since they had paid vacation*
16 **S6**: *They saw the sea*
17 **Emilie**: *Yeah they saw the sea how did they go see the sea (2)*
18 **S6**: *By bike*
19 **Emilie**: *By bike do you know the song on a bike (students shake head no) no because*
20 *you have at this time there are a lot of songs with exactly this theme of*
21 *vacation of bikes that came out uh so summer thirty-six think the French on*
22 *bikes because for the first time they had paid leave and they are going to go to*
23 *see the sea of course not all the French left for the sea unfortunately uh but*
24 *there we're talking above all about Parisians because Normandy is not very*
25 *far after all*

(Observation from 11 September 2006)

Notably in this excerpt, Emilie engages students in building a chain of meaningful associations from a political party (the *Front Populaire*) to a particular time reference, 'été 36', to paid vacation, to the sea and bicycles, to songs of the era that took up the theme of vacationing. Quite explicitly in lines 9–10, Emilie states that students should remember the particular phrase *'été 36'* and that if they use the phrase, French people will immediately be able to read the reference. The series of five questions Emilie poses between lines 12 and 19 serves to involve students in building this associative chain, and the network of associations are then all connected by Emilie in lines 21–23 in one form-meaning articulation ('think the French on bikes because for the first time they had paid leave and they are going to go see the sea'). She further qualifies the general image-phrase-meaning association by saying that this image of flocking to the sea really only included Parisians, rather than all of the French population. In this qualification, we again see Emilie's penchant for making sure that referents and their meanings were precisely presented to students. This moment of identifying a form and exploring its basic meanings was reinforced by another text, the image that appeared in the students' schedule for that week, which was a photo of some French people riding their bikes by the ocean accompanied by the subtitle *'Sur les routes de France grâce aux congés payés'* (On the roads of France thanks to paid vacation) (see Figure 4.2).

In contrast with a classroom in which a teacher and students consider a historical time period in terms of a year and an event (i.e. 1936 was the year that the Front Populaire-led government put into law rights to paid vacations for the French public), Emilie's orchestration of classroom

Figure 4.2 The French on Bikes in Summer '36

discourse and interaction promoted opportunities for much richer associations to be formed and extended students' access to both referential and symbolic dimensions of forms' meaning potentials (particular images, such as Parisians on bikes in this case, that are evocative in a cultural imaginary).

Identifying forms in text analysis activities

Other instances of identifying and exploring culturally meaningful forms appeared during text analysis activities in Emilie's class, usually once the *Identifications* exercises at the start of a class period had been completed. In these, patterns were again apparent in Emilie's instructional moves and are described in detail below. On some occasions, though, through the course of interacting around a text, moments Emilie could not have planned for arose, in which students' contributions to an ongoing analytic activity prompted her to focus the students' attention on identifying and specifying a culturally meaningful form. Two such instances are presented in Excerpts 6 and 7. In these examples and others like them in the data set, as students offered their responses to questions and their interpretations of texts and images during text analysis activities, Emilie would sometimes recast their versions of events and the way they named people, places and happenings. As in the *Identifications* activities, these interactions show Emilie focusing students' attention more precisely on a form, discarding imprecise or culturally implausible characterizations and replacing them with others. In some cases, all Emilie did was prompt students to offer something more precise, as in the following excerpt; at other times, she simply supplied more linguistically and culturally appropriate forms.

As the class discussed early phases of the war, for example, a student said that 10 May 1940 was 'the date that the Germans entered France' (line 2). Emilie responded, highlighting the significance of word choice as a symbolic act, asserting that the image of German troops 'arriving' in Paris is not in the French cultural imaginary and that an alternate referential term would be more likely used (lines 3–4). She emphasizes that there is an issue of connotation in play (line 3) and that *'entrer'* (to enter) is far too neutral a term and might even suggest that German forces were welcome in France, as she says in line 4 'that just means come in, enter'. Emilie does not replace the student's use of the word 'enter', though, with something more culturally appropriate. Instead, a classmate recasts the first student's statement in line 7, offering the word 'invade' to replace 'enter'. Emilie reinforces the image of soldiers 'invading' rather than entering Paris in lines 8–9 and contrasts the word *'envahir'* (to invade) with a third lexical item, *'invités'* (invited).

Excerpt 6 Entering or invading France

```
01 Emilie:  10 mai 40
02 S1:      Ça c'est la date que les Allemands uh ont entré en France
03 Emilie:  Oui plutôt que entrer ça veut dire entrer ça a une connotation très neutre alors que il
04          ne sont pas entrés ça veut juste dire venez entrez (motions with arms, waving as if
05          to welcome someone in)
06 Ss:      Hahaha
07 S2:      Les Allemands ont enva[hi la France
08 Emilie:                        [Oui d'accord là ils ont envahi la France ils n'étaient pas
09          forcement invités d'accord les Allemands envahissent la France d'accord
```

```
01 Emilie:  The 10th of May 40
02 S1:      That is the date that the Germans uh entered France
03 Emilie:  Yes rather than enter that means enter that has a very neutral connotation whereas
04          they did not enter that just means come in enter (motions with arms, waving as if to
05          welcome someone in)
06 Ss:      Hahaha
07 S2:      The Germans inva[ded France
08 Emilie:                   [Yes ok there they invaded France they weren't necessarily invited ok
09          the Germans invade France ok
```

(Observation on 11 September 2006)

Later in the same class period, Emilie recasts a student contribution lexically but also symbolically when the student asks for a way to say that Pétain was a German 'sympathizer':

Excerpt 7 Sympathizer versus collaborator

```
01 Emilie:  Voilà alors le Marechal Pétain c'est qui oui S1
02 S1:      Il était un héros de la première guerre mondiale
03 Emilie:  Mm-hm
04 S1:      Et um donc alors quand les Allemands ont envahi la France um le gouvernement uh
05          lui a donné beaucoup de pouvoir et il a signé armistice avec l'Allemagne et il était
06          um comment dit-on sympathizer
07 Emilie:  Il enfin on va dire plus tard voyez il a collaboré
08 S1:      Il a collaboré avec les nazis et donc il était le chef de la France occupée
```

01 **Emilie**: *There so Marechal Pétain who is it yes S1*
02 **S1**: *He was a hero from the first World War*
03 **Emilie**: *Mm-hm*
04 **S1**: *And um so then when the Germans invaded France um the government um gave him a*
05 *lot of power and he signed the armistice with Germany and he was um how do you say*
06 *sympathizer*
07 **Emilie**: *He well later people will say you see that he collaborated*
08 **S1**: *He collaborated with the Nazis and so he was the leader of occupied France*

(Observation on 11 September 2006)

When S1 explicitly requests a translation for the word 'sympathizer' (lines 5–6), Emilie seizes on the opportunity to replace 'sympathizer' with a more linguistically and culturally appropriate characterization of Pétain. In line 7, she makes clear that a different term, *'collaborateur'*, will be taken up in popular vocabulary. Her phrase *'on va dire plus tard'* (later people will say) suggests that it is not Emilie as the teacher that is offering her own preferred term to S1 for referring to Pétain but rather that she is identifying an alternative term that was widely used by French people after the beginning phases of the war and from that point onward. S1 immediately takes up this term in line 8. Here again an interactional moment from Emilie's classroom highlights how processes of specifying forms – by honing in on precise referential terms and by building basic form-meaning associations – were facilitated by Emilie's instructional moves.

These examples of identifying cultural references, from the more structured *Identifications* activities to more spontaneous occasions of drawing attention to particular forms, were the interactional foundation upon which all other interpretive and meaning-making activity occurred in Emilie's class. Identifying culturally and symbolically relevant forms in Emilie's class, then, involved the discovery of salient terms and settling on a particular articulation of these, sometimes through a questioning sequence and sometimes through Emilie's recasting of a student contribution. Identification also involved some basic processes of situating forms in relation to others. Through these interactions and processes, Emilie and her students were able to slowly weave webs of significance, connecting forms through a variety of semiotic relationships. These reference networks provided the skeletal framework that would then be elaborated and fleshed out through ongoing analytic and creative activities in the class, including regular analysis of a range of texts. Eventually, these frameworks were called into action, as students drew on their knowledge of and experiences with culturally and symbolically salient forms to make their own meanings in their creative writing projects.

Hypothesizing about the Meanings of Culturally Symbolic Forms

Identifications activities, which allowed students to begin exploring the meanings of certain culturally symbolic forms, were particularly structured interactional events, with Emilie tightly controlling which forms would be taken up and guiding, through her questions and comments, the direction of the class's general inquiry into these forms. Other activities presented more flexible and dynamic interactional spaces for students to produce hypotheses about the meanings of symbolic forms and to explore meaning in more depth. Usually these opportunities for advancing hypotheses and discerning what constituted plausible interpretations of cultural references were embedded in stretches of talk around interpretation and analysis of particular texts. In the same way that the *Identifications* terms were carefully chosen by Emilie to highlight particular reference points in discussing French experiences of the Occupation era, the texts Emilie selected for analysis and interpretation exercises in class were intentionally aligned with the forms and meanings that were developed through students' reading before class and in foundational discussions like the *Identifications* exercises.

On the day that the class first discussed the National Revolution and the rise of the Vichy government (14 September 2006), students carried out the *Identifications* activity described above (Excerpt 4), they listened and reacted to a propaganda clip produced by the Vichy government aimed at explaining what the National Revolution was, engaged in reciting aloud parts of the youth minister's speech from the clip, and discussed the role of young French people in the Vichy government's plans to transform France. At the end of class, Emilie also asked students to complete a chart comparing the Republic and the National Revolution, contrasting the two periods in terms of their respective mottos, the rights people had under each government, the place of religion and the symbols and historical references that each drew on in crafting their stances, practices and public discourses. After the class's exposure to this variety of texts and engagement in this range of analytic work, Emilie, in the final minutes of the class, provided one final video text and asked students to focus on how it was emblematic of the National Revolution.

During this short activity, students engaged in hypothesizing about the meanings of the commercial.

Excerpt 8 Hypothesizing about the meanings of a detergent advertisement

```
01 Emilie:  Alors maintenant ce que on va juste regarder un truc il nous reste trois minutes mais
02          vous allez voir vous allez essayer de comprendre comment c'est em-blém-a-tique de
03          la revolution nationale d'accord c'est une publicité et expliquez-moi pourquoi on
04          peut dire que c'est symbolique de l'époque (turns out lights and starts the clip)
05          d'accord
06 CLIP:    (black and white advertisement shows images of Lavor brand laundry detergent,
07          includes a song touting Lavor as new and as the best detergent)
08 Emilie:  Alors c'est la publicité pour quoi (turns lights back on) (4) c'est quoi comme produit
09          oui S1
10 S1:     Peut-être c'est un symbole de la nouveau régime parce que il y a laver toute la
11          société de les choses qui n'est pas très morales ou um qui qui n'aiment pas le travail
12          et le courage et c'est un symbole de cette uh cette uh laver cette action de laver
13 Emilie:  Oui il y a toute cette cette cette action de laver de purifier le pays on va purifier là on
14          va laver quoi d'autre (walks to the screen and points and reads) « lave seul blanc
15          comme neige » on lave mais on fait quoi également (1) on blanchit ça veut dire quoi
16          (1.5) au sens figuré
17 S2:     La pureté de les Français
18 Emilie:  On va baser ça sur une pureté la pureté de la race et donc on va exclure tout ce qui
19          n'est pas très blanc vous voyez uh vous-même vous avez ce terme de laver
20          également comment comment
21          vous traduisez en anglais (writing « la purification ethnique » on board)
22 S2:     Ethnic cleansing
23 Emilie:  Vous utilisez ce mot de laver en français c'est purifier mais là on va nettoyer on fait
24          le ménage dans la maison française et on enlève tout ce qui est sale tout ce qui n'est
25          pas assez blanc ça ça va être la révolution nationale

01 Emilie:  So now what we are going to just watch one thing we have three minutes left
02          but you are going to see you are going to try to understand how it is
03          em-blem-a-tic of the national revolution ok it is an advertisement and explain to
04          me why one can say that it is symbolic of the era (turns out lights and starts
05          the clip) ok
06 CLIP:    (black and white advertisement shows images of Lavor brand laundry detergent, includes
07          a song touting Lavor as new and as the best detergent)
08 Emilie:  So it's an advertisement for what (turns lights back on) (4) what kind of
09          product is it yes S1
10 S1:     Maybe it's a symbol of the new regime because there is washing all of society
```

11		*of the things that are not very moral or um that that don't like work and*
12		*courage and it is a symbol of this uh this uh washing this action of washing*
13	**Emilie**:	*Yes there is this whole this this action of washing of purifying the country*
14		*we're going to purify we're going to wash what else (walks to the screen and*
15		*points and reads) "washes as white as snow" we wash but what else do we do*
16		*(1) we whiten what does that mean (1.5) in the figurative sense*
17	**S2**:	*The purity of the French*
18	**Emilie**:	*We are going to base that on a purity the purity of the race and so we are*
19		*going to exclude all that is not very white you see uh you too you have this*
20		*term of washing too how how do you translate into English (writing « la*
21		*purification ethnique » on board)*
22	**S2**:	*Ethnic cleansing*
23	**Emilie**:	*You use this word washing in French it's to purify but there we are going to*
24		*clean we are tidying up the French house and taking out everything that is*
25		*dirty everything that is not white enough and that that is going to be the*
26		*national revolution*

(Observation from 14 September 2006)

Emilie asks students at the start of this excerpt to focus on how the advertisement is representative of the National Revolution era, emphasizing each syllable of the word 'em-blém-a-tique' as she pronounces it and stressing the word with arm gestures as well (line 3). In order for students to offer hypotheses, though, about the symbolic nature of the advertisement, they need to draw on their background knowledge of the National Revolution, all of which had been built up the previous night as they read about this phase of the war period and during the class period itself. By design, students were provided ample opportunity before viewing the short clip to build up a store of knowledge about what other relevant forms were in relation to this text and to construct some understandings of the Vichy government and the planks of its National Revolution platform. Without these understandings, hypothesizing about the advertisement would likely have been exceptionally challenging.

What characterizes the hypothesizing activity in this excerpt and others like it in the data set is that Emilie scaffolded students' hypotheses in particular ways. First of all, Emilie was always quite explicit in inviting students' explanations of the meaning of texts. Here in line 2, Emilie states quite clearly that she wants students to focus on the ways in which the commercial may be viewed as emblematic and symbolic of the National Revolution (lines 2–4). The student who first replies after the clip in line 9 has clearly understood the sort of textual analysis Emilie wants students to engage in, as she immediately comments on how the advertisement is a symbol of the new government and its intent to clean society of all that is not moral and all that is against the Vichy leaders' conceptions of work and courage. Another way Emilie routinely facilitated and built on hypothesizing about meaning was in taking up and recasting student contributions once they made them, as in lines 12 to 13 in this example. When S1 links the Vichy government (she calls it the *'régime'*), its moral principles and the advertisement for laundry detergent, Emilie pulls out a key term S1 has used, *'laver,'* and extends it (*'purifier'*, *'blanchir'*). Emilie also supported and expanded students' hypothesizing efforts by drawing their attention to salient elements of the texts they analyzed. This act of making an element of a complex perceptual field stand out, which can involve pointing, gaze and body orientation as well as verbal marking, Goodwin (1994) calls 'highlighting'. In this case, for example, in line 13–14, Emilie walks to the projection screen and traces with her finger the slogan that appears on the soap container in the ad. By doing this, Emilie extends S1's hypothesis, adding that more than just washing, the ad promotes 'whitening'; this detail allows Emilie to ask about what 'whitening' might mean in a figurative sense (line 15), which a student associates with themes of racial purity (line 16). In the remainder of the interaction, Emilie also relates the advertisement, its language and signs to a comparable term in English (lines 17–20) as well as a broader cultural narrative about 'tidying up the French house' under the Vichy government's National Revolution (lines 22–25). Emilie routinely invited students' hypotheses and then supplemented them in multiple follow-up moves, as we see in this example, such that much deeper interpretations emerged from a student's initial contribution.

Another example of the hypothesizing interactions that occurred regularly during textual analysis activities in Emilie's class is presented in Excerpt 9 below. While analyzed in more depth elsewhere for the ways that a constellation of discursive moves over the course of an entire text analysis episode promoted perspective-taking (Kearney, 2012), the piece of interaction presented in Excerpt 9 exemplifies in particular the way textual analysis activities became rich sites for students in Emilie's class to hypothesize about the referential and more deeply symbolic meanings of various forms and of whole texts. In the class's study of Pétain and his rise to power, Emilie projected a poster the Vichy government had produced and circulated among the French population in 1940 (see Figure 4.3). In the excerpt, students' hypothesizing is invited and then scaffolded in patterned ways by Emilie.

When she asks what students see in the image in front of and behind Pétain, S3 offers a hypothesis about what the use of color in the poster might suggest on a more figurative level.

Figure 4.3 Propaganda poster

Excerpt 9 Poster analysis

20	**S3**:	La couleur de um le ciel derrière um Pétain c'est uh très noir et um
21		maréchal Pétain c'est um très <u>clair</u> c'est <u>blanche</u> et um les couleurs de le
22		um de le (2) de uh je ne sais pas le scène
23	**Emilie**:	Mm-hm
24	**S3**:	Avant uh Pétain c'est très clair
25	**Emilie**:	Ouais vous avez tout un un contraste clair obscur et ce qui est obscur est
26		derrière (2) d'accord c'est donc physiquement c'est derrière ça veut
27		dire c'est derrière moi c'est de l'histoire la ruine de la France c'est
28		derrière moi <u>moi</u> je suis nous allons devant nous allons vers le futur donc

20	**S3**:	*The color of um the sky behind um Pétain it is uh very dark and um*
21		*Maréchal Pétain it is um very <u>light</u> it's <u>white</u> and um the colors of the um of*
22		*the (2) of um I don't know the scene*
23	**Emilie**:	*Mm-hm*
24	**S3**:	*Before uh Pétain it is very light*
25	**Emilie**:	*Yeah you have a a whole light-dark contrast and what is dark is behind (2) ok*
26		*it is so physically it is behind that means it is behind me it is history the ruin of*
27		*France is behind me me I am we are moving forward we are going toward the*
28		*future so*

(Observation from 11 September 2006)

While her interpretation is not completely fluent in linguistic terms and while the hypothesis she is making about color use in the poster is only implied, Emilie is able to take up S3's contribution and reformulate it in more fluent linguistic and analytic terms, saying that there is a 'light-dark contrast' and that 'what is dark is behind' (lines 25–26). Once she has rearticulated but also affirmed S3's partially developed hypothesis, Emilie also becomes involved in voicing, speaking through Pétain's voice in lines 27–28. As she does, she articulates a message that he and his government, through this image, may have intended for the French population. As Emilie speaks as Pétain, she also uses pronouns in such a way that students are repositioned and addressed directly as the population that may have looked on this poster in 1940. Throughout the poster analysis interaction, a cycle of hypothesizing repeats in the interaction in which Emilie first focuses students on describing what is literally depicted in the image and how content and composition begin to suggest figurative meanings as well. In the third part of the hypothesizing and interpretation cycle, Emilie then often propels students' hypotheses into the realm of considering ideological messages conveyed by signs and symbols in the poster. She achieves this largely through voicing and embodiment moves that promote a repositioning of herself and students into different subjectivities for animating and 'reading' the image. This crucial interactional process in Emilie's classroom is explored further in the next section, but it is worth noting here that forays into understanding ideological meanings were really contingent on there having been some interactional work already accomplished with regard to literal and figurative readings of texts.

A bit further in the poster analysis interaction, a different student asks Emilie a question about the poster, seeking information so that she can offer a hypothesis about it:

Excerpt 10 When was this portrait made?

```
40 S1:     Quand est-ce que cette portrait c'est est fait parce que c'est est-ce que ça
41         est fait um depuis le um uh le (annonce) de de Gaulle
42 Emilie: Oui en fait c'était fait juste après juste après son discours du 17 juin donc
43         vers soit 17 18
44 S1:     So ça peut être un un réaction contre de Gaulle ((pronounced strangely))
45         peut-être
46 Emilie: Mm-hm ah oui là vraiment c'est un message direct (2) d'accord c'est
47         bon ? maintenant devant au premier plan qu'est-ce qu'il y a
```

40	**S1**:	*When was this portrait it is made because it is is that made um since/after the*
41		*um uh the (announcement) of de Gaulle*
42	**Emilie**:	*Yes in fact it was made just after his speech of the 17th of June so around the*
43		*17th 18th*
44	**S1**:	*So it can be a a reaction against de Gaulle ((pronounced strangely)) maybe*
45	**Emilie**:	*Mm-hm ah yes there really it was a direct message (2) ok is that good? now in*
46		*front in the foreground what is there*

(Observation from 11 September 2006)

The overall analysis of the poster is guided primarily by Emilie's questions and invitations to students to advance interpretations of particular parts of the image. However, in Excerpt 10, S1 initiates a question about when the poster was made, suggesting in line 41 that she is interested in knowing whether it was produced after de Gaulle made a speech from London in opposition to capitulation to German forces. Upon receiving a response from Emilie (line 42), S1 is able to announce her hypothesis in line 44 that the poster is perhaps a reaction against de Gaulle and his speech from London about continuing to resist. This interpretation is strongly confirmed by Emilie in line 46, who calls the poster a 'direct message' to de Gaulle. S1's hypothesis, then, enriches the class's understanding of the poster by making it clear that it did not just have the French population as an audience but was also likely a targeted message to de Gaulle and any of his supporters.

Students were also drawn into hypothesizing when Emilie introduced hypothetical situations. For example, in discussing the military debacle, she proposed to students *'vous êtes soldat d'accord vous (êtes) avec votre troupe vous avez un chef qui vous dit ce qu'il faut faire et d'un seul coup vous regardez tout le monde est mort vous faites quoi'* ('you are a soldier, you are with your troop you have a leader who tells you what you have to do and then suddenly you look everyone is dead what do you do') (Observation from 11 September 2006). In similar fashion, Emilie suggested that students were among those fleeing Paris as the German forces advanced and again asked 'What do you do?'

Hypothesizing moments often launched and definitely furthered interpretive activity in Emilie's class. Students were actively engaged in constructing interpretations. These hypothesizing interactions, though, were also clearly intended to facilitate students' reinscription of signs, meanings and cultural narratives within the plotlines of their own writing assignments. This was evident in Emilie's explicit reminders to students as they worked with various texts that they should absorb images and impressions in order to shape the formation of their characters' stories. The moments in which Emilie projected students into hypothetical situations also likely afforded access to meanings and points of view that greatly facilitated the *Mémoires* writing project.

In negotiating and deepening textual and cultural meanings, students' contributions were key, and they did, with time, show more and more initiative in proposing hypotheses and interpretations rather than simply providing them when Emilie elicited them. At the same time, Emilie's instructional moves cannot be underestimated. Her role in supporting students' hypothesizing was to elicit, rearticulate, refine and extend student interpretations and often to transport these interpretations from the literal and figurative level to the ideological.

Repositioning Classroom Actors and Animating Cultural Texts through Voicing and Embodiment

Students' awareness of symbolic forms and increasingly deep understandings of the meaning potentials of these forms was further extended by Emilie's regular practice of animating cultural texts and perspectives through voicing, embodiment and repositioning herself and students in classroom discourse. This practice began very early in the semester as the class first delved into study of the World War II era in France (as is evident in the poster analysis in Excerpts 9 and 10 above). The following excerpts demonstrate how over the course of one class period, interactions like the *Identifications* activities, and others that facilitated meaning-making around culturally relevant forms, were enhanced and enriched by these moments of animating texts and particular voices, which brought meaning-making into the present moment and directly drew students into considering and potentially inhabiting unfamiliar subjectivities. When Emilie animated texts and perspectives through voicing and embodiment, she repositioned herself and her students and projected them into the plotlines of individual and cultural narratives.

Near the start of class on 11 September 2006, Emilie and her students were discussing the lightning war (*Blitzkrieg*) and military debacle, when the following episode unfolded:

Excerpt 11 What do you do in this case?

01 **Emilie**: La guerre éclair elle a fait cent mille morts elle a fait un million huit cent
02 cinquante mille prisonniers vous imaginez en quelques un temps très
03 limité vous faites cent mille morts et vous faites un million huit cent
04 cinquante mille prisonniers ah mon grand-père était donc était sur le front
05 il était dans le nord-est et ils étaient dans une forêt il y avait toute sa troupe

```
06         il y avait son commandant le général donc il y avait toute la hiérarchie et
07         d'un seul coup les Allemands ont bombardé bombardé bombardé mon
08         grand-père s'est réveillé fin il est sorti de sa stupeur il a regardé ils étaient
09         deux survivants tout le monde est mort autour de lui qu'est-ce que vous
10         faites dans ce cas-là vous êtes soldat d'accord vous (êtes) avec votre troupe
11         vous avez un chef qui vous dit ce qu'il faut faire et d'un seul coup vous
12         regardez tout le monde est mort vous faites quoi
13 S1:     Tu t'enfuis aussi
14 Emilie: Où
15 S1:     À l'Angleterre um uh je ne sais pas où
16 Emilie: On part ouais on part vers l'Angleterre ou bien
17 S2:     Um je ne sais pas le mot pour um uh um um vous dites que c'est la fin je je
18         surrender
19 Emilie: Oh je me rends se rendre [writes term on board] oui il peut y avoir ça ou
20         bien vous avez d'autres (unintelligible) ben mon grand-père il a dit moi je
21         rentre chez moi (2) qu'est-ce que je vais faire ici je ne vais pas attendre je
22         rentre chez moi et avec son ami ils ont dit bon on va rentrer dans notre
23         maison on va voir nos femmes nos enfants
```

01 **Emilie**: *The lightning war resulted in one hundred thousand dead and one million*
02 *eight hundred fifty thousand prisoners can you imagine in a very limited time*
03 *you kill one hundred thousand and you take one million eight hundred and*
04 *fifty thousand prisoners my grandfather was on the front he was in the*
05 *northeast and they were in a forest there was his troop his commander the*
06 *general so there was the whole hierarchy and suddenly the Germans attacked*
07 *attacked attacked my grandfather woke up well he came out of his stupor he*
08 *looked around and they were two survivors everyone was dead around him*
09 *what do you do in this case you are a soldier ok you (are) with your troop you*
10 *have a leader who tells you what to do and suddenly you look and everyone is*
11 *dead what do you do*
12 **S1**: *You flee too*
13 **Emilie**: *Where*
14 **S1**: *To England um uh I don't know where*
15 **Emilie**: *One leaves yeah one goes to England or*
16 **S2**: *Um I don't know the word for um uh um um you say it's the end I I surrender*
17 **Emilie**: *Oh I surrender to surrender yes there could be that or you have other*
18 *(unintelligible) well my grandfather he said me I'm going home (2) what am I*
19 *going to do here I'm not going to wait around I'm going home and with his*
20 *friend they said ok we're going to go home to our house we are going to see*
21 *our wives our children*

(Observation from 11 September 2006)

At this early point in the semester Emilie was, in interactions like this one, socializing students into routines that would become highly regular when it came to exploring the meanings of symbolic reference points. In this case, around the term 'la guerre éclair', Emilie first offers quite factual information (lines 1–4) before shifting to a narrative mode and telling the story of her grandfather who was on the front and experienced firsthand the effects of the lightning war. She paints a vivid scene that then becomes a setting and situation into which she begins to project the students themselves. In lines 9–10, she directly addresses students as 'you' but as 'yous' that find themselves in the same situation as her grandfather did. After repositioning students in this way, through setting up a particular narrative and using pronouns and direct address strategically, Emile directly asks students, in this situation 'what do you do?' (line 9). A student responds in line 12 that 'you flee' but uses a second person singular pronoun that makes it unclear whether she is referring to a generalized 'you' (as in 'one flees'). What is clear is that she has not adopted a first-person voice to speak through, although this seems quite understandable given that even though Emilie has projected students into the scene, her question would likely be interpreted by students or anyone else as a hypothetical one. Interestingly, though, in line 16, a second student responds to Emilie's question 'what would you do?' and does so by employing a first-person pronoun. She creates her own simple scene as she does not know the word for surrender and first describes that 'it's the end' before saying 'I I surrender'. Emilie provides the word S2 is looking for both orally and on the blackboard while also confirming that this would have been one possible decision for soldiers following the lightning war. She then turns to a voicing sequence (lines 18–21) in which she returns to her grandfather's story. In speaking through his voice, Emilie makes clear another option soldiers had as the German forces overwhelmed the French army – they could go home. But in addition to providing this information, Emilie is able, as a result of the direct adoption of her grandfather's voice, to bring students into a here-and-now orientation that allows her to animate his possible decision-making process as well as his concerns for seeing his family and returning home.

Later in the same class, Emilie turns the students' attention to the ramifications of the approaching German forces on the civilian population. One of the texts Emilie's students read regularly in preparation for class was a collection of first-person accounts called *Paroles d'Étoiles: Mémoire d'enfants cachés*. Written retrospectively by those who were children during the war era and who were separated from their families and hidden in non-Jewish households, this collection offered a variety of individual stories of experience and rich exposure to the kind of content and language that might appear in the genre of memoir writing. But these stories also could be considered together and discussed for the overall images and sentiments they tended to convey of various stages of the Occupation period. Based on their reading of particular stories the night before, Emilie asked her students about the sorts of images they had retained of Parisians' exodus from the city as German troops invaded. As the class shares images of this mass flight from Paris, several instances of projecting students into a scene and repositioning them in discourse emerge.

Excerpt 12 Projecting students into the exodus from Paris

```
01 Emilie:  Alors en résumé quels images est-ce que vous avez tiré de de l'exode d'après ces
02          témoignages qu'est-ce qui s'est passé pendant l'exode qu'est-ce que les gens ont fait
03          ceux qui s'enfuyaient vers le sud mais donc techniquement qu'est-ce qu'ils ont fait
04          qu'est-ce que vous voyez sur les routes de France (2)
05 S1:      Les morts
06 Emilie:  Des morts ouais et ceux qui n'étaient pas morts
07 S2:      Um des choses qui ne sont pas nécessaires qu'ils um comment ça se dit ils l'a
08          abandonné sur la route um
09 Emilie:  Donc imaginons d'accord on est en juin 1940 uh donc vous êtes toutes des femmes
10          dont les maris sont peut-être prisonniers et vous vous êtes des de vieux messieurs
11          d'accord qui n'êtes pas partis à la guerre vous participez à l'exode qu'est-ce que vous
12          faites concrètement vous partez avec quoi vous faites quoi oui S3
13 S3:      Um je pense que on passe on passe de la vie avec seulement um des objets
14          temporaires il est nécessaire qu'on mange et qu'on dormit et pour cette raison ils
15          ont fait des lits temporels peut-être avec des matelas oui mais tout c'est très
16          désorganisé et il n'y a rien à faire sauf marcher jour et jour et jour
17 Emilie:  Donc vous marchez d'accord on est tous d'accord vous marchez vous marchez si
18          vous êtes un peu plus privilégiés qu'est-ce que vous avez
```

(Lines 19–48 omitted. In this stretch, Emilie asks students in what ways those fleeing may have travelled, what they would have brought and left or abandoned and why. Students offer ideas in one-word or other short replies and Emilie continues to address students in ways that project them into the exodus scene.)

```
49 Emilie:  Vous avez pratiquement tous dit désorganisé panique le chaos pas chaos
50          (pronounced in English) la psychose ps ps la psychose donc c'est un mouvement de
51          panique on est sur la route on prend beaucoup de choses on laisse beaucoup de
52          choses voilà um dans le texte de Claudine elle vous dit le samedi 15 juin 1940
53          d'accord donc là on est un jour après l'invasion de Paris les maires du département
```

54	du Loiret ont l'ordre d'évacuer immédiatement la population le Loiret c'est une
55	région de la France et c'est de cette région uh dont ma famille est originaire donc
56	comme je vous ai raconté mon grand-père a été fait prisonnier il est parti en
57	Tchécoslovaquie ma grand-mère elle était dans le Loiret ma grand-mère elle a fait
58	parti de l'exode donc ma grand-mère elle avait vingt-huit ans elle avait deux petits
59	enfants qui avaient trois et cinq ans peut-être elle avait son père sa mère son beau-
60	père sa belle-mère qui étaient âgés et elle a mis donc dans un chariot parce que mes
61	grands-parents étaient fermiers ils étaient dans une ferme elle a pris une vache un
62	cheval des poules des canards et puis petit-à-petit chute on se débarrasse pas de la
63	belle-mère on a gardé la belle-mère peut-être qu'elle aurait dû la mettre um mais
64	des choses vraiment elle m'a raconté des choses apocalyptiques fin vous imaginez
65	vous êtes vous êtes jeunes vous avez vos enfants votre mari vous ne savez pas où il
66	est vous ne savez pas s'il est mort ou pas et vous devenez chargé vous êtes
67	responsable de tous ces gens et il fallait partir vous ne savez pas où et ils sont
68	arrivés à un pont d'accord vous comprenez un pont et ils l'ont traversé et juste
69	quand ils ont fini de traverser les avions ont bombardé et donc là ils étaient à ça de
70	la mort et ensuite donc vous comprenez quelque chose l'exode n'était pas organisé
71	du tout la psychose par définition n'est pas organisé et donc les gens partaient et
72	après on leur disiez revenez et ils rentraient non non repartez ils ne sont pas allés
73	loin uh vous avancez vous partez vous avancez vous partez pendant des jours
74	comme ça et puis à un moment donné l'armistice a été signe de toute façon tout le
75	monde est rentré voilà donc c'est ça cette fameuse débâcle au niveau de la
76	population donc souvenez-vous bien qu'il y a la débâcle militaire c'est-à-dire que
77	l'armée française est complètement démantelée éclatée atomisée vous avez donc
78	1,850,000 prisonniers vous avez 500,000 morts vous avez certains militaires qui
79	partent en Angleterre d'accord ça c'est la débâcle militaire et la débâcle au niveau de
80	la population c'est l'exode ça va est-ce que c'est clair oui je vais vous montrer juste
81	cinq minutes l'extrait d'un film qui s'appelle Jeux Interdits (6) (writes title on board)
82	et on vous montre en juin 40 comment c'était essayez de bien essayez de vous jeter
83	de plonger dans l'ambiance de l'époque est-ce que ça va le vocabulaire absorber les
84	images pour faire vos personnages ensuite
01 **Emilie**:	*So in summary what images have you taken of of the exodus from these*
02	*accounts what happened during the exodus what did people do those who fled*
03	*toward the south but concretely what did they do what do you see on the*
04	*roads of France (2)*
05 **S1**:	*The dead*
06 **Emilie**:	*Dead people yeah and those who weren't dead*
07 **S2**:	*Um things that aren't necessary that they um how do you say they*
08	*abandoned it on the road um*
09 **Emilie**:	*So let's imagine ok we are in June 1940 uh so you are all ladies whose*

10	*husbands are prisoners maybe and you you are some old gentlemen ok who*
11	*didn't go to war you are part of the exodus what do you do concretely you*
12	*leave with what you do what yes S3*
13 **S3**:	*Um I think that people get by with only um temporary objects it is necessary*
14	*to eat and to sleep and for this reason they made temporary beds maybe*
15	*with mattresses yes but everything is very disorganized and there is nothing*
16	*to do except walk day and day and day*
17 **Emilie**:	*So you walk ok we all agree you walk you walk if you are a little more*
18	*privileged what do you have*

(Lines 19–48 omitted. In this stretch, Emilie asks students in what ways those fleeing may have travelled, what they would have brought and left or abandoned and why. Students offer ideas in one-word or other short replies and Emilie continues to address students in ways that project them into the exodus scene.)

49 **Emilie**:	*You have all practically said disorganized panic chaos not chaos (pronounced in English)*
50	*hysteria ps ps hysteria so it is a panicked movement we are on the road we*
51	*take a lot of things we leave a lot of things so there um in Claudine's text she*
52	*tells you that Saturday June 15 1940 ok so there we are one day after the*
53	*invasion of Paris the mayors of the Loiret department have the order to*
54	*immediately evacuate the population of the Loiret it's a region in France and*
55	*it is this region that uh my family is from so as I told you my grandfather was*
56	*taken prisoner he left for Czechoslovakia my grandmother she was in the*
57	*Loiret my grandmother was part of the exodus so my grandmother she was*
58	*twenty-eight years old she had two small children who were three and five*
59	*years old maybe she had her father her mother her father-in-law her mother-*
60	*in-law who were elderly and so she put in a cart because my grandparents*
61	*were farmers they had a farm she took a goat a horse some chickens some*
62	*ducks and then little by little out of the wagon we didn't get rid of the mother-*
63	*in-law we kept the mother-in-law maybe she should have put her um but*
64	*things that were really she told me apocalyptic things can you imagine you*
65	*are you are young you have your kids your husband you don't know where he*
66	*is you don't know if he is dead or not and you become charged with you are*
67	*responsible for all of these people and it is necessary to leave you don't know*
68	*where and they arrived at a bridge ok do you understand a bridge and they*
69	*crossed it and just when they finished crossing planes bombed and so there*
70	*they were inches away from death and then so you understand something the*
71	*exodus was not at all organized hysteria by definition is not organized and so*
72	*people left and afterward people told them to come back and they came back*
73	*and no no leave again they didn't go far ok you move forward you leave you*
74	*move forward you leave for days like that and then at a certain moment the*
75	*armistice was signed anyway everyone went home so there that's the famous*

76	*debacle on the level of the population so be sure to remember that there was*
77	*the military debacle that is to say that the French army is completely*
78	*dismantled blown up atomized so you have 1,850,000 prisoners you have*
79	*500,000 dead you have certain soldiers who leave for England ok that is the*
80	*military debacle and the debacle on the level of the population it is the exodus*
81	*ok is it clear yes I am going to just show you five minutes the excerpt from a*
82	*film that is called Forbidden Games (6, writes title on the board) and it shows*
83	*you in June '40 how it was try to absorb the images to fashion your characters*
84	*then try to throw yourself plunge yourself into the ambiance of the era is it ok*
85	*the vocabulary absorb the images to create your characters later*

In Excerpt 12, Emilie addresses her students as a group of students sitting in a French classroom in 2006 during the first lines of the interaction (lines 1–4), and she refers to the people who participated in the mass exodus from Paris upon German invasion by using third-person pronouns. However, pronoun usage shifts in lines 9–12, where Emilie refers to students as 'you' but asks them to imagine (recall that this is a frequent marker in Emilie's class of a shift in perspective) themselves as particular social types ('women whose husbands are prisoners maybe' and 'elderly gentlemen who did not go off to war'). With these broad social positions in mind, Emilie also establishes the general scene in these lines that students should begin to envision, including a particular moment in time (June 1940) and a major event (the exodus). She then asks students in subsequent lines to further bring the scene to life by offering details. The first student's response to Emilie's question about what, as people in this position, they would have brought with them does not take up use of the first-person voice, but she does supply some details of the scene (lines 13–16). In the next stretch of talk (lines 17–31), Emilie continues to position the students as 'yous' that participated in the exodus, but the students still do not take up first-person pronouns in order to voice the experience; rather, lines 17–31 become a listing sequence as students contribute ideas of what objects might have been brought as Parisians fled the city. A student's comments in line 29–30 that some objects are abandoned prompts Emilie to step out of the ongoing projection of students into the past and this exodus scene in particular. After this brief detour, Emilie in lines 36–40 comes back to addressing students as 'you' and projecting them into the scene; however, her use of 'you' is more general than before, with no real association of 'you' with a particular historical actor or even a social type, as was the case earlier in the interaction. In lines 51–62, Emilie makes a brief reference to a text the class had read for homework and then connects this to her own family's story of fleeing the Loiret region. There is great descriptive detail in Emilie's story, establishing a scene within the broader exodus scene the class has been discussing. In lines 62–68, Emilie projects students into her own family's narrative, asking them to again 'imagine' (line 64) and then addressing them as 'yous' in the same situation as her grandmother (lines 64–68). Emilie then tells of a particular episode when her family was crossing a bridge. She does this to emphasize the disorganization of the exodus but also to provide an intertext for a clip the class will watch at the end of class from a film called *Jeux Interdits*, which also contains similar content. In the last stretch of interaction represented in the excerpt, Emilie provides a summary for students of what the debacle and exodus were. Then she announces the final activity for the day, a clip that shows 'how it was' (line 83) in June 1940. She connects their classwork to the *Mémoires* project, encouraging them to throw themselves, to plunge themselves (line 84), as they watch the clip, into the ambiance of the era and to use the images they see as material in creating their own characters and stories. Seeing how Emilie encourages her students in this way, we also can imagine how the interactions in her class made it easier for her students to reposition themselves later as they composed their assignments.

The two excerpts from 11 September 2006 constitute a multistaged projection of students into a past reality. Emilie achieves this projection through the repositioning of herself and students via consistent leveraging of linguistic resources to reposition classroom actors in discourse and various instances of voicing. The discourse features that Emilie leverages to achieve voicing and repositioning are most often shifts in pronoun reference (or we might say shifts in origo and deictic reference, which have to do with the point from which one speaks), use of direct address, use of the discourse marker 'imagine' to launch projections into a past reality and particular scene, and ventriloquation (speaking others' words), either by directly quoting or by proposing utterances they might say. Voicing and repositioning in these two excerpts and in general as discursive processes in Emilie's classroom are not just about an in-the-moment pedagogical strategy that she uses to help students' access, explore and hopefully understand others' voices and perspectives. Making the inherent heteroglossia of languages more readily apparent to students, ventriloquating others' voices and ultimately students' fashioning of a speaking/writing voice (in the *Mémoires* project) from their internalization and appropriation of that heteroglossia is a broader process of developing intercultural and symbolic competences. That is to say that in speaking through a range of voices to animate diverse subjectivities and perspectives, Emilie was able to model realizations of a range of meaning potentials that various linguistic and symbolic forms could take. She was also able to suggest how individuals' stories and plotlines associated with broader social types were constitutive of 'history'. In projecting students as occupying different subject positions through her classroom discourse, Emilie apprenticed them into new possible vantage points and ways of seeing experiences of the war period. Beyond helping them to perceive and interpret differently, Emilie's moves to reposition students encouraged them to also speak through a new voice and subject position, with some students adopting first-person pronouns to speak as a young mother fleeing Paris as the German forces advanced, a soldier standing up from the rubble of a bombing to find himself among the only survivors and other such positions.

Although not apparent in the previous excerpts, Emilie drew regularly on physical modes and material space in order to achieve the repositioning processes she also accomplished through use of words, images, texts and voicing strategies. Embodiment, or a focus on the role of the human body and its situation in space as one of the many meaning-making resources we have available to us, is of use in considering Emilie's interactional moves; this is because not only did certain gestures or movements serve as possible icons as students attempted to understand Emilie's language use and the texts they interacted with, but embodiment also advanced the process of repositioning classroom actors in discourse, an important element in the overall semiotic project in Emilie's classroom, since grasping and making meaning from new perspectives was essential. Returning to the classroom episode in which Emilie and her students analyzed a propaganda poster representing Pétain as a protector and savior of France in early phases of the Occupation period, I focus on the ways that, when used in conjunction with voicing, embodiment supported repositioning and exploration of various subjectivities in Emilie's classroom.

Excerpt 13 Body language

57 **Emilie**: Et à ça il va opposer le drapeau français ((planting the flag)) et qu'est-ce
58 qu'il montre sur sa droite
59 **S7**: La prospérité
60 **Emilie**: La prospérité
61 **Ss**: L'alimentation
62 **Emilie**: L'alimentation ((whistles)) on va manger enfin (1) quoi d'autre ça
63 évoque quoi ça ces céréales des fleurs ((rolling motion with arms))
64 **Ss** : La paix
65 **Emilie**: La paix d'accord le blé ((pointing to the wheat in the image)) espèce de uh
66 qui symbolise aussi un peu la paix la richesse de la France ne vous

67	inquiétiez pas la France est <u>riche</u> (1) et c'est ça qu'il vous propose
68	((hand stretched out to right like Pétain)) voyez son <u>geste</u> ((stretching hand
69	out like Pétain)) regardez tout son langage du corps ((pointing to different
70	parts of Petain's body)) <u>donc</u> derrière lui ((pointing with thumb behind
71	her)) le malheur (1) d'accord contre le malheur ((pointing to screen)) il
72	<u>plante</u> ((swift downward planting of an imaginary flag)) le drapeau
73	français et voici ce qu'il vous offre ça c'est le futur (1) ne vous inquiétez
74	pas maintenant on va passer sur le maréchal Pétain (2) qu'est-ce que
75	vous pouvez me dire sur donc cette représentation du maréchal Pétain
76	(1) il est où donc dans le tableau

57	**Emilie**:	*Going to match the French flag ((planting the flag)) and what does he <u>show</u>*
58		*on his right*
59	**S7**:	*Prosperity*
60	**Emilie**:	*Prosperity*
61	**Ss**:	*Food*
62	**Emilie**:	*Food ((whistles)) we are going to eat finally (1) what else that evokes what*
63		*that these cereals flowers ((rolling motion with arms))*
64	**Ss**:	*Peace*
65	**Emilie**:	*Peace ok wheat ((pointing to the wheat in the image)) a kind of uh that*
66		*symbolizes also a little peace the <u>wealth</u> of France don't worry France is <u>rich</u>*
67		*(1) and it is that that he offers you ((hand stretched out to right like Pétain))*
68		*look at his <u>gesture</u> ((stretching hand out like Pétain)) look at his whole body*
69		*language ((pointing to different parts of Pétain's body)) <u>so</u> behind him*
70		*(pointing with thumb behind her)) misfortune (1) ok against misfortune*
71		*((pointing to screen)) he <u>plants</u> ((swift downward planting of an imaginary*
72		*flag) the French flag and here is what he offers you that that's the future (1)*
73		*don't worry now we are going to move to Maréchal Pétain (2) what can you*
74		*tell me about this representation of Maréchal Pétain (1) he is where then in*
75		*the painting*

In the class's continued analysis of the propaganda poster, Emilie focuses in on Pétain himself, who is at the center of the image. She first draws students' attention to what he holds in his right hand, which he 'plants' against the misfortune and destruction represented behind him on that side of the image. While the flag is already firmly anchored in the static image, Emilie is able to animate the action of Pétain opposing all that has come before, what previously in the interaction the class has identified as the 'ruin of France'. Emilie then focuses students' attention on the other side of the picture, asking what Pétain is showing on his right-hand side (lines 57–58). Students offer some descriptive comments about what they see and sometimes articulate what they think the images of fields and food are intended to represent more figuratively (lines 59–64); Emilie too identifies in these lines particular details and the figurative meanings they are likely meant to symbolize (peace, France's richness). A brief voicing sequence in line 66, in which Emilie speaks as Pétain telling his citizens not to worry, transitions into a third-person commentary on what Pétain is offering 'you'. The 'you' in line 67 momentarily positions students as members of the French population, most likely, and then Emilie brings attention specifically to Pétain's body language (lines 68-69). Accompanying this explicit talk about body language, Emilie then starts to embody Pétain again (line 72), planting an imaginary flag. Another reinforcement of the repositioning of students as the 'you' to whom Pétain is making an offer (line 72) and another brief taking up of Pétain's voice (line 73) follow. Throughout this interaction, we begin to see the ways that Emilie often marshaled numerous semiotic resources and employed them together in her instruction in order to support an overall effect of repositioning students and making and interpreting meanings from multiple perspectives.

While it was most often Emilie who took on various personae through voicing and embodiment moves during classroom interaction, occasionally students did as well. On rare occasions, Emilie's repositioning of students in discourse (as people who lived during the war era, for example) prompted them to respond through a first-person voice. In other cases, she designed exercises that would require students to try on another's voice. An example of this is presented in Excerpt 14 below. As part of the class's study of the National Revolution, following the video clips from *L'Oeil de Vichy* Emilie had played that had to do with the role of young French people in the Vichy government's new vision for France, Emilie asked the students to look in their packet of readings for the text of a speech given by the youth minister, Mr Lamirand, and the following interaction ensued:

Excerpt 14 With a convincing tone

01 **Emilie**: Qui veut lire la première phrase avec le même ton solennel qui veut lire la
02 première phrase (1) en imitant le ministre avec ce ton solennel allez c'est pas
03 compliqué ça (1) bon S1 allez hup lisez la première phrase
04 **S1**: Oh
05 **Emilie**: Mais avec un ton convaincant uh comme Monsieur Lamirand à vous
06 **S1**: Le maréchal a convié tous les Français à faire ce qu'il a appelé la revolution
07 nationale c'est-à-dire une <u>vraie</u> révolution rompant délibérément et
08 définitivement avec ce qui a conduit la France dans l'état où elle se trouve

```
09                actuellement
10  Emilie:       Ben voila merci vous voyez vous parlez comme ça tout le monde signe on va tous
11                chanter dans les bois alors qu'est-ce qui vous choque déjà dès la première phrase
12                (3) il n'y a pas deux choses qui vous choquent (2) dans la première phrase la
13                première ligne oui S2
14  S2:           Um tu je ok um le maréchal a convie tous les Français à faire ce qu'il a appelé la
15                révolution nationale c'est-à-dire une vraie révolution rompant délibérément et
16                définitivement avec ce qui a conduit la France dans l'été où elle se trouve
17                actuellement
18  Emilie:       Voyez heureusement qu'il n'y ait pas de dictateurs féminins parce que là elles
19                sont encore pires voyez
20  Ss:           Hahahaha
21  Emilie:       Bon alors merci S2 alors dites-moi qu'est-ce qui vous semblent complètement
22                déjà ridicule

01  Emilie:       Who wants to read the first sentence with the same solemn tone who wants to read
02                the first sentence (1) imitating the minister with this solemn tone come on it's not
03                complicated (1) good S1 go ahead read the first sentence
04  S1:           Oh
05  Emilie:       But with a convincing tone uh like Mr. Lamirand take it away
06  S1:           The Maréchal has urged all of the French to do what he has called the national
07                revolution that is to say a true revolution breaking deliberately and definitively
08                with what drove France into the state that she currently finds herself
09  Emilie:       Well there it is you see you talk like that and everyone signs up we are all going to
10                sing in the woods so what shocks you already from the first sentence (3) there
11                aren't two things that shock you (2) in the first sentence the first line yes S2
12  S2:           Um you I ok um the Maréchal has urged all of the French to do what he has called
13                the national revolution that is to say a true revolution breaking deliberately and
14                definitively with what drove France into the state that she currently finds herself
15  Emilie:       You see luckily there weren't female dictators because there they are even worse
16                you see
17  Ss:           Hahahaha
18  Emilie:       Good so thank you S2 so tell me what seems completely ridiculous to you already
```
(Observation from 14 September 2006)

In this brief interaction, Emilie had planned for a student to animate the youth minister's voice by asking him to read a brief portion of a speech. She is clear in directing him to read the passage with emotion and with a convincing tone (lines 1, 2 and 5), which he then does in lines 6–8. His emphasis on the word *'vrai'* to highlight that the National Revolution was a 'true' revolution is particularly remarkable, as he begins to truly appropriate the words on the page in order to inflect them with what he believes to be an appropriately solemn and convincing tone. Interestingly, a second unplanned reading of the text emerges. After asking students to focus on the content of the line that has just been read by S1, a second student begins to speak but does not answer the questions Emilie has posed. Instead, after some false starts (perhaps marking her uncertainty about whether she is in fact expected to perform another reading aloud of the speech excerpt), she begins to recite the same sentence (lines 12–14). In her reading, S2 speaks more forcefully than did S1. She chooses to accent more words in the sentence, stressing 'deliberately' and 'definitively' quite emphatically in addition to stressing the word 'true'. S2's rendition presents the opportunity for Emilie to joke in line 15 that perhaps female dictators are harsher than their male counterparts. We might speculate as well about the effect of students' speaking through others' voices in this way. Far beyond a shift in pronoun use, the style and affect students employ to reaccent another's words may personalize meaning potentials of those forms and possibly lead students to form richer networks of meaning that include the sound and feel of words as they themselves produce them. Of course, such direct ventriloquation as well as experiences speaking through the voices of other individuals and social types, real and imagined, mirrors what students were asked to do in their global simulation writing projects (discussed in depth in the next chapter), so Emilie's instructional moves here were likely intended as well to prepare students for that work of meaning-making through narrative writing.

Repositioning students in classroom discourse so that they were projected into times, places, scenarios and subjectivities that were unfamiliar to them was a key interactional and pedagogical process in Emilie's class. Emilie achieved this by drawing on the rich semiotic material that she had brought into the classroom through the many varied texts students read before class and worked with during class time. But in the context of this designed semiotic network, Emilie engaged in meaning-making processes that drew on the discursive affordances of the network, and she drew on multiple modes simultaneously. Multimodality is the nature of semiosis in all meaning-making situations to some degree, but Emilie's deployment of a diversity of modes to advance her pedagogical purposes is worth noting, since in ML classroom environments, linguistic channels (whether spoken or written) are usually quite privileged. Harnessing the potential of other modes could prove extremely fruitful in ML education.

Developing a Metalanguage for Engaging in Interpretation

If we recall that one of Emilie's broad objectives in this course was to instill in students skills that would extend far beyond the classroom and the study of this particular historical period, language and content, her focus on equipping learners with a metalanguage and a general analytic approach for dealing with cultural texts and representations makes a great deal of sense. In a social semiotic view, acquiring these types of overarching awareness and ability are part of expanding one's perceptual and meaning-making capacities. In terms of instructional process and interactional moves, Emilie furnished this metalanguage and demonstrated analytic processes quite often through modeling and then provided space for students to practice with these. In the two classroom examples below, we first see the introductory phases of the propaganda poster analysis that has already figured several times in this chapter. In this excerpt, Emilie supplies analytic terminology and procedures for interpreting the poster, but these processes will clearly work as students approach other texts. In the second excerpt in this section, six days after the poster analysis, we see explicit discussion in Emilie's class of the power of representation and the representation of power, a conversation that permitted students to engage directly with larger issues of representation and meaning, namely that representations are not neutral and that they must be considered for their possible intended and ascribed meanings and the extent to which these are ideologically motivated. In this excerpt especially, we have clear evidence that in addition to learning how to perceive in new and more numerous ways and to engaging regularly in interpretive practices around texts to stretch one's abilities for semiotic action, overall awareness of the nature of signs, representations and what they do, the power that they exert is also an entirely appropriate goal in ML education and one that we can see evidence of having developed as students discuss texts like Marin's.

Excerpt 15 Providing a metalanguage and procedure for textual analysis

01 **Emilie**:   Voilà alors maintenant ce que j'aimerais que vous fassiez c'est que nous
02   analysions cet image-là parce que là ((pointing to screen)) on entre <u>dans la</u>
03   <u>propagande vichyste</u> vous allez voir le maréchal Pétain à partir du moment
04   où il devient <u>le chef de l'Etat</u> on ne parle plus de président on verra ça
05   jeudi il va devenir le <u>chef de l'Etat toute sa politique</u> ((rolling motion with
06   hands)) va être va être basée sur une propagande <u>intense</u> ((right forearm

07 falls like an ax)) et ça ((gesturing toward the screen)) c'est un des premiers
08 exemples de la propagande <u>pétainiste</u> ce que j'aimerais que vous fassiez
09 c'est que vous identifiez les détails iconographiques ((tapping on board))
10 et que vous les analysiez déjà donc au premier plan à l'arrière-plan à
11 gauche à droite au centre ((gesturing to different parts of the image))
12 d'accord? alors dites-moi on va déjà analyser l'arrière-plan qu'est-ce que
13 ça représente l'arrière-plan? est-ce que vous voyez ça si je
14 fais ça comme ça c'est bon oui peut-être mieux qu'est-ce
15 qu'il y a à l'arrière-plan derrière le maréchal Pétain donc à droite
16 ((sweeping hand across background of image))

01 **Emilie**: *There so now what I would like you to do is that we analyze this image*
02 *because here ((pointing to the screen)) we enter <u>into Vichy propaganda</u> you*
03 *are going to see Maréchal Pétain from the moment where he becomes <u>the</u>*
04 *<u>head of State</u> we no longer speak of a president we will see that on Thursday*
05 *he is going to become <u>the head of State his whole politics</u> ((rolling motion*
06 *with hands)) are going to be are going to be based on an <u>intense</u> ((right arm*
07 *falls like an ax)) propaganda and that ((gesturing toward the screen)) that is*
08 *one of the first examples of <u>Pétainist</u> propaganda what I would like you to do*
09 *is that you identify the iconographic details ((tapping on board)) and that you*
10 *analyze them so already in the foreground in the background to the left to the*
11 *right at the center ((gesturing to different parts of the image)) ok? so tell me*
12 *we are already going to analyze the background what does that represent*
13 *the background? can you see it if I do that like that it's good yes maybe better*
14 *what is there in the background behind Maréchal Pétain then on the right*
15 *((sweeping hand across background of image))*

As Emilie sets up the class's discussion of the propaganda poster, she supplies them with a metalanguage and an analytic process for viewing and interpreting what they see. She furnishes certain elements of the metalanguage verbally and on the blackboard, and she supports the communication of this metalanguage to students by gesturing in front of the projected image of the propaganda poster as she reads terms from the board that refer to areas of the image (lines 10–11). But she also offers broader terms; she identifies the image multiple times as falling within the genre of 'propaganda' (lines 2, 7 and 8) and she uses the term 'iconographic details' both verbally (line 9) and on the blackboard to give an analytic name to what they will identify and discuss in the image. Emilie then goes on to explain explicitly what the interpretive process will entail (lines 9–10), namely two major steps – identifying iconographic details and then analyzing them. That she then lists the areas of the image suggests that this is a systematic process and that focusing on composition is itself important, although she does not explicitly say so. In the remainder of the interaction, which she launches in lines 11–15, Emilie then actually models and walks students through the overall analytic procedure she is suggesting to them. This apprenticeship in how to 'read' texts was not unnoticed by students. As the interview excerpt at the start of this chapter attests, students remarked the level of analytic attention Emilie accorded to the analysis of this particular text. Within the collaborative analysis the class constructs in the rest of the interaction, the students' engagement in identifying and then analyzing signs and symbols is a further indicator that Emilie's direct instruction about interpretive processes had an effect.

A short time after the analysis of the propaganda poster, the class engaged in discussion of a portion of Louis Marin's text on the representation of power and the power of representation. In the excerpt that follows, we see students articulating their understandings of how images can exert power, and ultimately a student connects Marin's text on representation to the class's previous work with the analysis of the poster of Pétain.

Excerpt 16 Power of representation

01 **Emilie**: D'après le texte de Marin pourquoi est-ce que les régimes dictatoriaux utilisent
02   les images la prolifération des images du chef oui S1
03 **S1**: Um je pense qu'il y a beaucoup de de raisons mais uh c'est parce que um le chef
04   d'un régime ne peut pas être uh dans toutes uh tous les endroits à le même
05   temps um et si il y a beaucoup de images um du chef uh uh on peut ou si si si tout
06   le si quelqu- si tout le monde a a l'opportunité de de voir um l'image de la chef
07   chaque jour um l'image a un type de pouvoir um la même? elle (2) le même? uh

[Lines 8–13 omitted in which Emilie and S1 negotiate how to say 'the image has a kind of power in itself'; Emilie eventually offers 'l'image a un type de pouvoir en elle-même']

14 **Emilie**: Voilà bien ouais S2
15 **S2**: L'image manipule mais le peuple um Marin dit un pouvoir qui paralyse fascine
16   inspire la crainte c'est quelque chose qui peut changer les um les têtes de tout
17 **Emilie**: Ça peut changer ça peut conditionner ça peut changer la perception des choses
18   mais surtout quand on dit fasciner paralyse ça c'est quel sentiment quelle émotion
19   si je vous dis j'étais fascinée paralysée
20 **Ss**: La peur
21 **Emilie**: Oui vous avez aussi la peur d'accord on va jouer aussi sur la crainte d'accord oui
22   S4

23	**S4**:	Mais il dit aussi uh uh [manipule] du chef ou uh être magnifié idéalisé c'est uh
24		c'est uh l'image du chef uh idéal qui a le pouvoir uh la socié- les gens ne savent
25		pas uh le chef uh uh ce qui est [derrière] une
26		personne mais avec tous les images il est uh quel- quelque chose d'autre qui est
27		idéal pour les gens
28	**Emilie**:	Oui c'est ça en fait ce ne sont pas des attributs humains que vous allez montrer
29		(1) dans le contexte du maréchal Pétain on ne montre pas un vieil homme
30		avec des rides (1) qui est décrépit non là vous avez un image du surhomme (2)
31		c'est le chef que vous voyez (1) d'accord c'est le pouvoir qu'on va voir et donc qui
32		paralyse qui fascine et en même temps qui est toujours là qui est partout pour
33		que vous ne l'oubliez pas alors dites-moi qui est omnipresent par definition qui
34		est omniprésent fascine pétrifie mais que l'on aime
35	**S2**:	Dieu
36	**Emilie**:	Fascine pétrifie mais que l'on aime
37	**Ss**:	Dieu
38	**Emilie**:	Dieu et ben voilà encore une fois on rentre dans ce dans ce champs sémantique il
39		est comme dieu il va se substituer à dieu
40	**S2**:	C'est comme ces portrai- ces portraits du maréchal um avec le what›s the word
41		for the flag
42	**Emilie**:	[Le drapeau
43	**Ss**:	[Le drapeau
44	**S2**:	Oui le drapeau et il était au centre de de l'image et il parait comme Christ
45	**Emilie**:	Oui
46	**S2**:	Comme tout brille et tout ça
47	**Emilie**:	La gloire d'accord le chef dans sa gloire mais là vous allez avoir et donc
48		malheureusement qui dit omniprésence (5.5) [writing on board] si vous êtes
49		omniprésent en général qu'est-ce que dieu fin dieu est supposé être omni- fin
50		dieu est par définition omniprésent mais qu'est-ce qu'il est également il est
51		omni-
52	**S5**:	Omniscient
53	**Emilie**:	Omniscient ben voilà (5) [writing on board]
54	**S2**:	Oh ça (induce) la peur du peuple la peur qu'ils pensent qu›il va savoir tout (qu'ils)
55		et que pour les collaborateurs (unintelligible)
56	**Emilie**:	Voilà vous regardez le chef il est omniprésent mais le chef vous regarde le chef
57		vous entend et c'est tout attention oui S6
01	**Emilie**:	*According to Marin's text why do dictatorial regimes use images the proliferation*
02		*of images of the leader yes S1*
03	**S1**:	*Um I think there are a lot of of reasons but uh it is because um the leader of a*
04		*regime cannot be uh in all uh all places at the same time um and if there are a lot of*
05		*images um of the leader uh uh people can or if if every if someone- if everyone has*

06   has the opportunity to to see um the image of the leader everyday um the image has
07   a kind of power um the same? (2) the same? uh

[Lines 8–13 omitted in which Emilie and S1 negotiate how to say 'the image has a kind of power in itself'; Emilie eventually offers 'l'image a un type de pouvoir en elle-même']

14 **Emilie**: There you go good yeah S2
15 **S2**: The image manipulates but the people um Marin says a power that paralyzes
16   fascinates inspires fear it is something that can change the um the heads of all
17 **Emilie**: That can change that can condition that can change the perception of things but
18   especially when we say to fascinate paralyses that is what sentiment what emotion
19 **Ss**: Fear
20 **Emilie**: Yes you have fear too ok we are going to play on fear as well ok yes S4
21 **S4**: But he says also uh uh [manipulates] of the leader or uh to be magnified idealized it
22   is uh it is uh the image of the ideal uh leader who has power uh socie- people do not
23   know uh the leader uh uh what is [behind] a person but with all the images he is uh
24   some something else that is ideal for people
25 **Emilie**: Yes that's it in fact it is not human attributes that you are going to show (1) in the
26   context of Maréchal Pétain they are not going to show an old man with wrinkles (1)
27   that is decrepit no there you have an image of a superhuman (2) it is the leader that
28   you see (1) ok it is power that we see and therefore that paralyzes fascinates and
29   that at the same time is always there that is everywhere so you don't forget it so tell
30   me who is omnipresent by definition is omnipresent fascinates petrifies but that we
31   love
32 **S2**: God
33 **Emilie**: Fascinates petrifies but that people love
34 **Ss**: God
35: **Emilie**: God and so here you go once again we return to this to this semantic field he is like
36   God he is going to substitute himself for god
37 **S2**: It is like these portai- these portraits of the Maréchal um with the what's the word
38   for flag
39 **Emilie**: [Flag
40 **Ss**: [Flag
41 **S2**: Yes the flag and he was in the middle of of the image and he seemed like Christ
42: **Emilie**: Yes
43: **S2**: Like everything shining and all that
44 **Emilie**: Glory ok the leader in his glory but there you are going to have and so
45   unfortunately what rhymes with omnipresence (5.5) [writing on board] if you if you
46   are omnipresent in general what does God well God is allegedly omni- well God is by
47   definition omnipresent but what else is he he is omni-
48 **S5**: Omniscient

49	**Emilie**:	*Omniscient well there it is (5) [writing on the board]*
50	**S2**:	*Oh that causes fear of the people fear that they think that he is going to know*
51		*everything (that they) and that for the collaborators (unintelligible)*
52	**Emilie**:	*There it is you see the leader he is omnipresent but the leader is watching you the*
53		*leader hears you and that's it be careful yes S6*

(Observation from 18 September 2006)

In this excerpt, Emilie asks a straightforward question about why dictatorial regimes proliferate images of the leader (lines 1–2). In response, several students offer reasons, some citing Marin's text directly and others paraphrasing the way he describes the powers representations can exercise (e.g. substituting for a leader who obviously cannot physically be everywhere at once, inspiring fear and self-surveillance, etc.). S1 even comments on the way that images take on a power of their own (lines 3–13), and another, S4, implies that images become more powerful than the actual person since they are idealizations (lines 21–24). Emilie then poses a second question about who else fascinates, paralyzes and petrifies (lines 29–31). Students quickly guess 'god,' which leads S2 to make a connection with the poster the class analyzed days before (lines 37–38) in which Pétain also presents himself in god-like fashion. Emilie carries the comparison further, prompting students to say that he who is omnipresent is also omniscient, and concludes their discussion by saying that the leader is watching 'you' (line 52). The discussion students and Emilie had in relation to the text they read on the representation of power provides us with evidence that broader consideration of semiotic processes were in play in Emilie's class; beyond analysis of particular texts, she made space for them to reflect explicitly on the nature of representation and how it operates not just to make meanings but to exert power.

Conclusion

The chapter opened with a student remarks, raising questions about how teachers can help learners understand cultural texts from unfamiliar points of view. It then offered a detailed analysis of several examples from classroom discourse and interaction, in which Emilie and her students read, listened to, viewed and engaged with cultural texts. The excerpts and analysis illustrated practices surrounding the interpretation of cultural texts that were typical in Emilie's class and formed the basis for claims about the meaning-making practices that more broadly underpin development of semiotic awareness and symbolic competence, such as (1) identifying culturally symbolic forms and reference points (words, phrases, images); (2) hypothesizing about possible meanings of these forms; (3) animating cultural narratives, one type of symbolic form, through voicing and embodiment; (4) repositioning the students or teacher in classroom discourse to project them into the plotlines of cultural narratives and (5) developing a broader approach to the interpretation of meaning and a metalanguage for this analytic process. Broadly speaking, becoming symbolically competent in this class involved first identifying symbolic forms and then exploring and mapping the meaning potentials of those forms – trying out their social semiotic affordances. As the examples in this chapter illustrate, through the class's collaborative analyses of particular instances of use (e.g. linguistic and other symbols appearing in a specific text or representation), through the projection of students as participant examples (Wortham, 1992) of figures and social types relevant to the historical period, and through students' own use of symbolic forms (e.g. in reciting excerpts from a speech), particular acts of meaning served as points of entry into broader cultural meanings. Put differently, instantiations of symbolic forms (words, image, cultural narratives) in texts and in classroom interactions opened access to considering how these forms might mean more broadly, for particular groups with various perspectives and agendas. This consideration helped to move the class from the analysis of forms as symbolic representations to performing meanings as symbolic action in some cases and locating symbolic power in others. It is also worth noting that as Emilie and her students engaged with symbolic meaning-making around representations of different types, they simultaneously worked out linguistic expressions as they dealt with understandings of content. In many of the excerpts from classroom interaction in this chapter, we see that language forms (words, phrases, whole texts) are indeed intertwined with cultural meanings, as is often claimed in the profession. But what becomes abundantly clear is that form-meaning relationships are better considered in ML education as complex, dynamic networks, the meaning potentials of which students discover to some extent as already existing (that is, in terms of the fairly conventionalized or culturally shared meanings symbolic forms have) but which they also can begin to personalize as they build their own abilities to mean in French using symbolic forms. These were experiences with meaning-making from new points of view and through new linguistic and symbolic resources that were extended and complemented by the narrative writing assignment that anchored the global simulation project discussed in the next chapter. In Chapter 5, we see a different type of learning opportunity that students were afforded but through which they similarly continued to form networks of referential and symbolic meaning that connected both individual and broader social scales of meaning.

Note

(1) Recall that observations did not take place at all class meetings, so there were certainly more *Identifications* activities that took place on days I was not present.

5 Realizing Meaning Potentials Through Narrative Writing

> *It is more, yes, a knowledge of oneself through the learning of the knowledge of the other. It's more that. It's also affirming oneself...in class we have seen with Sydney who at the beginning, because she didn't have, because she wasn't at ease speaking, finally she realized that French is just a vehicle, but that also gave her the chance to express herself. It's that too. It's finding a voice. It's finding a place in the class but equally to then realize that one has a place in society.*
> Emilie talking about a student, Sydney
> (Interview 19 December 2006)

> *Alyssa explains in our interview that the French collaboration was 'the best kept secret in the Western hemisphere'. She goes on to say that she was in France with her father during the summer, and as they walked through the city, she marveled out loud at how the spires on the cathedrals on the Ile de la Cîté survived the World War II bombings. Her father replied that he did not think there was much bombing in Paris and that the French had capitulated pretty quickly. So, for her, the Occupation dossier was interesting because 'it wasn't learning to communicate things that I already knew in French; it was really learning in French.' I suggest to Alyssa that as Americans, especially of younger generations, we tend to know very little about what happened between the beginning and the end of World War II in France. Alyssa adds that it is often a very positive view of the Americans and the British 'who were being very heroic' and the rest is 'a blind spot'.*
> (Interview 17 November 2006)

In the classroom under study, a rich textual environment was in place where symbolic forms and cultural narratives were available for analysis and interpretation at every turn[1]. Intercultural learning and development of symbolic competence for this group, however, was not only about learning to recognize a web of forms and meanings as they are realized through particular cultural texts and in cultural imaginaries or only about learning to interpret meaning from cultural representations by accessing another point of view. Intercultural learning was also very much about learning to perform, create and reframe meanings and, in a broader way, to possibly reconsider oneself and one's perspectives, as Alyssa's comments above indicate occurred for some students in Emilie's class.

At least part of language learning is a process of finding one's voice in another language. If we conceive of voice as never wholly belonging to one speaker (Bakhtin, 1986), we begin to see that in learning a language, one does not merely translate his or her voice into new words and expressions but also begins to construct and consistently renew a voice by drawing on a whole new array of other voices and stories that resound in all language, as students in this class did and as Emilie's remarks above suggest. When Kramsch (1995) writes that 'foreign language...learners have to be addressed not as deficient monoglossic enunciators, but as potentially heteroglossic narrators' (p. 90), she is speaking about the transformative potential of ML learning and the possibility for language learners to become something other than solely speakers of their native culture and worldview or full-fledged members of a foreign culture. Rather, learners' engagement with other cultures creates a space for the potential transformation of both native and foreign cultures and for learners themselves to emerge as potentially transcultural beings.

In this chapter, several examples of students making meaning through their extended writing projects are presented. By writing through both social and individual voices and by drawing on the range of cultural referents, meanings and narratives that were available to them, students were able to spin new meanings and to realize meaning potentials. I explain how students in Emilie's class came to develop the ability to integrate cultural and symbolic meanings and sometimes to express new ones, to turn forms to their own intended meanings, a key component of being critically, culturally aware and being symbolically competent. Specifically, I describe and analyze the meaning-making practices surrounding the recontextualization of symbolic forms and the performance and reshaping of symbolic meanings that occurred in Emilie's class as students engaged in the extended writing assignment for which they authored the first-person fictional accounts of characters who lived through World War II in France. Excerpts from students' work reveal several meaning-making practices central to the development of critical cultural awareness and symbolic competence, including: (1) drawing on a network of symbolic forms, (2) resignifying cultural references to transform their meanings, (3) interweaving 'small stories' and broader cultural narratives, and (4) creating intertextual relations. Evidence of creative meaning-making in students' writing is complemented at the end of the chapter with excerpts from interviews with students, in which the impact that this project had on them and their perceptions of the culture learning process is apparent.

In discussing the students' writing, I address the way that students spun new meanings by making connections across various cultural symbols, texts and narratives. Intertextuality, or the way that meanings are forged when texts are brought into relation with each other, can be a powerful narrative device in making meaning. Drawing on the multiple cultural texts that were available was very apparent in the class's activity, and making connections across cultural narratives was a way for a denser web to be woven and for the polyvocal and polysemic nature of culture to be accessed. The *Mémoires* project also offered the opportunity to engage not only with the overarching narratives associated with French perspectives on this era, but also with personal and individual stories that nuance the bigger picture. Bruner (1991) argues that in fact, large and small stories cannot be separated since 'the particulars of narratives are tokens of broader types' (p. 6). Bruner goes on to say that 'particularity achieves its emblematic status by its embeddedness in a story that is in some sense generic' (p. 7), emphasizing that what we might call 'small stories' have meaning only because they fit with what we might call 'large stories'. The pieces of students' work presented in this chapter support the claim that in intercultural learning, spinning new meanings and making connections among semiotic resources are just as important as developing an awareness that a semiotic network even exists and cultivating a flexibility in interpreting meaning.

With so many texts at their disposal, and with Emilie urging them to absorb as much content and language as possible from these texts, it is not surprising that my analysis of students' written work found it to be highly intertextual. Lemke (1992) posits thematic, orientational and organizational types of intertextuality based on the ways that texts can be related to each other through their patterns of content, their points of view (or stance) and their structure and purposes (as in our recognition that genres are categories of texts that share some elements of structure or purpose, for example) respectively.

In the students' *Mémoires* work, intertextuality was apparent along all three dimensions. Themes that were present in the other texts the class encountered were often integrated (and in fact, certain themes were heavily suggested by the prompts Emilie gave students, like in the fourth chapter of the students' *Mémoires*, where the theme of 'betrayal' had to figure in some way). One particular text the class used, *Paroles d'Étoiles* (a collection of writings by Jewish people who were children at the time that the war broke out), offered an organizational intertext since it was the main model of the memoir genre that the class encountered and analyzed. It is likely that other primary source texts the class studied also served as models for organizing a narrative of the war experience. Because students encountered the same texts and because of the constraints set up by the assignment (i.e. being written as a memoir, responding to particular prompts for each chapter, etc.), the themes and organization were similar across students' work; however, students clearly drew on the texts they encountered as part of the class's work in different ways, highlighting some themes and not others within the broader topics suggested in the prompts, borrowing certain forms and conventions of memoir writing apparent in the *Paroles d'Étoiles* texts and not others. The most striking differences, though, were apparent in the realm of orientational intertexts. Stance and point of view were embodied in the individual voice of the character of each story and were achieved in different ways by the students. This is not to say that there were not orientational intertexts apparent in the students' writing in general or that similar stances were not taken up across students' stories. Yet, bringing to life the voice of their characters was very much about creating a highly particular stance and orientation to historical events, and while students drew from the range of stances they encountered in the texts the class worked with, each character's point of view was unique. While all of the students' compositions dealt with similar thematic content and were all in the genre of 'memoirs,' then, the selection of events and reference points students would weave their characters' stories around and the stance characters had toward them distinguished their accounts.

Writing Through a Culturally Different Voice and Exploiting Affordances of Semiotic Resources

The creative writing component of the global simulation project provided an opportunity for students to explore and construct meanings through the telling of the stories of the war from a particular point of view and through a particular voice. In an article that focuses on the development of academic literacy among second language learners, Boughey (2000) likens a writer's voice in a piece of writing to a soloist that is backed by a choir. In this particular metaphor for writing, the choir is the collection of voices that accompanies and supports the main authorial voice. This conception clearly borrows from more linguistic conceptions of voice, such as Bakhtin's (1981) notion of heteroglossia, where a multiplicity of voices and linguistically constructed personae are believed to resound in all language use. In Bakhtin's work, a multiplicity of voices is the source of a diversity of meanings. Writing about the utterance, Bakhtin (1986) claimed

[T]here can be neither a first nor a last meaning; it always exists among other meanings as a link in the chain of meaning, which in its totality is the only thing that can be real. In historical life this chain continues infinitely, and therefore each individual link in it is renewed again and again, as though it were being reborn. (p. 146)

The 'links in a chain' metaphor here is similar to the 'web of texts' and 'network of meanings' that I have been discussing throughout this book. That Bakhtin writes about the historicity of this chain of meanings is also particularly salient in the context of the class under study, since the students and teacher were in fact engaged in interpreting historical meanings and narratives (although, as Kramsch & Whiteside [2008] have argued, historicity is a dimension of language and meaning that all ML learners need to be engaged with regardless of curricular content). When the students wrote the fictional memoirs of the character they created, they were penning a narrative that was meant to enter into dialogue with others of its kind. That is to say that in writing their characters' memoirs, students had to pay attention not only to what was possible (i.e. by including relevant contextual details and by avoiding cultural anachronism – contradiction of the historical facts) but also to what was plausible and believable and to suggest that in composing the fictional memoirs of their invented characters, students could draw on the cultural narratives they encountered in their coursework (and elsewhere, arguably) as resources in constructing meaning. A familiarity with the themes and stances existing in relation to various reference points and across a range of cultural texts about the war was therefore necessary.

The written work of students that is presented below illustrates the ways that they were able to develop and demonstrate symbolic and intercultural competence as they constructed plausible historical settings (by referencing salient reference points) and then voiced a fictive, but again plausible and meaningful, experience through a narrating voice that needed to make sense among other individual and social voices. The students' writing necessarily required them to reposition themselves, to adopt and reshape culturally unfamiliar voices and to create meaning in the process. Two students' work on the *Mémoires* project is described in order to convey the complexity of the narrative worlds the students imagined and to illustrate what this exercise in weaving new stories contributed to students' intercultural learning. What became apparent in analyzing their work was, first, the development of very particular stances as they created a new voice; and second, the intertextuality (a weaving of a variety of narratives and texts) that allowed students to construct their stories. That is, students were able to render their characters' stories credible ('historically and cultural precise' as Emilie often said) by drawing on semiotic resources and cultural narratives that they learned about from other source texts (written texts, film clips, Emilie's stories, etc.), which then served as the basis for their imagining of a new story. This procedure is evident across all of the students' texts, since in analyzing them, I was able to identify themes and storylines that strongly echoed a story told in class or encountered in a reading, and even particular wordings that resembled a way of talking that the students had experience with as a result of the class (i.e. a particular wording used by Emilie to describe certain historical events, phrases from texts). This is to say nothing of the texts and narratives students drew on that were not part of the course material; that is, their understanding of this period of history was also likely to have been shaped by other texts external to the environment of the French class itself.

In all, analysis of students' projects revealed that development of personal meaning potentials in students was, on one hand, reflected in their increased facility with realizing the meaning potentials of forms and signs in ways that were close to the usages they encountered for these forms in their coursework. On the other hand, at times, they turned semiotic resources to their own symbolic, meaning-making purposes. This was perhaps a more agentive kind of decision-making as they wrote. Ultimately, this allowed students to try on new roles and perspectives and to create complexity of meaning, which are central pedagogical goals when we talk about cultivating students' symbolic and intercultural competences.

Two *Mémoires* Projects

The two students whose work is discussed below had very different experiences with the *Mémoires* part of the global simulation project. Katie, on the one hand, said that she enjoyed the creative writing involved and found that it did help her to think about the situation of someone living at the time. Brina, on the other hand, expressed the most reservations of all the students I interviewed about composing the fictional memoirs. She said,

> I think that the *Mémoires* offered an opportunity to sort of ask yourself in a at least semi-realistic way how you personally might react in the situation and might feel rather than just reading about the people who were affected and saying 'oh my goodness they must have felt such and such a thing at such and such a time' you had to actually sort of try as best you could to stick yourself in that situation which was

very hard to, I mean I always worried that if somebody actually who went through this read this they would [laughs in a scoffing way] be like 'this is absurd' because like I have no idea...to sort of assume these feelings that I think really are probably indescribable. (10 November 2006)

So while Brina found the project to be useful in achieving a deeper engagement with those experiences that people living at the time may have had, she also believes that truly understanding this period of history is impossible without actually having lived it and that, even had one been there, the era and events, to some degree, defy understanding (recall the initial directions Emilie distributed to the class about the global simulation project in which the notion of writing to 'understand' this historical period was put in quotes). Brina in this excerpt makes reference to gaining access to the feelings that those living at the time might have experienced, signaling an opinion that was shared by many of her classmates – that writing the *Mémoires* forced them to consider emotional experiences of the war. This kind of affective engagement appears to be productive, even if attempting to think, view and feel from another perspective is only semi-realistic, as Brina suggests.

Katie told me that in writing her *Mémoires* project, she attempted to create a character that very much resembled herself and whose life mirrored her own in many ways. She said that it was interesting to see how different her life would have been had she been born 65 years ago in France and that she tried to make choices as the character that she would have made herself. When I asked whether there was anything uncomfortable about adopting this persona, Katie said there was something 'weird' about thinking that if it really had been her living through this historical era she might have turned in her Jewish neighbors to the authorities. She said 'That's a strange kind of thing to think about yourself' (30 November 2006).

In the following section, I analyze these two students' *Mémoires* projects in terms of the way they brought various reference points together and included certain signs and forms to create a plausible historical and narrative world through their writing. I then examine the ways they made meanings with semiotic resources in these created environments – specifically, how they applied and sometimes stretched meaning potentials through their particular acts of meaning. These instances, taken together, build patterns of rich intertextuality and stance-taking such that distinct authorial voices are constructed and some elements of the students' overall intercultural learning process are suggested, such as how the act of 'perspective-taking' may have had broader implications for their intercultural learning and development of symbolic competence. The projects of these two particular students were selected for detailed analysis because while they both demonstrate the patterns that I found across all of the students' work (drawing on the rich narrative environment present in Emilie's class while also developing a particular story and stance for their invented characters), Katie's and Brina's reactions to the project and their approaches to writing, as gauged in my interviews with them, were quite different. In presenting the written work of two students who showed such divergent opinions and approaches regarding the project, I would like to suggest that similar results (i.e. the production of credible and meaningful historical fictions) emerged precisely because the classroom ecology Emilie set up afforded learning opportunities to all students.

The References, Stories and Stances in Brina's Project

Table 5.1 summarizes Brina's project wherein, despite her assertion in our interview that 'nothing really happened' to her character, a particular perspective on the uncertainty of everyday life for everyday people during the war emerges nonetheless. In our interview together, Brina said of her project:

> I sort of tried to show that even when nothing you know crazy was happening you know you weren't describing you know ravaged bodies on the soil there was still this you know daily, quotidian element of the stress.

While Brina opted not to author a story that recounted traumatic events, mostly because she felt uncomfortable with assuming what those who really did experience horrific calamities felt, she wove an entirely credible historical fiction. This was because she was able to establish a credible narrative world and to create meaningful and compelling stances for her protagonist. The main plot developments of her character's memoirs, chapter by chapter, are outlined in Table 5.1.

A first example serves to illustrate the way that Brina's *Mémoires* project realized meaning potentials not only by using the network of references she had available but also by stretching those networks in meaningful ways. In the first and second chapters of her character's memoirs, Brina integrates the theme of Maréchal Pétain's increasing presence in daily life. In the first chapter, for example, she writes

Table 5.1 Overview of Brina's *Mémoires* writing project, entitled *'C'est ainsi que nous avançons'*

Chapter titles	Synopsis
Préface	The story is characterized as being about everyday life and everyday people, and as 'at once personal and universal'. The 'editor' writes 'what is important is not to judge the events of the past but to be touched by its stories and, consequently, to decide to carry on in such a way that history does not repeat itself.'
Chapitre 1 : 'La vie avant la guerre' (Life before the war)	The introductory chapter presents the main character, Mercedes – a 22-year-old young woman who was married and the mother of a small child at the start of the war. The character's family is described and an explanation is offered for why neither the father nor husband of the character leave for war. Finally, the character relates her mixed emotions concerning Pétain, whose speech she has heard.
Chapitre 2 : 'Les Incertitudes et les Soucis' (Uncertainties and Worries)	Mercedes describes a changed Paris from which a large number of citizens have fled and which German forces occupy. Her family worries about her brother who had gone to fight and a neighbor whose husband also went to the front. Mercedes mentions that Pétain's portraits are everywhere. She worries and feels uncertain. Anti-Semitism in Paris is becoming more visible.
Chapitre 3 : 'La propagande qui inspire' (Propaganda that inspires)	Mercedes describes the radio speeches she hears and the posters she sees and says that the population became 'intoxicated' and 'boiled over with hatred' at this point in the Occupation. Mercedes describes her daily concerns – about her husband potentially leaving to work in Germany under the Compulsory Work Service, about waiting in line for food. She is suspicious of one of her neighbors. The first stretch of dialogue of the memoirs is presented: a conversation between Mercedes and Madame Armand, a florist working on the ground floor of the building.

Chapter titles	Synopsis
Chapitre 4 : 'Si on pouvait le refaire à nouveau...' (If we could do it over...)	Mercedes' brother comes home from the front. She also has an uncomfortable encounter with a woman while in line for food. The woman spews anti-Semitic remarks and Mercedes goes along with them to avoid endangering herself. She sees a Jewish girl who is crying as this occurs though and feels guilty.
Chapitre 5 : 'Et tout d'un coup...' (And suddenly...)	Mercedes' husband wants to do something to resist the occupying forces and the regime and suggests that the couple take care of a Jewish friend's child in order to protect him from possible discovery and deportation. They come up with a story to explain who the child is. The husband also announces that another family in the building – the Fechners – have disappeared. Mercedes suspects that another neighbor has denounced them.
Chapitre 6 : 'Une sorte de fin' (A kind of ending)	The war is over, but as people come back to Paris, there is little to celebrate given the losses they have suffered and the still difficult circumstances of living in the city. Mercedes says that everyone was haunted by something. She also says that it was difficult to identify who the collaborators and the resistants were after the war since some people pretended to have been part of the resistance. She mentions that one of her neighbors (Henri Fechner) returned to the building and then describes the reuniting of the child the couple had protected with his family. Mercedes closes her memoirs by stating that nothing would be the same.

Excerpt 17 Reaction to Pétain's speech

01 Après avoir entendu le discours de Pétain, beaucoup de gens se sont sentis
02 soulagés – ils voyaient Pétain comme un protecteur, quelqu'un qui les
03 sauverait et qui sauverait la France. Je voulais ressentir la même chose; après
04 tout, Pétain semblait tellement calme et optimiste. Mais j'avais des sentiments
05 mêlés; mon frère me disait toujours qu'il fallait se méfier de l'eau qui dort.

01 *After having heard Pétain's speech, a lot of people felt*
02 *relieved – they saw Pétain as a protector, someone who would save them and*
03 *who would save France. I wanted to feel the same thing; after all, Pétain*
04 *seemed so calm and optimistic But I had mixed feelings; my*
05 *brother always told me that still water runs deep.*

The class's discussions of Pétain in early weeks of the Occupation dossier were extensive, and students encountered a variety of texts that provided diverse perspectives on this central historical figure, including written texts like official documents and other articles; visual texts like propaganda posters, film clips and photographs; and aural texts like Pétain's speeches and class discussions, to name just a few. Brina clearly drew from the class's analysis of the *'Don à la patrie'* poster (as evidenced by the use of specific terms like 'protecteur' and 'sauver' that were also present in the class's analysis of the poster), and references the omnipresent propaganda of the Vichy government in Chapter 2, a theme that was also discussed in relation to the Marin text the class read on the power of representation and the representation of power.

When Brina's character identifies a group of people that saw Pétain as a protector and potential savior (lines 1–2), she is not only integrating relevant symbolic forms associated with Pétain but is also referencing a particular stance toward the Vichy government that certain members of the French population may have held; in fact, Emilie explicitly explained during class interaction that sentiment toward Pétain was largely positive in early stages of the war, since most French people did not want to be involved in a military confrontation and were relieved when the armistice with Germany was signed. The character, Mercedes, though, does not share their relief, even though she wants to (line 3); rather, she takes up a position of quiet distrust (line 5), a decidedly different and atypical kind of stance toward Pétain and his government. This particular stance represents an important choice on Brina's part in distinguishing her character's voice and making meaning through the narrative. The class's discussions and the texts they encountered posited the vast majority of the French population to be in favor of Pétain (or at least in favor of the cessation of combat that came with his taking power) during the early days of the Occupation. Taking up a distrustful stance toward Pétain at this point in the war tells us a great deal about Brina's character as an individual, especially because this lack of trust is juxtaposed in her writing with the prevailing social voices of the time, those who were 'relieved' (line 2) in hearing Pétain speak.

What becomes apparent in this first example from Brina's written work is that even in telling the story of one character, multiple stances on the same historical figures and happenings enter into dialogic relation, informing and distinguishing each other. In all of the students' *Mémoires* projects, the presence of other characters was the most common way in which multiple stances were introduced, but many students made their characters' point of view apparent by contrasting it with other social voices, as Brina does in this example. The multiple voices, then, that populated Brina's work, and all of the other students' work too, begin to give us an idea of the complex view of this historical era that students were constructing and their need to rely on a solid network of semiotic resources in order to accomplish these meanings textually. In addition to expressing an understanding of the broad cultural narratives that circulated and social voices that were present during the war by drawing upon them to populate the character's narrative world, the students' writing was also inhabited and propelled narratively by individual voices and stories, providing an opportunity to construct particular stances and very situated points of view on the war and the Occupation. These stances, once established, provided fertile ground for forging meanings within the text of each chapter students wrote, in ways that sometimes realized meaning potentials of words, phrases, metaphors and whole cultural narratives in more or less conventionalized ways (i.e. ways students had seen them used in other texts and contexts), but that at other times were quite novel. What Brina's work in Excerpt 17 illustrates as well is that just because a character performed a particular stance, other often contrasting positions were also likely to be present, which suggests that in telling one character's story, it was impossible for students to stay cloistered in relating only that particular take on the narrated events.

Especially for those students who tried to make decisions for their character as they might make them for themselves, which was the case for many students, writing through this imagined persona and its individual voice provided access to 'the story of the war' that was highly personal. But even for those students who, like Brina, did not claim such a strong resemblance between their character and themselves, the process of decision-making was still thought to be revealing in understanding experiences of the war. Moreover, this mix of individual and social voices in writing the memoirs, and the interplay of various narratives did not lend to the creation of a monolithic vision of history or of historical players in the students' writing. Rather a din of voices resound in students' work and a complex of intricate nuances were created. This brief excerpt from Brina's *Mémoires* project already begins to illustrate the complexities of perspective-taking and the impact that such an activity can have on intercultural learning and development of symbolic competence.

Brina's character, Mercedes, continues to take up a stance marked by distrust and suspicion toward all of the people around her in subsequent chapters of the memoirs, but her stance shifts after a particular incident that is a turning point in the narrative. In providing the prompt for the fourth chapter, Emilie asked students to include a story of betrayal wherein the character could be either the betrayer or the betrayed. (Most students incidentally chose to be the betrayer). Brina's character betrays her own beliefs under the pressure to conform to public anti-Semitism while simultaneously betraying those Jewish people around her by agreeing with the hateful remarks made by a woman she meets in the food line. The betrayal is felt viscerally when Mercedes looks into the crowd and sees a little girl wearing a yellow star of David crying as she stares at Mercedes. Following this instance, in Chapter 5, Mercedes and her husband decide to protect the son of a Jewish couple they know by temporarily adopting him as their own. The character's stance toward the events that surround her were marked by a kind of distance and self-preservation in the beginning chapters of the memoirs, but after the betrayal she commits, Mercedes seems to shift her perspective. The title of the chapter describing her act of betrayal is *'Si on pouvait le refaire à nouveau...'* ('If we could do it over again...'), after all, relating her character's regret and textually marking an orientational and thematic shift in the writing. That an extended dialogue is presented in this chapter is salient as well. As uncomfortable as it may have been to write, Brina was able to make the anti-Semitic female character speak, and the effect of the scene is that the suspicion that Brina's character harbors at all times for those around her is turned back on her, as the woman she meets in line ends their discussion by saying that maybe Mercedes has something to hide herself. It is at this point in the story, with a plot turn provoking a change in stance, that Mercedes begins to empathize with those around her who experience even worse hardship because there is discrimination and hate piled on top of the common difficulties the population had in finding food and getting on with everyday life. I would like to suggest in analyzing students' work that it is potentially their stances toward the historical era, toward those who lived through the war, toward those who talk about it today, and toward the world more generally that can shift as a result of delving so deeply into individual experiences and actively making meaning around them (even if they are fictions) because these imaginations are themselves real, subjective and emotional experiences. It might be that this chapter on betrayal shifted Brina's stance toward empathy as it did for her character. This episode in the story of Brina's character is emblematic of the kind of shift in stance we hope occurs when we view intercultural learning and ML education more broadly as potentially transformative.

The narrative that Brina created suggests that her understandings of culture, history and of this particular moment in history were developing. First there is evidence that Brina was aware that a unified 'French' position on the war does not exist. This is apparent across her memoirs, but also in Excerpt 17 presented above. There is also evidence, in her writing as well as that of the other students in the class, that she was able to call into action her knowledge of contextual details and elements of various cultural storylines in order to create a credible account. She integrated relevant reference points and symbolic touchstones that rendered the account recognizable as pertaining to the World War II era and as a piece of writing that attempted to make sense of this period of human existence. A further understanding that seems to be apparent in analyzing the story Brina authored is that decisions did not simply revolve around getting through the difficulties of everyday life. Even though she claimed that 'nothing really happened' to her character in our interview, she was quick to qualify that no major traumatic event, like being sent to a concentration camp or losing her husband in the war, occurred. The episode her character relates about her act of betrayal, where a decision in the moment haunts her afterward (as suggested by the title for Chapter 4), seems to significantly impact the trajectory of the character's story, moving away from an exclusive focus on her own life and survival to helping others. While Brina says she focused mostly on the stress of everyday life under the Occupation, this episode seems to show that she considered the more emotional and personally traumatic dimensions of existence during this time period. Writing the memoirs of her character then was not only a vehicle for applying the knowledge she had of cultural 'facts' or even assembling a network of relevant symbolic references and cultural narratives, but also an exercise in attempting to inhabit another point of view and make decisions from another perspective, all in an effort to make sense of and make meaning around a troubling era.

The References, Stories and Stances in Katie's Project

Table 5.2 presents Katie's *Mémoires* project, in which a young girl very much like herself comes to striking realizations of her own naiveté.

The narrative that Katie constructs is one that is rich in its inclusion of symbolic reference points and its construction of thematic and orientational intertexts. As in Brina's written work, the memoirs of Katie's character, Séverine, are also characterized initially by a description of her position in relation to the new Vichy government and Pétain. In the second and third chapters of Séverine's memoirs, there is extensive evidence that Katie was drawing on the semiotic network she had developed through engagement with a broad range of texts in Emilie's class.

Excerpt 18 I was a Pétainiste

01 Je l'ai cru. Quelle raison est-ce que j'aurais eu de douter de lui? Je peux
02 encore entendre ses mots : « J'assume à partir d'aujourd'hui la direction du
03 gouvernement de la France. Sûr de l'affection de notre admirable armée qui
04 lutte avec un héroïsme digne de ses longues traditions militaires contre un
05 ennemi supérieur en nombre et en armes; surs que, grâce à sa magnifique
06 résistance, elle a rempli ses devoirs vis-à-vis de nos alliés; sur de l'appui des
07 anciens combattants que j'ai eu la fierté de commander, je fais à la France le
08 don de ma personne pour atténuer son malheur. » J'étais Pétainiste, et je ne
09 pouvais pas imaginer l'alternative.

01 *I believed him. What reason would I have had to doubt him? I can still*
02 *hear his words : "I assume as of today the head of the*
03 *French government. Sure of the affection for our admirable army that*
04 *struggles with heroism worthy of its long military tradition against an enemy*
05 *superior in number and in arms; sure that, thanks to its magnificent*
06 *resistance, it fulfilled its duty to our allies; sure of the support of former*
07 *soldiers who I had the pride of commanding, I make to France the gift of my*
08 *person in order to reduce her suffering." I was a Pétainiste, and I couldn't*
09 *imagine the alternative.*

In this passage, a very famous speech by Pétain that the class had read, heard and discussed in depth surfaces verbatim in Séverine's story. Beyond the speech itself, which is clearly referenced in this excerpt, Emilie's animation of one particular line, *'Je fais à la France le don de ma personne pour atténuer son malheur, (I give to France the gift of my person to ease her pain)'*,

Table 5.2 Overview of Katie's *Mémoires* writing project, entitled '*Qui ne dit mot consent: Une histoire de propagande, de rumeurs, et de foi perdue pendant la Deuxième Guerre Mondiale* (He who says nothing consents: A story of propaganda, rumors and lost faith during the Second World War)'

Chapter titles	Synopsis
Préface	The editor introduces a letter received from the main character in which she asserts that individual stories like hers make up the 'official history of the war' and that both well-known and ordinary moments are described, especially because the ordinary ones are in danger of disappearing. She also writes about the power of words and their ability to rewrite history. The character writes that in 'animating' history through her memoirs some might think that she is exaggerating, but that is of little importance. In thinking back to the war now, the character writes that faces and voices mix together.
Chapitre 1 : 'Au Début' (In the Beginning)	The main character (Séverine), a 20-year-old young woman, and her family are introduced, and she describes her happy but uneventful life before the war. Séverine describes Pétain and particularly his voice. At the beginning of the war, she believed what he said. She also says that at the start of the war, she considered de Gaulle to have abandoned his homeland in its time of need.
Chapitre 2 : 'La Méduse' (The Medusa)	This chapter opens with a discussion of the portraits of Pétain, whose eyes seemed to follow Séverine everywhere. She then describes how, just a few years before the war, a certain level of contentedness reigned in France, but now the Vichy government had reacted strongly against the socialist measures of the previous regime and blamed the Jews for disorder in the country and the war itself. Séverine describes the way that the Vichy government considers youth to be at the base of its revolution and her reaction to considering herself as defined by her youth. She describes herself as mostly indifferent to what was going on beyond her 'small world'. She does attest to having a negative reaction though to the 'pastoral scenes' that the regime pushed on the public, since she was a city girl. A conversation that Séverine overheard between her brother and a friend who wanted to go work in Germany is related, but the brother decides to stay in Paris. The chapter closes with Séverine evoking again the image of Pétain who looked over the family as they went about their life in occupied Paris.

(continued)

Chapter titles	Synopsis
Chapitre 3 : 'L'autruche' (The Ostrich)	The chapter opens with the image of a young Séverine as an ostrich with her head in the sand, attempting to 'maintain a facade of normalcy' while people began to disappear around her. One day at the store where she worked, she noticed that another salesgirl was missing, and on her way home, Séverine notices all of those people who are missing from her everyday life. When she gets home, her twin brother brings to her attention the fact that all of these people were Jewish.
Chapitre 4 : 'Le gris' (Gray)	Séverine relates in this chapter the story of a neighboring family that is arrested during the Vel d'Hiv round-up and her silence and lack of resistance as the event unfolded. The chapter is a philosophical kind of contemplation of the nature of betrayal, guilt and difficult circumstances.
Chapitre 5 : 'Le Héros' (The Hero)	Feeling guilt and anger about the Vel d'Hiv and how it touched the lives of a family living in her building, Séverine searches desperately for an opportunity to right the wrong she believes she has committed. When she overhears that a family in the building, the Fechners, may be denounced, she asks her brother for help in saving them. Much to her surprise, he tells her not to try to be a hero. She has felt her brother's distance and not understood it, but years later she realizes that there were many kinds of resistants, not just those who everyone knew from their public acts, but also ones like her brother who quietly aided those he could, and still others who resisted by not reporting those who were more actively resisting.
Chapitre 6: 'Après la guerre' (After the war)	In this final chapter, Séverine considers the period after the war. She briefly evokes the image of Parisians dancing in the streets, but quickly replaces this hazy memory with a much clearer one of a woman whose head was shaved as a crowd threw objects and insults at her for allegedly having committed a variety of detestable acts during the war – like sleeping with German soldiers and denouncing her Jewish neighbors. Séverine then describes the return of a neighbor in the building, Henri Fechner, but says that the biggest mystery of all was her brother and his participation in the resistance, which she never had the courage to ask about, even after the war. The memoirs close with a broad meditation on the impact of the war on Séverine and the French people more generally.

which was spoken by Emilie in a kind of mocking tone during the class's analysis of a propaganda poster produced by the Vichy government early in the war, serves as a contrast for the particular stance that Katie's character will take up. Pétain's speech, the poster bearing a line from the speech as a title (see Figure 4.3) and the discussion in class surrounding the speech and the poster, then, serve as a set of intertexts for the story Katie writes, but Katie's character's stance toward Pétain and his speech is also constructed. She achieves this by framing the quote from the speech with statements of her unwavering support of Pétain at this point in the war (lines 1 and 8–9). Interestingly in line 1, her question 'What reason would I have to doubt him?' aligns her character with sentiments that were common among many in the French population at the time, while also setting up the narrative possibility that Pétain could, should or would be doubted by her character or others as time passed.

In the next paragraph of this first chapter of Séverine's memoirs, the social voice to which Katie's character conforms (i.e. a Pétain supporter at the start of the war), is reinforced when she writes

Excerpt 19 De Gaulle

01 Je croyais qu'il ressentait la même chose que moi: la présence des Allemands
02 n'était pas nécessairement mal, et ils étaient préférables au chaos. Quand j'ai
03 entendu le discours de Charles de Gaulle à la radio, je me suis fâchée. « Il a
04 fui »,ai-je pensé, « il ne sait rien du coût de continuer la lutte ». Je voulais
05 seulement que le calme revienne.

01 *I thought he felt the same thing as me: the presence of the Germans*
02 *wasn't necessarily bad, and they were preferable to chaos. When I heard*
03 *Charles de Gaulle's speech on the radio, I got angry. "He fled",*
04 *I thought, "he knows nothing of the cost of continuing the fight". I just*
05 *wanted the calm to return.*

The character's voice and the social one it references are both being developed in these two paragraphs. In Excerpt 19, Séverine begins by stating that she thought her brother shared her belief that the German presence in Paris was not such a bad thing given the chaos that preceded it (lines 1–2). The position Katie's character takes up here is very much in line with some of the excerpts from *Paroles d'Étoiles* that the class had read about initial reactions to the Occupation. There are also echoes of a comment that Emilie made during the class's analysis of the propaganda poster, when Séverine writes, 'il a fui,' in talking about de Gaulle (line 3).

During the discussion of the *'Le don à la patrie'* poster, Emilie, speaking as a Pétainiste, calls de Gaulle a traitor for having fled and vividly animates the voice of a Pétain supporter. The resurfacing of the verb *'fuir'* (to flee) and the stance that is taken up in these paragraphs of desiring a return to calm over all else, suggest that the analysis of the poster and other texts informed Katie's construction of her character's story.

A second example illustrates the pervasive intertextuality in Katie's *Mémoires* project. In Katie's title for the second chapter, 'La Méduse,' there is a suggestion of myriad potential intertexts in the class's work. A strong visual theme had developed as the class studied the Vichy government and its preoccupation with surveillance. As was described in Chapter 4, the class spent time explicitly talking about the power of representation and the potential impact of a proliferation of images of a leader on a population. The film clips that the class often watched came from the documentary called *L'Oeil de Vichy* (The Eye of Vichy), and during one of the *Café de retrouvailles* activities, Emilie had written *'Souriez l'œil de Vichy vous regarde'* ('Smile the eye of Vichy is watching you') on the board. But a particular symbol related to sight and viewing is evoked by Katie's choice of title – that of the medusa – perhaps echoing the strong visual theme that had been consistently associated with the Vichy government and this period of history in general. Clearly there is a visual dimension to this Greek myth – that looking at the medusa would freeze a man to stone – but this particular image was also encountered in the first paragraph of the novel the class read, *La Cliente*, perhaps constituting the most likely source of this image in Katie's work:

Excerpt 20 Passage from *La Cliente* (Assouline, 2000: 19)

01 On n'en finira jamais avec cette histoire. Elle nous hante, elle nous obsède,
02 impossible de nous en débarrasser. Plus d'un demi-siècle que la méduse nous
03 colle à la peau.

01 *We will never finish with this story/history. It haunts us, it obsesses us,*
02 *impossible for us to get rid of it. More than half a century that the Medusa*
03 *has stuck with us.*

Emilie brought up the idea of the medusa briefly in class, right around the time that students were to begin reading the novel, which was also around the time that students would have been writing the second chapter of their characters' memoirs. In her mention of the medusa at the end of a lesson on the omnipresence of Pétain in French society at the start of the war, Emilie asked if the class was familiar with the Greek myth and then provided further information about how this myth is applied in a particular way when speaking about the war from a French perspective.

Excerpt 21 La Méduse

01 **Emilie**: Avant qu'on parte j'aimerais juste (3) faire mention de méduse
02 est-ce que vous connaissez le mythe grec de méduse la gorgone
03 **S1**: Médusa
04 **Emilie**: Médusa c'est quoi (2.5) S2
05 **S2**: Si on regarde méduse on devien- dans une pierre
06 **Emilie**: Mm-hm oui c'était donc un monstre une gorgone et si jamais vous
07 la regardiez vous étiez pétrifiés (1.5) d'accord souvenez-vous de ça
08 c'est un terme qu'on retrouvera vous savez vous avez un livre à lire
09 la Cliente et ce sera un des thèmes récurrents ((making a cycle-like
10 motion with hands)) la méduse très souvent les historiens très
11 souvent comparent l'occupation à la méduse (3) si vraiment vous
12 voulez êtes pétrifiés (1) donc souvenez-vous de ça parce que là
13 lorsqu'il met regarder l'histoire dans les yeux vous vous êtes
14 pétrifiés fascinés ((rolling motion with hands and looking down at
15 Marin text)) vous avez également ça fait ref- ça fait penser à la
16 fameuse méduse les victimes de méduse qui ne bougeaient plus

01 **Emilie**: *Before we leave I would just (3) like to make mention of medusa*
02 *do you know the Greek myth of medusa the gorgon*
03 **S1**: *Medusa*
04 **Emilie**: *Medusa what is it (2.5) S2*
05 **S2**: *If you look at the medusa you beco- in a stone*
06 **Emilie**: *Mm-hm yes so it was then a monster a gorgon and if ever you looked*
07 *at her you were <u>petrified</u> (1.5) ok remember that it's a term that we*
08 *will find again you know you have a book to read the Client and this*
09 *will be one of the recurring themes ((making a cycle-like motion with*
10 *hands)) the medusa very often historians very often compare the*
11 *occupation to the medusa (3) if you really want to look history in the*
12 *eyes you are petrified (1) so remember that because there when he*
13 *put you are petrified fascinated ((rolling motion with hands and*
14 *looking down at Marin text) you also have that makes ref- it makes*
15 *you think of the famous medusa the victims of the medusa who no*
16 *longer moved*

(Observation from 18 September 2006)

In this piece of classroom interaction, Emilie is making a particular intertextual connection between the Greek myth of the medusa and historians' very particular terminology for advancing a perspective on the war, while also weaving in a reference to Marin whose text also had introduced the notion that seeing and being seen can have powerful effects (petrifaction and terrifying fascination among others). Emilie explicitly advises students that the medusa is a term and reference point they will find over and over again (line 8) and even calls the medusa a theme (line 9), which may have signaled to students that this might be an appropriate avenue to pursue in their compositions.

In Katie's work, employing the image of the medusa as a title for her second chapter announces the strong visual element that continues in the chapter itself and makes a broader statement on the nature of considering history. The first paragraph of Katie's second chapter reads

Excerpt 22 His eyes followed me

01 Ses yeux me suivaient. Comme La Joconde, que j'avais vue quand j'étais
02 petite, son visage paraissait me regarder. Je le voyais partout: dans les rues,
03 au marché, aussi chez moi. On vendait son portrait dans les magasins, et
04 chaque famille était encouragée à en acheter. Bien sur, nous l'avons fait.

01 *His eyes followed me. Like the Mona Lisa, that I had seen when I was young,*
02 *his face seemed to look at me. I saw him everywhere: in the streets, at the*
03 *market, also in my home. His portrait was sold in the stores, and every family*
04 *was encouraged to buy one. Of course, we did.*

The first line of the chapter (line 1) is simple but has great impact. Katie is describing in rich detail, here, the effect that seeing Pétain's image everywhere might have on a person. As Séverine describes all of the places she saw Pétain's image in succession (lines 2–3), a dizzying effect is created, and we get a real sense that she is being followed, even into her own home. She makes the point though (lines 3–4) that escaping Pétain's gaze was unavoidable if one desired to avoid raising suspicion. In this excerpt, Katie is reconstructing one of the themes that recurred in other class activities and texts – that of watching and being watched. That this aspect of her character's experience is linked to the image of the medusa seems to suggest that meanings are really made in the space between texts. That is to say that in connecting her character's experience of being watched with the symbol of the medusa, a sense of danger, menace and discomfort are produced around the particular story of Séverine but also around the history of this period more broadly.

Katie closes her second chapter that has a strong visual theme by coming back to the image of Pétain's 'all-knowing gaze' (line 2).

Excerpt 23 Pétain's All-Knowing Gaze

01   Nous travaillions, nous allions au marché, nous dînions tous les soirs, et nous
02   écoutions les discours politiques à la radio, sous le regard omniscient du
03   Maréchal Pétain, mais la tension était palpable.

01   *We worked, we went to the market, we ate dinner every night, and we listened*
02   *to the political speeches on the radio, under the all-knowing gaze of Maréchal*
03   *Pétain, but the tension was palpable.*

In lines 2–3, Pétain surveys the family as they eat dinner. The family goes about its daily life (lines 1–2), but the sense of danger or 'tension' (line 3) is also apparent. That Katie chose to remind us of Pétain's ever-present gaze by placing the family in their salon is not a coincidence either. This scene appears to be drawn directly from another film clip from *L'Oeil de Vichy* that the class watched, where the Vichy government's vision of the ideal family sat around their table listening to the radio, above which was perched a portrait of the Maréchal. Katie's development of a theme in the second chapter of her character's memoirs is highly complex. Drawing on a variety of symbols and texts the class had encountered and the storylines and stances apparent in those texts, Katie is able to create a coherent and meaningful chapter. Beyond recounting the events of Séverine's life, a consistent message about the danger and threat of being watched is conveyed.

The depth of the intertextuality apparent in Brina's and Katie's work, and in other students' work, has certainly not been discussed in full, simply because the links between texts the class encountered and the ones students authored are too numerous and perhaps impossible to relate in their full connectedness. Tracing every link that students made in this dense web of texts would indeed be impossible, but the variety of textual links that have been presented in relation to students' writing certainly begins to give an idea of just how dense the web of stories and meanings was in this class. What is clear is that the rich textual environment in this class created a space where many voices and many narratives resounded and echoed each other, and when it came time to narrate the experience of the war from a particular point of view, students were entirely capable of doing so in a credible way by anchoring their plots in relevant reference points, drawing on the symbols and cultural narratives they encountered through their class work and distinguishing their characters' voice among the many others that inevitably came to populate their fictions. What is striking, and potentially very promising, about this kind of project is the space that is opened up as well for students to develop their understandings of other points of view and to potentially shift their own personal stances. In encountering a variety of perspectives on the war (and thus the world too), students in this class had the opportunity to also revise their own perspectives, their own versions of history and their own way of seeing themselves and the world. My interviews with students confirmed that for at least some of them, this was the case. Beyond shifts in one's own stance toward the world, however, and a reconsideration of one's place in it, the analysis presented in this section suggests the rich meaning-making that students can engage in when they are provided with a textually rich environment that makes available a wide range of symbolic reference points, cultural narratives and voices. The students' *Mémoires* projects demonstrate not only that students understand the narratives and texts they encountered in class but that they could draw on them to make meaning themselves.

From Katie's preface, which she also constructs in highly dialogic fashion (as a conversation between the editor and the author and protagonist of the memoirs collection) speaks to the explicit awareness that some students developed of the symbolic and personal power of words and other semiotic resources:

Excerpt 24 Katie's preface

01 Le pouvoir des mots est un sujet auquel je pense souvent. Est-ce qu'il y a d'autres choses
02 qui restent à part les mots? Maintenant, j'ai mes souvenirs de la guerre. Les autres en ont,
03 et nos souvenirs forment une histoire officielle de la guerre. Nous donnons des perspectives
04 différentes sur les mêmes évènements, comme l'armistice, le Vel d'Hiv, et la libération
05 de Paris, mais sur les autres moments? Nous ne vivions pas juste seulement dans ces
06 moments célèbres: la vie quotidienne se déroulait malgré tout. Et c'est ça, le quotidien,
07 qui est en danger d'être oublié. C'est cela ma raison d'avoir écrit cette histoire. Il y a eut
08 mille petites trahisons et sacrifices qui se sont passés pendant la guerre sans qu'on les
09 remarque, et il faut que quelqu'un les préserve. Sinon, on pourra prétendre qu'ils ne se
10 sont jamais passés et la vérité sera à jamais perdue. J'ai vu pendant la guerre comment
11 le pouvoir des mots se manifeste, comment les discours et la propagande pouvaient
12 réécrire l'histoire que nous aurions considérée comme forte. Alors j'ai décidé de préserver
13 ma propre histoire, incluant les deux: mes impressions sur nos souvenirs partagés et les
14 petits moments qui n'influençaient pas la grande histoire du monde, mais qui ont
15 changé ma vie. En écrivant, j'espère capturer les émotions et les présenter.

01 *The power of words is something I think about often. Is there anything else that exists besides*
02 *words? Now, I have my memories of the war. Others have them, and our memories form an official*
03 *history of the war. We offer different perspectives on the same events, like the armistice,*
04 *the Vel d'Hiv, and the liberation of Paris, but about the other moments? We didn't just live these*
05 *well-known moments: everyday life unfolded despite everything else. And it is that, the everyday,*
06 *that is in danger of being forgotten. That is precisely my reason for having written this story.*
07 *There were a thousand small betrayals and sacrifices that happened during the war without*
08 *anyone remarking them, and it is necessary that someone preserve them. If not, we could pretend*
09 *that they never happened and the truth will be lost forever. I saw during the war how the power of*
10 *words manifests itself, how speeches and propaganda could rewrite the history that we would*
11 *have seen as strong. So I decided to preserve my own story, including both: my impressions on our*
12 *shared memories and the small moments that did not influence the larger history of the world, but*
13 *that changed my life. In writing, I hope to capture emotions and to present them.*

At several points, in this piece of writing that Katie composed after having written all of the other chapters of the *Mémoires*, Katie articulates the power of words and the meaning in drawing on them to make sense of the past and ourselves. She also writes quite directly about the way words are used to manipulate and exercise power. Katie's awareness of the interconnectedness of situated, individual meanings and culturally shared, symbolic significances is also apparent, indicating that the *Mémoires* writing project did indeed alert her to the nature of the fact that personal and collective meaning-making feed each other but that they also appear quite different at times, even when rooted in the same source phenomena. As we read the words of her protagonist, we can only guess that some of what she expresses reflects her own understandings that came about as a result of having completed this historical fiction writing project.

Students' Take On Perspective-Taking

To support the analysis of students' in-class interactions and their written work, in this section, I share excerpts from interviews with students in which they shared their views of their own learning activity in Emilie's class, particularly with respect to the global simulation project. What they expressed on intercultural learning in this class deepens our understanding of the nature of students' engagement during the project.

Part of the process of intercultural learning for this group of students is exposure to a rich semiotic environment and a variety of perspectives in the rich textual environment that Emilie created, but mere exposure to these does not necessarily translate to ability to deploy meaning-making resources or to understanding or acceptance of an unfamiliar point of view. A major element in these students' intercultural learning process was the active practice of perspective-taking, or the projection of oneself into an unfamiliar cultural frame of reference and regular engagement with a range of meaning-making practices. While students never called this activity perspective-taking, their repeated use of the term 'perspective' in my interviews with them and the strikingly similar characterizations of their intercultural learning process suggest that this is an appropriate term. The student remarks discussed below all emerged as responses to the same question about the class's global simulation project, suggesting that this pedagogical approach, the fundamental goal of which is for students to simulate an unfamiliar reality, may be particularly well-suited to intercultural learning, especially in the ML setting where students are physically (and in this case, temporally) far removed from the target-language culture. Two students' perspectives on the writing component of the global simulation, Katie's and Brina's, were integrated with analysis of their written work in sections above, but their classmates' views support the claim that the environment that was created and the pedagogical intervention that was directed by Emilie seemed to have had some common effects across students' experiences.

Sydney discussed perspective-taking in terms of accessing states of mind. In describing the class's work surrounding the French experience of World War II, she said 'you had to go into their mind' in order to write first-person fictional memoirs (Interview 16 November 2006). Sydney characterized her experience of the class's activity as being plunged into history. She explained that she automatically projected herself into historical situations and proceeded to ask herself questions about what she would have done, how she would have been, what she would have wanted. She saw these as eminently cultural questions that led to her 'immersion' in the culture. She then explained that this process of projecting herself into an unfamiliar cultural context was not uncomfortable for her. In fact, she said that this kind of approach is 'the most natural thing to do if you want to answer those kinds of questions'.

Heather offered further insight into the process of adopting an unfamiliar cultural perspective when she described her learning during the global simulation as an act of repositioning. Heather says that adopting another cultural frame of reference was helpful in learning about French perspectives on the war:

having to really put yourself in that position and try and understand what people were going through I think gave you a much better understanding than just thinking you know 'I can't believe the French would go along with something like the Nazis'. (Interview 17 November 2006)

Heather says that this process of repositioning was a little bit uncomfortable for her, especially the in-class *Café de retrouvailles* activities, where students took on their personae, since she is 'not really into acting'. Despite this discomfort, she said she learned a lot from the project. Heather's remarks begin to reveal one of the main characteristics of perspective-taking cited by several students; rather than judging the 'other' from an outsider's perspective, putting oneself 'in that position' seems to lead to a deeper understanding, suspension of judgment and, in some cases, to empathy. Jeannette described the writing of her character's memoirs as an exercise in analyzing the emotions and thought processes of someone without passing judgment, 'to better understand how things can happen and how things can escalate' and to highlight the 'gray area' of morality (Interview 8 December 2006). Nearly all of the students in the class wrote about the complicating factors and dilemmas that make up history and the inability to categorically cast judgment on historical players when they wrote the final composition of the memoirs writing project, which was in fact the preface to the collected chapters.

Brina agreed with many of her classmates that not passing judgment on historical actors or events was a result of the project, and she emphasized that this awareness came about because students were able to better understand the difficult decision-making processes of those who lived through the war experienced. She said

Reading *La Cliente* and just talking about decision-making I guess provided a real sense of not being too judgmental and understanding that there was no...often it was a lose-lose situation there was no easy way to make a decision and just not I mean I guess we learn this in various classes but not to be overly critical or judgmental of historical players and particularly not of sort of the common people who you know whether they had brothers or fathers on the front or you know were in a concentration camp you know God knows what was happening to them. (Interview 10 November 2006)

Katie's experience especially with the global simulation further reveals the potential effects of adopting another cultural perspective in order to understand it. When Katie talks about the *Mémoires* writing project, she says that she created a character that was like herself, and that she constructed her character's story by asking herself what she would have done in the same situations. When asked whether this was an uncomfortable exercise, as noted above, Katie said that there was something strange about thinking that she would have turned her Jewish neighbors in to the authorities and commented that this was a strange thing to think about oneself. She seemed to be proud, however, that she was able to project herself honestly into an unfamiliar context and face this troubling realization, since she said that many of her classmates ended up with characters who were resistants in the end, which she evidently found too facile of a conclusion. Katie's approach to the *Mémoires* project is a strong example of a student projecting herself into the voice of an unfamiliar speaking subject and of the impact that this experience can have for students' visions of themselves.

In the process of intercultural learning, then, perspective-taking appears to be a main cognitive, emotional and textual/interactional process for gaining access to and trying on new ways of seeing the world. Narrative writing as a method of encouraging perspective-taking was particularly effective in this class. Sydney, for example, told me that she was comfortable 'using a story to discover things or to explore other options,' (Interview 16 November 2006) and while some students said it was time-consuming and difficult to write these compositions, they overwhelmingly agreed that in the end, the writing component not only greatly improved their written French, but allowed them to engage with the course content in a deep way.

Part of perspective-taking, according to the students, involved accessing and experiencing the thoughts and emotions of physically, culturally and temporally distant personae, and in some cases, students transformed their understandings and shifted their own perspectives. Grace described the global simulation and the cultural learning that occurred during the activity as not being only about the application of facts: 'It was good in like grasping sort of the emotions of the period while the facts were I guess sort of better for learning the actual historical [aspects]' (Interview 17 November 2006). Brina too attested to having constructed a 'personal connection' through the memoirs writing project 'to something that I mean is generally difficult to relate to…and you feel emotionally upset I mean I did just reading about it but to sort of do that next little step "what would I do if it was me"' (Interview 10 November 2006). The affective dimension of perspective-taking also appears to be a key element in rendering this learning experiential and self-reflective and moving it beyond the accessing of thought processes alone.

In discussing the global simulation particularly, the students in this class showed evidence of having transformed their understandings and having shifted their perspectives. Jeannette explained how her view of this period of history changed over the course of the project. She says she had always thought of France as a victim, but she came to see the Vichy government and other agentive 'actors' of the time period differently, to consider the gray areas and the complexities of this historical era and to explore divergent opinions and experiences. She added, 'I just thought it was really interesting because I'm really interested in like social movements and like what motivates people to make certain political decisions' (Interview 8 December 2006). That her attitudes about World War II transformed is significant since in many ways the main question in intercultural learning is, as Lantolf (1999) writes, 'if, and to what extent, it is possible for people to become cognitively like members of other cultures; that is, can adults learn to construct and see the world through culturally different eyes' (p. 29). Students' work in the class, as they interpreted representations and then created their own representations of history in the writing project, shows that indeed they were able to construct and see the world through culturally different lenses; but they did more than that. The type of transformation they experienced and that we often envision as a prime goal in intercultural learning in ML education involves an integration of the insights gained from adopting new perspectives into learners' broader worldviews and their sense of actual and possible selves. As Jeannette remarked, she was able to make connections between the class's study of World War II and her broader personal interests in social movements, power and control, while still other students attested to making discoveries about themselves as a result of the course.

Katie also described how her perspective changed when it comes to this historical period. She said she had spoken with her family about all of the things she learned that she did not know before because 'you never really hear about France and World War II' (Interview 30 November 2006). She went on, 'There's this whole set of events that like we've never heard of in America like le Vel d'Hiv or whatever and it's just such a big deal in France and it's kind of like the collective like history and nothing we ever learn about or consider important.' Katie told me that both her father and brother are history buffs who are particularly interested in World War II, so it is a topic that she had heard about in some detail before arriving in her French class. Her transformed understandings as a result of taking this course are further exemplified as she talks about having previously viewed all of the French as collaborators during the war. Through this class, she came to develop a more nuanced understanding and, in many ways, to occupy a third place, as Kramsch (1993) would say, suspending her 'American' beliefs to consider other perspectives on the French experience of the war.

Analysis of my conversations with students in interviews confirms the importance of learning to understand and having the opportunity to adopt other perspectives, speak through different voices and claim new stances in the process of intercultural learning. Such shifts in perspective, which were especially encouraged by the global simulation project, were viewed by students as providing access through interpretation of signs to new meanings, new and/or transformed views of events and people, and potentially transformed views of themselves as well.

Conclusion

In this chapter, analysis has focused on students' developing abilities in drawing on their growing repertoires of semiotic resources in order to make meaning in creative narrative writing. In presenting analysis of two students' projects and students' perspectives on their experience with learning through the global simulation approach, I have attempted to build an argument for the success of a semiotically conscious and narrative approach to intercultural teaching in Emilie's class.

In creating a character and a credible narrative world, shaping a voice and telling a story, students were able to try on another view of the world and to construct meaning with that point of view as an anchor. A great resource in achieving these meanings were the many cultural texts that the students encountered in their class and all of the textual and interactional supports students had as they first established form-meaning connections. There is extensive evidence of intertextuality, complexity of meaning and a proliferation of voices and perspectives, lending support to the claim that students were indeed caught in webs of meaning as Emilie intended and were then able to spin their own. They did so by handily balancing the tension between using symbolic forms in recognizable, culturally conventional ways while also embedding these in novel stories and sometimes stretching typical meaning potentials. Students were involved as they wrote in a process of decision-making, selecting forms, events, symbols, images and plot developments to craft a coherent text of their own. This selection was made from an infinite range of possibilities, but in order to be read as a credible, plausible historical fiction, there were limits to what students could choose to include and how they could employ symbolic forms. This decision-making process cultivated in learners an awareness that there are options in expressing oneself and that making choices as a language user makes a difference in meaning. This meta-awareness contributes to one's symbolic competence precisely because it starts to bend symbolic power in a language learner's favor, a shift that we see quite vividly in the writing of Emilie's students, who came to adopt a 'variationist frame of mind' (Kramsch, 2007) and to marshal a repertoire of semiotic options to their learning purposes.

Note

(1) Much of this chapter is a revised version of an analysis presented in Kearney (2008), an unpublished doctoral dissertation.

6 Sense-Making in a Web of Meanings: Implications for Theory, Research and Practice

Through the metaphor of a web, this chapter brings the meaning-making practices presented in Chapters 4 and 5 together into an overall conceptual model for developing deeply meaningful competence in ML education. The benefit of the web metaphor is discussed along with components and dynamics of the model. Several insights about the nature of meaning that are important for the ML classroom are then highlighted, namely that (1) meaning is relational and multilayered (spanning timescales and social scopes from the individual to the collective); that (2) the ability to make sense of events, the world, and ourselves hinges on reading and making form-meaning connections (semiosis); that (3) meaning is made from particular points of view and through the symbolic resources available; that (4) when we study new MLs we gain access to new semiotic material and processes, potentially seeing the world from new vantage points; and that (5) we can do so critically, gaining perspective on familiar and unfamiliar cultures while also potentially forging new ground in between. The chapter discusses the way this model enters into dialogue with existing theories of the development of intercultural and symbolic competences before turning finally to the practical issues in translating a social semiotic view of intercultural learning into teaching practice and ideas for future directions. Ultimately, it is a pedagogy of potentials – engaging learners with meanings on a continuum from personal to cultural – that I hope to summarize and reinforce.

A Web of Meanings

The idea of a web as a metaphor for meaning-making has been attractive to those interested in language and culture for some time. Geertz (1973) eloquently writes,

Believing, with Max Weber, that man is an animal suspended in webs of significance he himself has spun, I take culture to be those webs, and the analysis of it to be therefore not an experimental science in search of law but an interpretive one in search of meaning. (p. 5)

Like Geertz, those who adopt a complex, dynamic systems perspective on language (e.g. Larsen-Freeman & Cameron, 2008) and a social semiotic view of ML education (e.g. Kramsch, 2009; van Lier, 2004b) envision interrelated meanings in similarly networked fashion and interpretive and generative action around these (semiosis) as central to understanding social life, especially in unfamiliar cultures. The notion of a web is indeed attractive for a number of reasons. Webs are three dimensional and dynamic. They have a center but invite movement away from that point, making multiple positions and vantage points possible. Webs are constantly made and unmade, or at least certain strands and sections are. Connections between nodes on a web can be strong or tenuous, more or less elastic. In the construction of webs, the coordination of many internal and external resources is required of the web maker. Yet, these qualities alone do not make the web metaphor work when we discuss meaning-making. Certain precisions need to be made in order to transform what appears at first glance to be an apt comparison into a full-blown conceptual tool that can enhance our thinking about semiosis and about the development of intercultural and symbolic competence in ML education more specifically.

Webs are a fitting metaphor for cultures, as Geertz suggests, but in considering semiosis, the metaphor must account for the organizational and structural aspects of meaning-making as well as processual elements. In addition, the idea of a web has to function at multiple levels. That is, we can adopt a view of culture as a web, but we also need to be able to zoom in and to consider mini-webs within the larger system[1]. Semiosis, at its most basic, can be thought of as occurring first at a micro level: signs are brought into relation with each other to form texts or acts of meaning. At a second level, texts or acts of meaning are brought into relation with each other to form cultures, much broader swaths of the web. In this way, culture is clearly assumed to be an eminently discursive phenomenon since it is constituted by texts. It is important to recall that 'texts' have to be understood in very broad ways. Of course, texts and acts of meaning include the written and oral forms we produce with language; however, assemblage of signs to produce visual, corporeal and material 'texts' is also central to human meaning-making. The way we dress, occupy space, gesture and talk, for example, might all function together as an articulation of signs to produce meanings about ourselves as a particular kind of person at a particular point in time.

That many texts are multimodal is also crucial to attend to in thinking about the way that semiosis unfolds in moment-to-moment interaction and on broader scales. There are, of course, likely to be many levels of meaning-making that fall on a continuum of particular instances of texts (specific acts of meaning) all the way to very large cultures and their shared, highly conventionalized meanings. This is what Matthiesson (2009) refers to as a cline of instantiation.

At the micro level, each node in a web, each point of connection between radial strands are texts or acts of meaning, where multiple signs are deployed together usually in different modes to achieve some referential and symbolic (and probably social and practical) action and meaning. These nodes are perhaps enduring, perhaps more ephemeral. They are necessarily connected to other nodes and a broader, networked environment. Connections may be established (shared by many) or novel (recently made and not necessarily shared). Acts of meaning can be viewed from different vantage points in the web. For example, one could view one text and point of view from the vantage point of another perspective and text. Infinite possible vantage points yield innumerable ways of bringing acts of meaning into relation. More broadly, the more one travels the web of connected acts of meaning, the better sense one has of the overall network, and certain routes, positions and acts of meanings may become internalized, a part of an individual's personal meaning-making repertoire. The web is what is 'out there', something that is shared but that clearly will not look the same to everyone. Indeed, it is much too vast and dynamic for anyone to ever fully (or even more than just only very partially) 'know' and travel. But comprehensive knowledge of a universe of interrelated meanings is not the objective; it is more the ability to function with more and more choice and agency that we aim for, especially in educational realms and intercultural education more specifically.

The meaning-making activity of one university-level French class during its study of occupied France serves as a convenient example of how this web metaphor can function conceptually. In Emilie's class, the coordinated deployment of signs formed the many texts and acts of meaning the class worked with. These texts were diverse, ranging from encyclopedic-type recountings of history in their informational packet of readings, to the family stories Emilie told, to primary source documents like memoirs, transcripts of speeches and legal documents, to images and film clips and to historical fictions, like the novel the class read. The class's work often consisted in considering these texts precisely in terms of the signs they brought together and how they deployed them to make particular meanings. At another level, the textual environment or the overall semiotic environment that Emilie designed and coconstructed with her students made intertextuality – the relation of texts and acts of meaning – inevitable. Texts were brought into relation with each other to form deeper, more complex understandings of cultural meanings. The students' extended writing project as well as in-class discussions provided rich opportunities for connecting texts and comparing and contrasting their acts of meaning.

To recap, principles about meaning that are highlighted by this metaphor and that must be foundational in our reconceptualization of intercultural learning in ML education are, first, that meaning is relational – that it requires us to think in terms of the interrelatedness of social actors, semiotic resources and dimensions of context. Because meaning is relational, countless and diverse affordances are possible for making meaning. We also need to keep in mind that meaning is complex and always multilayered. Instances and broader meaning potentials are always connected such that all acts of meaning not only make a particular meaning, they also invoke and possibly reshape broader shared meanings. Connecting meaning at various social scales has been a longstanding challenge in ML education, but a social semiotic view greatly clarifies the relationship of meaning at the level of particularity, the level of broad convention and many levels in between. Meaning is also only understandable in relation to forms. Making form-meaning connections is the action, the process of semiosis. A broad range of forms must be considered in ML education, including the familiar linguistic forms we most often entertain in our classrooms (words, grammatical structures, lexical chunks, certain larger texts like letters, newspaper articles, short stories and books), but meaningful forms also include other semiotic modes as well as the coordinated use of multiple modes at once; and forms such as cultural narratives, which are clearly indexed by language use and other semiotic resources but that themselves constitute forms in their own right. Grasping the broad range of forms and signs that are available in particular semiotic environments creates the possibility of making sense of the world from a range of points of view. All meaning is made from particular perspectives, and subjective, historically shaped and equally future-oriented positions must be part of our understanding of how meaning is made. When we begin to connect acts of meaning with the perspectives and positions they represent, critical dimensions of meaning-making, especially in ML classrooms, becomes apparent. As learners broaden their awareness, knowledge and active engagement with semiotic material and practices, they gain access to other ways of viewing and constructing the world, and consequently, they become more able to question the way things are and to gain transformative kinds of power for themselves and possibly for changing the world they live in.

Renegotiating 'Negotiation of Meaning'

At the start of this book, I began to lay out an argument for reconsidering meaning-making in ML education. What we need are broader conceptions of meaning in ML education, conceptions that move beyond the merely referential to embrace the symbolic dimensions of meaning. A social semiotic perspective has much to offer us in this endeavor, and having laid out in detail the meaning-making processes that took place in one classroom and how these seemed to positively impact students' intercultural learning and development of symbolic competence, it now is possible to discuss how a social semiotic view of ML education, namely in construing language learning as potential expansion of one's meaning-making repertoire, enters into dialogue with theories of intercultural learning and symbolic competence.

Byram's (2012) recent work emphasizes the need to clarify the relationship between language awareness, cultural awareness and intercultural competence. He also points out the need for language awareness to be developed at the level of the self and at the level of broader social grouping, what he calls 'social analysis – the use of language in society – and self-analysis, analysis of the significance of language and culture for the self' (p. 8–9). An ecological and social semiotic view of ML learning environments specifically posits the development of perceptual abilities (in terms of both process – ways of perceiving – and content – particular perceptions) as central to learning and developing in new semiotic environments. This kind of growth seems to relate quite naturally to Byram's awarenesses at both social and personal levels; language and cultural awareness are collapsed in a social semiotic view, making it a bit easier to consider awareness-raising as an integrated process in the ML learning enterprise rather than there being two separate foci. Social semiotics' construct of meaning potentials further addresses Byram's challenge to relate development of both linguistic and cultural awareness and experience in a model of intercultural competence; this is because meaning potentials clearly connect individual instances of language use and situated meanings to much broader shared meanings and puts these in reciprocal relationship along a cline of instantiation. Forms and meanings then are always connected regardless of level. Considering the main elements of Byram's (1997) model of intercultural competence, a social semiotic perspective on intercultural learning seems well-matched with the knowledge, skills, attitudes and critical engagement Byram has long supported as key. What is new in a social semiotic interpretation of the model is that a clear process – semiosis through acts of meaning and stretching one's personalized meaning potential – connects and brings to life these dimensions.

Kramsch's (2006, 2011) theory of symbolic competence is already quite connected to and informed by a social semiotic perspective; however, what this research and analysis have offered is a way of seeing how precisely symbolic representation, symbolic action and symbolic power – which are extremely useful touchstones for talking about culture-in-ML-education – work in conjunction in acts of meaning at the individual or textual level as well as at broader levels of interrelated and networked acts of meaning. Particular texts can be analyzed in ML classrooms for the ways they represent, including which signs are assembled and what these signs can refer to and likely refer to. Interaction with texts and analysis of them is transported to focus on symbolic action when they are interpreted for what they do and how they use signs to do it. Finally, symbolic power enters into interactions around acts of meaning when a teacher and her students begin to engage with the question of what agenda a representational text or act of meaning advances and whose interests such a move serves. In Emilie's class, instructional scaffolds such as re-positioning students and animating texts through voicing and embodiment greatly facilitated students' access to representations both as symbolic action and symbolic power. Her quite direct instruction delineating a standard process for approaching the interpretation of cultural texts and the class's explicit discussion of the representation of power and the power of representation point to the benefit at times of unambiguous talk about the way forms and particular acts of meaning facilitate the wielding of symbolic power, and not always in oppressive ways. Especially because we tend to put stock in the claim that ML learning in general naturally leads to deeper personal or cultural understandings and intercultural competence in learners, as if these followed automatically from encounters with new languages, the need for explicitness and planfulness in culture pedagogy cannot be understated.

Returning briefly to the web metaphor, what this book has attempted to show about semiotic processes in the ML classroom environment and how these relate to others' theories of semiosis in language education and theories of intercultural learning and development of symbolic competence can be summarized metaphorically as supporting students to (1) see the web, (2) learn to crawl and (3) spin new meanings. This research shows how rich learners' engagements can be if affordances are present as a result of the semiotic environment that is designed and the interactions and engagement that are facilitated. Put differently, these dimensions are first, raising awareness of a new network of signs and meaning and second, focusing in on identifying particular semiotic resources in that network. As we saw in Emilie's classroom, this involves the precise articulation of what forms are, naming them and then attaching referential meanings. Second, 'learning to crawl', means that learners gain the opportunity and skills to explore meaning potentials more deeply, moving more toward the symbolic. This dimension engages learners in investigating how forms are deployed in particular texts and how they constitute particular acts of meaning, by whom, for what purposes, with what effect and in what broader universe of potential meanings and perspectives. Finally, 'spinning new meanings' refers to creating opportunities for learners to realize meaning potentials, to 'textualize' as Kramsch (2002) suggested, and possibly resignify symbolic forms. This is where intercultural learning is truly felt; adoption of a perspective becomes experiential and writing or speaking through other voices and subjectivities, especially through long-term projects, can awaken and engage the human, emotional and moral core of a learner.

Given these processes, what we need as teachers in ML education is to create classroom ecologies that are rich in semiotic material and that are designed to enhance learners' semiotic tools and strategies, which the next section turns to in more detail.

Translating a Social Semiotic Model of Intercultural Learning into Practice

Language teachers often have the intuitive sense that their students, in learning a new language, come to mean in new ways – that something happens as learners discover and appropriate linguistic and other semiotic forms and use them with increasing agency and style over time and with the right opportunities. Pinpointing more exactly what this transformative process entails and identifying curricularly and pedagogically how it can be facilitated and supported through ML education has been to date quite elusive. The chapters of this book have thus far attempted to make more visible and transparent what some of these learning processes and instructional pillars might be by describing and analyzing in detail the effective practices that took place in one teacher's classroom. Yet, many practical questions remain. In this section, I return to some of the challenges laid out in Chapter 1 and directly address the practical implications of the model presented above. I do so in an effort to broaden my discussion of what ML teachers can do to facilitate meaning-making practices that promote deep engagement with culture in the classroom and what challenges they will likely face in attempting to do so. I attempt to anticipate and respond to questions about possible limitations of the broad model, such as its applications to earlier stages of ML learning, to instruction of younger learners, or to the teaching of nonhistorical content. I also try to lay out some concrete, while still flexible, strategies that will be practical to all teachers of MLs. I conclude with a consideration of possible directions for future research, which would further elaborate the range of practical options available to ML teachers while also providing additional empirical bases from different teaching and learning contexts to substantiate and/or revise existing theoretical models.

In this research, I set out to better understand certain challenges ML educators face, namely in defining meaning, conveying it, engaging their students with meanings and meaning-making and supporting them in creating meanings. The semiotic processes suggested in the previous section represent a solid starting point in addressing these challenges, but teachers will clearly have to consider the realities of their own instructional contexts and their learners' characteristics and intents in order to tailor these processes to their specific settings. To reiterate, in general what teachers need to aim to foster through their pedagogy is (1) awareness among students of linguistic and other signs and how semiosis operates in their worlds and in their own personal lives and (2) engagement in semiotic processes of signification and interpretation, which involves interpretation and production of texts or acts of meaning.

Following van Lier's (2004b) insights on the ecology of ML classrooms, it can be helpful to consider pedagogical supports as being implemented at three levels potentially: macro, meso and micro. At the macro level, we should be thinking about curriculum, how content is organized and overall pedagogical approach. In some cases, there is perhaps a project-based curriculum in place or a particular approach like the global simulation that will create an overall structure and environment in which semiotic practices can become focal. In the early stages of ML education, even at very young ages, a language awareness curriculum as practiced through initiatives like the *Elodil* project (http://www.elodil.com), for example, could frame the kind of deep engagement with meaning I have advocated in this book. Major tasks and assignments are also important to consider at this broad level, and these are necessarily interlaced with learning objectives. In Emilie's class, examples of this level of consideration are the overarching *Mémoires* writing project that anchored the global simulation and even the *Café de Retrouvailles* activities, which took place on a weekly basis as well. Establishing a position on language choice – L1 or L2 or both – for engaging in meaning-making and determining when and how to draw on these in dealing with symbolic forms, texts and cultural representations is a further macro-level consideration. Some teachers may make determinations based on factors like students' language proficiency, the linguistic complexity of a text and the relative complexity of a learning task, or practical considerations like time. These factors aside, there is no reason to believe that intercultural learning of substance is superior when it occurs through the medium of learners' more familiar languages or the new ML they are studying. It is reasonable to expect that certain forms of interpretation or production of symbolic meaning are beyond the proficiency level of students at introductory levels in particular; yet, we should begin from the assumption that all learners, at all proficiency levels, can engage in symbolic meaning-making.

On a meso level, van Lier (2004b) recommends that we should be thinking about designing 'individual tasks…consisting of a series of steps or activities that occur sequentially or in collaborative construction' (n.p.). The writing of individual compositions that build on each other to incrementally craft a complete narrative arc and all of the planned activities that took place during class sessions, which also built on each other cumulatively, are examples from Emilie's course of meso-level pedagogical scaffolds. This is in line with Byrnes *et al.*'s (2010) work, for example, which lays out a case study of a genre-based ML writing curriculum that, to be effective, relies on certain pedagogical practices in addition to planned curricular progressions and clear curricular goals and modes of assessment. Specifically, these authors draw from Rothery (1996) to suggest four instructional stages that drive their pedagogical approach; these align closely with the research presented in this book and might inform discussion of culture pedagogy more generally in ML education. These stages are: (1) 'negotiating field' or building content knowledge and knowledge of perspectives that are relevant to whatever text students will ultimately produce; (2) 'deconstruction,' during which students examine model texts in the genre of interest to analyze textual features and 'how texts construe and realize culture' (p. 124); (3) 'joint construction,' during which the teacher and students construct a text together in that genre, with the teacher providing scaffolding moves; and (4) 'independent construction,' where students create texts in the genre on their own, with assistance from the teacher more in the form of feedback. Establishing the 'field' or context for interpreting and making symbolic meaning can be achieved at a curricular level, but in terms of instructional decisions, teachers need to think about what types of learning activities around which texts will help students to become aware of symbolic and cultural reference points, to be able to perceive relevant forms among others. Emilie achieved this largely through her *Identifications* activities, but any teacher might ask herself 'What reference points should students be aware of and how can I guide them to build understandings of these initially in terms of referential meanings and increasingly in terms of their symbolic ones?' It is at this phase especially that a teacher might decide to draw more heavily on students' L1 in order to build background knowledge and use referential and symbolic forms learners already know to connect with the new ones they are encountering. Analysis of particular texts (written visual, oral, multimodal, etc.) and multiple cycles of this around a set of symbolic forms constitute a type of 'deconstruction phase' in which students' interpretations can be invited and recast by the teacher. This need not be as elaborate as the text-analysis activities in Emilie's class; activities that involve more concrete semantic mapping, for example, would facilitate the task of identifying forms and hypothesizing about symbolic meanings for students with more beginning level proficiencies. Indeed, a semantic webbing approach is part of Byrnes' et al.'s instruction at all levels of college German, and a similar technique of semantic mapping is used in the *Cultura* project (Furstenberg *et al.*, 2001). Here too it is possible to imagine semantic webs that are multilingual as opposed to purely in the L2, especially if both L1 and L2 texts are included in the corpus of texts that delimit the field of interest or that make up the set of texts the class will analyze. Producing texts, whether as a collaborative effort or by individual students, must still be supported instructionally through in-class tasks that prepare students for writing, speaking, visually composing or making meaning otherwise, but if a semantic field has been firmly established and teaching has focused consciously on the analysis of particular instances of symbolic forms in context, learners are likely to be able to understand the meaning potentials of these forms to such a degree that they can practice deploying them on their own and for a range of purposes. Here too, the textual products students create need not look like the extended narrative writing project Emilie engaged her students in. Rather, image-word combinations, shorter texts or brief oral texts could all be appropriate textual products if they are appropriately anchored in a meaningful field and purpose.

At the micro level of planning for a classroom ecology that is supportive of and conducive to developing students' meaning-making repertoires, we need to think about interactional moments in classrooms; the nature of the back-and-forth discourse among teacher and students, students and other students, students and texts, etc.; and the particular instructional moves that a teacher could make to facilitate meaning-making practices. Moves that Emilie routinely made in her classroom discourse were to mark discourse when she planned on projecting students into a past or hypothetical reality, for example, by saying 'imagine' and then setting a scene. Her extensive voicing and embodiment moves were also consistent supports that facilitated perspective-taking as students analyzed particular texts, affording meaning-making from various points of view. Recall as well that Emilie planned scaffolding patterns into classroom discourse during *Identifications* activities by socializing students early on into a 'who, what, when, where, how' type of routine in discussing symbolic terms. Similarly, during textual-analysis types of activities, Emilie often structured discourse between herself and students to follow a cycle of focusing first on literal, then figurative, then ideological meanings and achieved this movement through targeted questioning. All of these instructional moves made it possible for students to better understand expectations about how to participate in classroom discourse, but they also served as a model for students of how to strategically engage with meaning-making. Not only did Emilie's modeling of interpretation of texts provide an example of reading acts of meaning, but students were always highly involved as she modeled, so they did not just see a demonstration but were actively involved in coconstructing these processes with her.

Another point of view is to conceive of pedagogical support in terms of phases, with planning, instruction and assessment informing and feeding back on each other. From this perspective, we might first focus on planning for a semiotic approach to intercultural learning. Articulating objectives around meaning and meaning-making would be an important first step. Depending on the nature of a particular course and what students' needs are, an objective might simply be that they be able to identify widely recognized cultural symbols in a range of texts and contexts. Beyond goals of identification and awareness, teachers might articulate learning objectives that are more focused on engaging students in the interpretation of texts and the production of acts of meaning. Alongside objectives, teachers need also to think about materials and texts in terms of these objectives, but also in terms of the forms and meaning potentials they include and reference and what sorts of meaning-making processes they naturally involve or could involve. Attention must be accorded to constructing an overall classroom ecology, including the selection of texts for their semiotic material. The richness of the textual environment and the semiotic network it sets up is key. All of these planning elements imply that teachers will need knowledge about signs, texts, voices, perspectives, dominant and counternarratives, and this could require research on the part of teachers, whether they are highly familiar with a culture or not. No one person could possibly be knowledgeable about the infinite number of meaningful texts out there in the world that could be included in a ML classroom, so for all teachers, the planning task involves delimiting a textual world and then researching the interrelations of the texts and materials that will make up a curricular unit, with an eye to the kinds of connections that can be made and the affordances for meaning-making that are created by bringing these texts into relation. More than any particular body of knowledge, a pedagogical stance and the establishment of a process and routines for engaging students in meaning-making around texts are central to the success of a semiotic approach to intercultural teaching.

Considering instruction itself, teachers will need to attend, as suggested above, to the way that instructional moves shape opportunities for meaning-making. Spending time planning out routine interactions will certainly go a long way in preparing teachers for instruction, but they will also need to be able to work contingently in the moment as they engage learners in interaction around texts. This kind of skill requires eliciting and then building on student contributions. In some cases, students' hypotheses about and interpretations of texts may be completely implausible, for example, but a teacher who seeks to support the development of symbolic competence will need to know how to recast and reorient these kinds of student contributions in more plausible directions. One of Emilie's strategies was also to raise students' awareness around the issue of plausibility in activities like the 'What doesn't fit?' exercise that asked students to identify and explain inaccuracies in generating acts of meaning. Making space for students to form their own connections among texts and contexts is also an element of instruction that cannot always be planned for. For example, if a student raised a comparison between the text the class was analyzing and one he knew from his own personal experience, Emilie often enthusiastically encouraged the student to explain rather than attempting to adhere rigidly to her own plan for making connections among texts. Overall, through instruction, teachers who adopt a social semiotic approach will attend to raising awareness among students of a semiotic field in which they will make meanings; will engage students in identifying signs by clarifying reference points and referential meanings; will support exploration of symbolic meaning potentials, deepening form-meaning connections through analysis and interpretation of texts in context; and will create opportunities for students to generate meanings, to 'textualize' signs in ways that realize and possibly stretch meaning potentials.

This last instructional element leads to questions of assessment or, put differently, the extent to which a teacher can evaluate whether students are able not only to read and interpret signs but also to make meaning-making decisions with semiotic resources. Projects or assignments that allow students to demonstrate their ability to make choices with language and other semiotic material will produce tangible artifacts for a teacher's consideration; more fleeting classroom moments, however, are also sites in which learners can certainly demonstrate their abilities to forge meaning. The short classroom exercise during which Emilie asked a student to recite the first lines of a propaganda speech, for example, afforded the opportunity for students to inflect these lines with their own meanings. van Lier (2004c) explains that assessment in an ecological view of language education, our means of evaluating learning or development, will necessarily depart from traditional or what have come to be common practices:

> The quality of educational experience is that which the learner remembers long after the test scores are forgotten. It cannot be measured in test scores, but it can be evidenced objectively in terms of diversified perception and action, the ability to cope under stress, increasing control of one's own physical, social and symbolic environment, the establishment of mutually rewarding relationships, and the development of one's talents and interests in a supportive environment. (n.p.)

Clearly, there is a need in instructional environments to assess students within the confines of a semester or an academic year and even on more narrow scales, such as within curricular units or at the ends of particular lessons. However, as van Lier, points out, the true impact of our teaching lies in the enduring effect that instruction and interaction in our classrooms has on students. In the case of symbolic competence, if students carry with them out of our classrooms more developed analytic skills or enhanced awareness about the nature of symbolic representation, for example, a social semiotic approach to intercultural learning has been successful. If they also come to form deeper and denser networks of form-meaning connections and the ability to draw on this more expansive repertoire to spin their own meanings, we can equally claim the effectiveness of our approach. However, we often will never know how these awarenesses or skills are called into action long after students have left our classes. We can focus, however, during the time students are with us, on creating opportunities for them to demonstrate their abilities to make meanings.

Possible practical challenges in implementing a social semiotic approach

While I studied Emilie's classroom and in the many discussions I have had with teachers sharing insights I have gained from that experience, I am often faced with questions about the particularities of her teaching context. That is, often teachers wonder if the kind of social semiotic approach I advocate, one that involves engaging learners in interpretation of texts and production of meaningful texts, is really one that will work in completely different contexts. For example, how can such an approach work in early stages of ML learning, when students really know few linguistic forms and structures and proficiency is just starting to develop? Or, how could very young learners be engaged in such an approach when their experience of the world is necessarily somewhat limited given their age? And, what of other than historical content? Textual analysis and global simulation seem to fit quite well when studying a historical period like the Occupation of France during World War II, but it can sometimes be difficult to imagine what a social semiotic approach would look like if other content were at the heart of a curriculum. These are among the most common questions I am asked when I share this research and approach; by way of an illustrative example, I attempt to address all of them.

If we adopt the overarching structure of the global simulation and the generic notion of a 'the village' project, it becomes possible to show how some of these commonly expressed concerns can be addressed. Magnin (1997) describes 'the village' global simulation in ML classrooms as possibly including the following:

> [A] site and a time period are chosen. Each villager selects an identity starting with a name, age and occupation. The professions will be those needed to support the population of the village. A historical past can be invented for the village with a local hero whose biography can be written. Students imagine the claim to fame of the village (cheese, car factory, monument), folklore and customs, the architecture of the houses. A newspaper can be created to report the local events. This simulation can end on a positive note such as the visit of a high-ranking official or a major festive celebration. It can also end on a creative note such as the historiography of the village by a famous writer. (n.p.)

Imagining an elementary school French classroom (young ML learners, who are also likely to have relatively little linguistic proficiency in the new language) instead of the university-level context that served as the main example of a social semiotic approach to intercultural learning in this book, let us assume that the teacher would like to engage her students in a 'village' simulation, set in the present day (rather than a historical era). Magnin's description of possibilities for this particular simulation begins to point to the affordances of this general curricular structure for an elementary school classroom, yet certain concerns still arise. Distinct from the project in Emilie's class, the challenges in working with students who do not yet have a great deal of linguistic proficiency might include issues of selecting texts, thinking about how to engage learners during classroom interactions and the nature of whatever final product students create that also serves as the thread holding the simulation together. To counter these concerns, a teacher would need to contemplate and plan carefully the nature of the textual environment. One strategy would be to provide more visual than verbal texts, to favor short texts over lengthy ones, and to mix in L1 texts with those in the L2. Another would be to attempt some balance of text complexity and task complexity. In the village global simulation, these texts could include pictures and signs from a variety of locations in a French village, sample newspapers or newsletters from small towns in France and other short texts like brief descriptions of French villages posted on the towns' actual websites. A focus on multimodality and the ways that much more than the verbal communicates meaning would be key for learners that were still developing linguistic proficiency. It is important to keep in mind that learners need not fully understand all of the forms in a text or even most of them in order to begin making meaning around them. Indeed, as Kramsch (2009) shows, very early on in the language learning process, students form personally symbolic associations around L2 forms. At introductory levels, various forms of free association and play with symbolic forms could be beneficial in raising learners' awareness of these forms in general and could set the stage for analyzing these forms in particular texts and representations in later lessons. As noted above, semantic webbing exercises could also prove a beneficial pedagogical measure in introductory-level classes in order to provide the time and space for students to familiarize themselves more with forms and to explore the way forms enter into relation with each other before they move to embedding these in their own creations with language. In the case of the village global simulation example, an initial exercise might ask students to respond with word or image associations when they hear the titles of several newspapers, for instance. Or students could be assigned to analyze the immediate cotext accompanying relevant forms, in a corpus-based analysis or concordancing approach, in a series of related articles in order to get a sense of commonly associated forms and the meanings that might typically accompany a particular form, in what contexts, when representing what perspectives and so on. Various genres within newspapers are potentially already familiar to students, so activities in which students are asked to form hypotheses about meanings are likely to be facilitated by generic intertextuality. That is, they may be able to propose interpretations about texts from an editorial section of a French newspaper if they know some forms, functions and meanings associated with the editorial genre in English-medium newspapers.

In terms of the kinds of goals the teacher might have, she could focus on supporting learners in becoming more adept in identifying visual and linguistic signs and hypothesizing about their meanings. During classroom interactions, analysis of visual, aural and short verbal texts might involve hypothesizing in a form quite different from in Emilie's class. For example, in the analysis of village newspapers, students might be asked to provide one-word hypotheses of what people do in the village (for work, for fun, etc.) based on the content they can discern from paging through the newspaper, skimming headlines and considering the sections it includes and the pictures and other images it contains. Alternatively, such hypothesizing and interpreting could take place in students' L1. This is in line, in any case, with meaning-making among multilinguals who do not switch among compartmentalized linguistic systems but rather that move fluidly along their singular meaning-making repertoire that happens to include features of multiple languages (Garcia, 2009). As semiotic resources grow in L2 features, we would expect that more meaning-making could occur in that medium.

When it comes to what students might create in such a global simulation and the opportunities they would have for making-meaning in a 'village' project, students could create their own imagined village in between two real villages in France. A key decision for the teacher would be to decide on the narrative plot that would propel all other analytic and creative activities. For example, she could announce that the class would work on creating a visitors' center for their village and planning its grand opening. Students' could take up various roles in relation to this plan and be responsible for preparing different elements of the center and event. A multitude of texts could be created to be housed in the visitors' center and in relation to the opening event (e.g. histories of the village, maps, collages, brochures, an announcement of the grand opening) and regular role-playing interactions could be set up in class to advance the planning of the center itself and of the culminating grand opening day. The linguistic demands of these texts could be managed by planning multiple exercises at the start of the unit that establish the relevant semiotic field for students, as described above, and then deliberately attending to the progressive building of students' knowledge of and experience with symbolic meaning potentials. In more simple fashion, students' engagement with learning about French villages and creating their own imagined village might lead to pairs or small teams of students designing and proposing a new symbol for the town (e.g. a stamp, a village monument, a logo for the village website); in doing so, learners would necessarily need to draw on relevant background knowledge and an appropriate semiotic field of resources, yet they would equally have room to create and make semiotic choices, all in a way that minimizes demands on linguistic proficiency. As with all global simulation projects, the possibilities are truly endless. The point here is to begin suggesting some of these precisely to emphasize that regardless of the age of learner or level of proficiency or the exact nature of curricular content, designing a classroom environment rich in texts and meaning-making processes is always possible and putting a social semiotic approach into action is always within reach. This example has begun to show how the general pedagogical approach of global simulation could still work in other circumstances and how, importantly, a curricular environment and the interactional processes at the core of a social semiotic approach to intercultural learning and development of symbolic competence can be facilitated.

Future Directions

As the brief examples in the previous section start to make clear, implementing a social semiotic approach in classrooms is a main objective for expanding the meaningfulness of ML education and the meaning-making that occurs in ML classrooms. In order to be able to expand a social semiotic approach into many more classrooms and fuel the profession with a pedagogy of potentials, generating a range of examples that can spark teachers' and curriculum planners' ideas about adapting the approach to their specific contexts will be beneficial. More focus on classroom-based empirical studies could contribute quite productively in this regard, offering more diverse windows into the practices of teachers who attempt to employ such an approach. At present, there really are no in-depth descriptions of such classrooms besides what I have presented in this book. Research in classrooms will also be crucial to pushing forward our knowledge of a fuller range of effective practices within such a social semiotic approach in a variety of learning contexts. These studies will also help to refine our theoretical notions of how semiosis occurs and can occur in ML classrooms. van Lier (2004b) writes that

> The ecological approach to education asserts the ultimately the quality and the lasting success of education are primarily dependent on the quality of activities and the interactional opportunities available to learners in the educational environment. Research therefore needs to focus on effective classroom practices in the contexts (diverse and varied) in which they occur. (n.p)

Pursuing this type of agenda in research on ML education, then, has quite important potential in making practical and theoretical impact. What is at stake is no less than our ability to foster through ML education the empowerment of learners to not only read the world but to remake it, if they have the knowledge, tools, opportunities and desire to do so.

Note

(1) This recalls Larsen-Freeman's (1997) work in that dynamic systems are seen to be nested and fractal in nature.

References

Agar, M. (1994) *Language Shock: Understanding the Culture of Conversation*. New York: William Morrow and Company.
Allen, H.W. and Paesani, K. (2010) Exploring the feasibility of a pedagogy of multiliteracies in introductory foreign language courses. *L2 Journal* 2, 119–142.
American Council on the Teaching of Foreign Languages (2010) Use of the target language in the classroom. See http://www.actfl.org/news/position-statements/use-the-target-language-the-classroom-0.
American Council on the Teaching of Foreign Languages (2013) World-readiness standards for learning languages. See http://www.actfl.org/sites/default/files/pdfs/World-ReadinessStandardsforLearningLanguages.pdf.
Assouline, P. (2000) *La Cliente: Roman*. Paris: Gallimard.
Austin, J. (1962) *How to do Things with Words* (2nd edn). Oxford University Press.
Bakhtin, M.M. (1981) In M. Holquist (ed.) *The Dialogic Imagination: Four Essays by M.M. Bakhtin*. Austin: University of Texas Press.
Bakhtin, M.M. (1986) In C. Emerson and M. Holquist (eds) *Speech Genres and Other Late Essays*. Austin: University of Texas Press.
Bakhtin, M.M. (1993) *Toward a Philosophy of the Act* (V. Liapunov, Trans.; M. Holquist and V. Liapunov, eds). Austin: University of Texas Press.
Belz, J. (2002) Second language play as a representation of the multicompetent self in foreign language study. *Journal of Language, Identity and Education* 1 (1), 13–39.
Belz, J.A. (2003) Linguistic perspectives on the development of intercultural competence in telecollaboration. *Language Learning & Technology* 7 (2), 68–99.
Belz, J.A. and Reinhardt, J. (2004) Aspects of advanced foreign language proficiency: Internet-mediated German language play. *International Journal of Applied Linguistics* 14 (3), 324–362.
Belz, J.A. and Thorne, S.L. (2006) Internet-mediated intercultural foreign language education and the intercultural speaker. In J.A. Belz and S.L. Thorne (eds) *Internet-mediated intercultural foreign language education* (pp. viii–xxv). Boston, MA: Heinle.
Benveniste, E. (1966) *Problèmes de linguistique générale*. Paris: Gallimard.
Bhabha, H.K. (1994) *The Location of Culture*. New York: Routledge.
Boughey, C. (2000) Multiple metaphors in an understanding of academic literacy. *Teachers and Teaching: Theory and Practice* 6 (3), 279–290.
Bourdieu, P. (1991) *Language and Symbolic Power*. Cambridge, MA: Harvard University Press.
Bourdieu, P. and Passeron, J. (1990) *Reproduction in Education, Society and Culture*. London: Sage Publications.
Brody, J. (2003) A linguistic anthropological perspective on language and culture in the second language curriculum. In D.L. Lange and M. Paige (eds) *Culture As the Core: Perspectives on Culture in Second Language Learning* (pp. 37–51). Greenwich, CT: Information Age Publishing.

Brooks, F. (1993) Some problems and caveats in 'communicative' discourse: Toward a conceptualization of the foreign language classroom. *Foreign Language Annals* 26 (2), 233–242.

Brooks, N. (1960) *Language and Language Learning. Theory and Practice.* New York: Harcourt, Brace, and World, Inc.

Bruner, J. (1991) The narrative construction of reality. *Critical Inquiry* 18 (1), 1–21.

Butler, J. (1997) *Excitable Speech: The Political Promise of the Performative.* New York: Routledge.

Byram, M. (1991) Teaching culture and language: Towards an integrated model. In D. Buttjes and M. Byram (eds) *Mediating Languages and Cultures: Towards an Intercultural Theory of Foreign Language Education* (pp. 17–30). Clevedon: Multilingual Matters.

Byram, M. (1994) *Teaching-and-learning Language-and-Culture.* Clevedon: Multilingual Matters.

Byram, M. (1997) *Teaching and Assessing Intercultural Communicative Competence.* Clevedon: Multilingual Matters.

Byram, M. (2012) Language awareness and (critical) cultural awareness – relationships, comparisons and contrasts. *Language Awareness* 21 (1–2), 5–13.

Byram, M. and Feng, A. (2004) Culture and language learning: Teaching, research and scholarship. *Language Teaching* 37, 149–168.

Byram, M., Morgan, C. and colleagues (1994) *Teaching-and-Learning Language-and-Culture.* Clevedon: Multilingual Matters.

Byram, M., Nichols, A. and Stevens, D. (eds) (2001) *Developing Intercultural Competence in Practice.* Clevedon: Multilingual Matters.

Byrnes, H. (2002) The cultural turn in foreign language departments: Challenges and opportunity. *Profession* 2002, 114–129.

Byrnes, H. (2006) Perspectives. Interrogating communicative competence as a framework for collegiate foreign language study. *Modern Language Journal* 90, 244–246.

Byrnes, H. (2008) Articulating a foreign language sequence through content: A look at the culture standards. *Language Teaching* 1, 103–118.

Byrnes, H., Crane, C., Maxim, H. and Sprang, K. (2006) Taking text to task: Issues and choices in curriculum construction. *ITL: International Journal of Applied Linguistics* 152, 85–110.

Byrnes, H., Maxim, H. and Norris, J. (2010) Realizing advanced L2 writing development in a collegiate curriculum: Curricular design, pedagogy, assessment. *Modern Language Journal* 94 (supplement), i–vi, 1–235.

Canagarajah, S. (2011) Translanguaging in the classroom: Emerging issues for research and pedagogy. *Applied Linguistics Review* 2 (2011), 1–28.

Caré, J.-M. (1992) Simulations globales. *Le Francais dans le Monde* 252, 48–56.

Caré, J.-M. (1993) Le Village: Une simulation globale pour debutants. *Le Francais dans le Monde* 261, 48–57.

Chaudron, C. (1988) *Second Language Classrooms: Research on Teaching and Learning.* Cambridge University Press.

Collings, N.Y. (2007) Cultural learning in the absence of culture? A study of how students learn foreign language and culture in a tertiary classroom. In D. Palfreyman and D.L. McBride (eds) *Learning and Teaching Across Cultures in Higher Education* (pp. 55–73). New York: Palgrave Macmillan.

Cook, V. (1991) The poverty-of-the-stimulus argument and multi-competence. *Second Language Research* 7 (2), 103–117.
Cook, V. (1992) Evidence for multi-competence. *Language Learning* 42 (4), 557–591.
Damen, L. (1987) *Culture Learning: The Fifth Dimension in The Language Classroom*. Reading, MA: Addison-Wesley Publishing Company.
Damen, L. (2003) Closing the language and culture gap. In D.L. Lange and M. Paige (eds) *Culture as The Core: Perspectives On Culture in Second Language Learning* (pp. 71–88). Greenwich, CT: Information Age Publishing.
Darvin, R. and Norton, B. (2015) Identity and a model of investment in applied linguistics. *Annual Review of Applied Linguistics* 35, 36–56.
de Bot, K., Lowie, W. and Verspoor, M. (2007) A dynamic systems approach to second language acquisition. *Bilingualism: Language and Cognition* 10 (1), 7–21.
Debyser, F. (1980) *L'Immeuble, Roman-Simulation en 66 Exercices*. Paris: BELC.
Debyser, F. (1996) *L'Immeuble*. Paris: Hachette FLE.
Duff, P. and Polio, C. (1990) How much foreign language is there in the foreign language classroom? *Modern Language Journal* 74 (2), 154–166.
Dupuy, B. (2006) 'L'Immeuble': French language and culture teaching and learning through projects in a global simulation. In J. Hammadou-Sullivan (ed.) *Project Based Learning in Second Language Education: Past, Present and Future* Volume 5 (pp. 195–214). Greenwich, CT: Information Age Publishing, Inc.
Ellis, R. (1992) Learning to communicate in the classroom. *Studies in Second Language Acquisition* 14 (1), 1–23.
Erickson F. (2006) Definition and analysis of data from videotape: Some research procedures and their rationales. In J. Green, G. Camilli, P. Elmore, A. Skukauskaite and E. Grace (eds) *Handbook of Complementary Methods in Education Research* (pp. 177–191). Mahwah, NJ: Lawrence Erlbaum.
Fauconnier, G. and Turner, M. (2002) *The Way Ee Think*. New York: Basic Books.
Fox, R. and Diaz-Greenberg, R. (2006) Culture, multiculturalism, and foreign/world language standards in US teacher preparation programs: Toward a discourse of dissonance. *European Journal of Teacher Education* 29 (3), 401–422.
Furstenberg, G., Levet, S., English, K. and Maillet, K. (2001) Giving a virtual voice to the silent language of culture: The CULTURA project. *Language Learning & Technology* 5 (1), 55–102.
García, O. (2009) *Bilingual Education in the 21st Century: A Global Perspective*. Malden, MA: Blackwell.
García, O. and Sylvan, C. (2011) Pedagogies and practices in multilingual classrooms: Singularities in pluralities. *Modern Language Journal* 95 (3), 385–400.
Geertz, C. (1973) *The Interpretation of Cultures*. New York: Basic Books, Inc.
Goffman, E. (1967) *Interaction Ritual: Essays on Face-to-Face Behavior*. New York: Basic Books.
Goodwin, C. (1994) Professional vision. *American Anthropologist* 96 (3), 606–633.
Graman, T. (1988) Education for Humanization: Applying Paulo Freire's pedagogy to learning a second language. *Harvard Educational Review* 58 (4), 433–448.
Guest, M. (2002) A critical 'checkbook' for culture teaching and learning. *ELT Journal* 56 (2), 154–161.
Hall, J.K. and Verplaetse, L. (eds) (2000) *Second and Foreign Language Learning Through Classroom Interaction*. Mahwah, NJ: Lawrence Erlbaum Associates.
Halliday, M.A.K. (1978) *Language as Social Semiotic*. London: Edward Arnold.

Jernigan, C. and Moore, Z. (1997) Teaching culture: A study in the Portuguese classroom implications for the national standards. *Hispania* 80 (4), 829–841.
Kang, H. (2010) The relative efficacy of explicit vs. implicit feedback in the learning of a less-commonly-taught foreign language. *International Review of Applied Linguistics* 47(4), 303–324.
Kanpol, B. (1999) *Critical Pedagogy: An Introduction*. Westport, CT: Bergin & Garvey.
Kearney, E. (2008) Developing worldview(s): An ethnography of culture learning in a foreign language classroom. Unpublished doctoral dissertation, University of Pennsylvania, Philadelphia. Available from ProQuest Dissertations and Theses database (UMI No. 3328597).
Kearney, E. (2009) Images as a resource for culture learning in the foreign language classroom. In M. Navarro Coy (ed.) *Practical Approaches to Foreign Language Teaching And Learning* (pp. 33–66). New York: Peter Lang Publishing.
Kearney, E. (2010) Cultural immersion in the foreign language classroom: Some narrative possibilities. *Modern Language Journal* 94 (2), 332–336.
Kearney, E. (2012) Perspective-taking and meaning-making through engagement with cultural narratives: Bringing history to life in a foreign language classroom. *L2 Journal* 4 (1), 58–82.
Kinginger, C. (2008) Language learning in study Abroad: Case studies of Americans in France. *The Modern Language Journal Monograph Series*. Volume 1.
Kramsch, C. (1993) *Context and Culture in Language Teaching*. Oxford University Press.
Kramsch, C. (1995) The cultural component of language teaching. *Language, Culture and Curriculum 8* (12), 83–92.
Kramsch, C. (1997) The privilege of the non-native speaker. *PMLA* 112 (3), 359–369.
Kramsch, C. (1998) *Language and Culture*. Oxford University Press.
Kramsch, C. (1999) Thirdness: The intercultural stance. In G. Vestergaard (ed.) *Language, Culture and Identity* (pp. 41–58). Aalborg University Press.
Kramsch, C. (2002) Language and culture: A social semiotic perspective. *ADFL Bulletin* 33 (2), 8–15.
Kramsch, C. (2006) From communicative to symbolic competence. *Modern Language Journal* 90, 249–252.
Kramsch, C. (2009) *The Multilingual Subject: What Foreign Language Learners Say About Their Experience and Why It Matters*. Oxford University Press.
Kramsch, C. (2011) The symbolic dimensions of the intercultural. *Language Teaching* 44 (3), 354–367.
Kramsch, C. (2014) Teaching foreign languages in an era of globalization: Introduction. *Modern Language Journal* 98: 296–311.
Kramsch, C. and Whiteside, A. (2008) Language ecology in multilingual settings. *Applied Linguistics* 29 (4), 645–671.
Kramsch, C., Zarate, G. and Lévy, D. (2008) Introduction générale. In G. Zarate, D. Lévy and C. Kramsch (eds) *Précis du plurilinguisme et du pluriculturalisme* (pp. 15–23). Paris: Editions des archives contemporaines.
Kress, G. and van Leeuwen, T. (1999) Visual interaction. In A. Jaworski and N. Coupland (eds) *The Discourse Reader* (2nd edn) (pp. 362–384). London: Routledge,
Lakoff, G. (1987) *Women, Fire, and Dangerous Things: What Categories Reveal About the Mind*. Chicago, IL: University of Chicago Press.
Lantolf, J. (1999) Second culture acquisition: Cognitive considerations. In E. Hinkel (ed.) *Culture in Second Language Teaching* (pp. 29–46). Cambridge University Press.

Larsen-Freeman, D. (1997) Chaos/complexity science and second language acquisition. *Applied Linguistics* 18 (2), 141–165.

Larsen-Freeman, D. (2003) *Teaching Language: From Grammar to Grammaring*. Boston: Heinle.

Larsen-Freeman, D. (2012) The emancipation of the language learner. *Studies in Second Language Learning and Teaching* 2 (3), 297–309.

Larsen-Freeman, D. (2014) Saying what we mean: Making the case for second language acquisition to become second language development. *Language Teaching/FirstView Article*, April 2014, 1–15.

Larsen-Freeman, D. and Cameron, L. (2008) *Complex Systems and Applied Linguistics*. Oxford University Press.

Lemke, J. (1992) Intertextuality and educational research. *Linguistics and Education* 4, 257–267.

Levine, G. (2004) Global simulation: A student-centered, task-based format for intermediate foreign language courses. *Foreign Language Annals* 37 (1), 26–36.

Levine, G. (2011) *Code Choice in the Language Classroom*. Bristol: Multilingual Matters.

Levine, G. (2014) The discourse of foreignness in U.S. language education. In J. Swaffar and P. Urlaub (eds) *Transforming the Foreign Language Curriculum in Higher Education: Critical Perspectives From the United States* (pp. 55–76). New York: Springer.

Lo Bianco, J. (2014) Domesticating the foreign: Globalization's effects on the place/s of languages. *Modern Language Journal* 98 (1), 312–325.

Long, M. and Crookes, G. (1992) Three approaches to task-based syllabus design. *TESOL Quarterly* 26 (1), 27–56.

Magnan, S. (2008) Reexamining the priorities of the National Standards for Foreign Language Education. *Language Teaching* 41 (3), 349–366.

Magnin, M.C. (1997) The Building: An adaptation of Francis Debyser's writing project. A global simulation to teach language and culture. In G. Walz (ed.) *China-US Conference on Education: Collected Papers* (pp. 55–62). Greensboro, NC: ERIC Clearinghouse.

Marin, L. (1981) *Le Portrait du Roi*. Paris: Editions de minuit.

Matthiessen, C. (2009) Meaning in the making: Meaning potential emerging from acts of meaning. *Language Learning* 59 (s1), 206–229.

Mills, N. (2011) Situated learning through social networking communities: The development of joint enterprise, mutual engagement, and a shared repertoire. *CALICO Journal* 28 (2), 345–368.

Mills, N. and Péron, M. (2008) Global simulation and writing self-beliefs of intermediate French students. *International Journal of Applied Linguistics* 156 (2009), 239–273.

Mishler, E. (1995) Models of narrative analysis: A typology. *Journal of Narrative and Life History* 5 (2), 87–123.

MLA Ad Hoc Committee on Foreign Languages (2007) Foreign languages and higher education: New structures for a changed world. *Profession* 2007, 234–245.

Moran, P. (2001) *Teaching Culture: Perspectives in Practice*. Boston: Heinle & Heinle.

Nieto, S. (2002) *Language, Culture and Teaching: Critical Perspectives For a New Century*. Mahwah, NJ: Lawrence Erlbaum Associates.

Ochs, E. and Capps, L. (2001) *Living Narrative: Creating Lives in Everyday Storytelling*. Cambridge, MA: Harvard University Press.

Ochs, E. and Taylor, C. (2009) The 'Father knows best' dynamic in dinnertime narratives. In A. Duranti (ed.) *Linguistic Anthropology: A Reader* (2nd edn) (pp. 435–451). Malden, MA: Blackwell.

Ortega, L. (1999) Language and equality: Ideological and structural constraints in foreign language education in the US. In T. Huebner and K.A. Davis (eds) *Sociopolitical Perspectives In Language Policy and Planning in the USA* (pp. 243–266). Philadelphia, PA: John Benjamins.

Osborn, T. (2005) *Critical Reflection and The Foreign Language Classroom*. Greenwich, CT: Information Age.

Osborn, T. (2006) *Teaching World Languages for Social Justice: A Sourcebook of Principles and Practices*. Mahwah, NJ: Lawrence Erlbaum Associates.

Paesani, K. and Allen, H. (2012) Beyond the language-content divide: Research on advanced foreign language instruction at the postsecondary level. *Foreign Language Annals* 45 (s1), s54–s75.

Palpacuer-Lee, C. (2010) Images, discourses, and representations at the art museum: Intercultural openings. *Proceedings of the Intercultural Competence Conference* 2010 (1), 304–334.

Pennycook, A. (1990) Critical pedagogy and second language education. *System* 18 (3), 303–314.

Pennycook, A. (2007) 'The rotation gets thick. The constraints get thin': Creativity, recontextualization and difference. *Applied Linguistics* 28 (4) 579–596.

Phipps, A. and Levine, G. (2012) What is language pedagogy for? In G. Levine and A. Phipps (eds) *AAUSC 2010: Critical and Intercultural Theory and Language Pedagogy* (pp. 1–14). Boston, MA; Heinle.

Pomerantz, A. and Bell, N.D. (2007) Learning to play, playing to learn: FL learners as multicompetent language users. *Applied Linguistics* 28 (4), 556–578.

Pufahl, I. and Rhodes, N. (2011) Foreign language instruction in US schools: Results of a national survey of elementary and secondary schools. *Foreign Language Annals* 44 (2), 258–288.

Reagan, T. (2002) 'Knowing' and 'learning' a foreign language: Epistemological reflections on classroom practice. In T. Osborn (ed.) *The Future of Foreign Language Education in The United States* (pp. 45–62). Westport, CT: Greenwood Publishing.

Reagan, T. and Osborn, T. (1998) Power, authority, and domination in foreign language education: Toward and analysis of educational failure. *Educational Foundations* 12, 45–62.

Reagan, T. and Osborn, T. (2002) *The Foreign Language Educator in Society: Toward a Critical Pedagogy*. Mahwah, NJ: Lawrence Erlbaum Associates.

Risager, K. (1991) Cultural references in European foreign language textbooks: An evaluation of recent tendencies. In D. Buttjes and M. Byram (eds) *Mediating Languages and Cultures: Towards an Intercultural Theory of Foreign Language Education* (pp. 181–192). Clevedon: Multilingual Matters.

Risager, K. (2006) *Language and Culture: Global Flows and Local Complexity*. Clevedon: Multilingual Matters.

Risager, K. (2007) *Language and Culture Pedagogy: From a National to a Transnational Paradigm*. Clevedon: Multilingual Matters.

Risager, K. (2008) Toward a transnational paradigm in language and culture pedagogy. Paper presented at the American Association of Applied Linguists Annual Conference, Washington, D.C.

Rothery, J. (1996) Making changes: Developing an educational linguistics. In R. Hasan and G. Williams (eds) *Literacy in Society* (pp. 86–123). London: Longman.

Saussure, F. (1916/1959) *Course in General Linguistics*. In C. Bally and A. Sechehaye (eds) W. Baskin (Trans.), New York: McGraw Hill.

Scarino, A. (2014) Language as reciprocal, interpretive meaning-making: A view from collaborative research into the professional learning of teachers of languages. *Modern Language Journal* 98 (1), 386–401.

Schieffelin, B., Woolard, K. and Kroskrity, P. (eds) (1998) *Language Ideologies: Practice and Theory*. New York: Oxford University Press.

Sercu, L., Bandura, E., Castro, P., Davcheva, L., Laskaridou, C., Lundgren, U. *et al.* (2005) *Foreign Language Teachers and Intercultural Competence: An International Investigation*. Clevedon: Multilingual Matters.

Stanton, D. (2005) On linguistic human rights and the United States 'foreign' language crisis. *Profession* 2005, 64–79.

Swaffer, J. and Arens, K. (2005) *Remapping the Foreign Language Curriculum: An Approach Through Multiple Literacies*. New York, NY: Modern Language Association.

Thorne, S. L. (2003) Artifacts and cultures-of-use in intercultural communication. *Language Learning & Technology* 7 (2), 38–67.

Toth, P.D. (2004) When grammar instruction undermines cohesion in L2 Spanish classroom discourse. *The Modern Language Journal* 88 (1), 14–30.

Toth, P.D. (2011) Social and cognitive factors in making teacher-led classroom discourse relevant for L2 grammatical development. *The Modern Language Journal* 95 (1), 1–25.

van Lier, L. (2004a) *The Ecology and Semiotics of Language Learning: A Sociocultural Perspective*. Boston: Kluwer Academic Publishers.

van Lier, L. (2004b) The ecology of language learning: Paper presented at the UC Language Consortium Conference on Theoretical and Pedagogical Perspectives, March 26–28, 2004. See http://uccllt.ucdavis.edu/events/ULCCTPP/leo.php.

van Lier, L. (2004c) The semiotics and ecology of language learning: Perception, voice, identity and democracy. *Utbildning & Demokrati* 13 (3), 79–103.

Waninge, F., Dörnyei, Z. and de Bot, K. (2014) Motivational dynamics in language learning: Change, stability, and context. *Modern Language Journal* 98 (3), 704–723.

Ware, P.D. and Kramsch, C. (2005) Toward an intercultural stance: Teaching German and English through telecollaboration. *Modern Language Journal* 89 (2), 190–205.

Waring, H. (2008) Using explicit positive assessment in the language classroom: IRF, feedback, and learning opportunities. *Modern Language Journal* 92 (4), 577–594

Warner, C. (2014) Mapping new classrooms in literacy-oriented foreign language teaching and learning: The roles of the reading experience. In K. Arens, J. Swaffar and P. Urlaub (eds) *Transforming the Foreign Language Curriculum in Higher Education: Critical Perspectives from the United States* (pp. 157–175). New York: Springer.

Weedon, C. (1987) *Feminist Practice and Poststructuralist Theory* (2nd edn). Oxford: Blackwell.

Wiley, T. (2007a) The foreign language 'crisis' in the United States: Are heritage and community languages the remedy? *Critical Inquiry in Language Studies* 4, 179–205.

Wiley, T. (2007b) Beyond the foreign language crisis: Toward alternatives to xenophobia and national security as bases for US language policies. *The Modern Language Journal* 91 (2), 252–255.

Woolard, K. and Schieffelin, B. (1994) Language ideology. *Annual Review of Anthropology* 23, 55–82.

Index

acts of meaning 62–63, 66–68, 98, 144, 152, 177–183, 186–187, 192–198, 201–202
ACTFL standards 16, 24–28
affordances 48, 57–60, 64, 80, 96, 99, 104, 138, 144, 149, 179, 181, 187, 190

Bakhtin 40, 42, 69, 98, 147, 149–150
Byram 32–40, 180

cultural narratives 41, 71, 80–83, 86, 98, 101–102, 125, 144, 146–148, 150–151, 157, 159, 167–168, 179

ecological theory 57–64, 99, 193
embodiment 59, 101, 123, 125, 133, 135, 144, 181, 186

global simulation 70–77, 79–81, 84, 93–95, 97–99, 137, 145, 149–152, 149–152, 169–174, 183, 189–192

Halliday 58, 66, 69
heteroglossia 40, 87, 98, 133, 147, 149
hypothesizing 53, 118–125, 144, 185, 191

Intercultural communicative competence 33–40, 176–177
intertextuality 83, 97, 147–152, 160–161, 164–167, 179, 191

Kramsch 6, 9, 13–15, 20, 23, 26, 29, 32, 37, 40–50, 52, 55–58, 61–69, 102–103, 147, 150, 174–175, 177, 181–182, 190

language ideologies 5–11, 14
language play 54–55

meaning-making repertoires 4, 6, 14, 29, 49–50, 55, 57, 63, 67–68, 79–80, 99, 174, 185, 188, 191

meaning potentials 3–4, 31–32, 37, 39, 50, 55, 59, 63–69, 98–99, 101–104, 111, 115, 125, 133, 137, 144–147, 151–153, 157, 174, 179–180, 182, 185–187, 192
MLA report 26, 41, 98
modern languages curriculum 3, 5, 17–18, 20–21, 23, 26, 51, 53, 55, 59, 183–184, 189, 192

narrative practices 45, 96–99

pedagogy of potentials 4, 176, 192
perspective-taking 52, 121, 153, 158, 169–172, 186

semiosis 58, 60, 95–96, 138, 176–181, 183, 193
social semiotic view of language learning 57–68, 79, 102, 138, 144, 176–177, 179–182, 187, 190, 192
subjectivities 25–26, 47–49, 54–56, 58, 60, 78, 123, 125, 133, 137, 182
symbolic action 47–48, 62, 65, 144, 181
symbolic competence 26, 32–33, 40, 45–50, 52–59, 62–64, 95–96, 133, 144, 146–147, 153, 158, 175–177, 180–181, 187–188, 192
symbolic power 29, 46–49, 53, 144, 175, 181
symbolic representation 47–48, 65, 144, 181, 188
symbolic self 47, 49, 61,

third place 33, 37, 44–45, 174

van Lier 33, 57–62, 78, 102, 177, 183–184, 188, 193
voicing 97, 101, 112, 123, 125, 132–135, 144, 181, 186

For Product Safety Concerns and Information please contact our EU Authorised Representative:

Easy Access System Europe

Mustamäe tee 50

10621 Tallinn

Estonia

gpsr.requests@easproject.com